Routledge Revivals

Overcoming Foundations

First published in 1989, *Overcoming Foundations* offers a challenge to both postmodernism and traditional doctrines of knowledge and value by undertaking a systematic philosophy without foundations. United by a concern for overcoming foundations without overcoming philosophy, the essays in this book discuss a wide range of issues in epistemology and ethics, incorporating analysis of major thinkers of the past and present and drawing critically on Hegel's argument. The book unveils the dogmatic assumption of the futility of philosophy's traditional quests for universal truth and ethics and lays out the strategy for achieving autonomy of reason and valid norms of conduct without foundational appeals.

After examining how a critique of foundations can be executed without making new foundational claims, Winfield considers how philosophy must operate in order to think truth without given conceptual schemes and to achieve rational autonomy. Finally, the author explores the implications of a reason free of foundations for the history of philosophy and the debates embroiling contemporary thought. The essays outline an independent theory of justice, rethinking morality, and the structures of civil society and democratic government. Overcoming Foundations advances a much ignored philosophical alternative, a systematic contribution to epistemology, ethics, and social and political philosophy.

Overcoming Foundations
Studies in Systematic Philosophy

Richard Dien Winfield

First published in 1989
by Columbia University Press

This edition first published in 2024 by Routledge
4 Park Square, Milton Park, Abingdon, Oxon, OX14 4RN

and by Routledge
605 Third Avenue, New York, NY 10017

Routledge is an imprint of the Taylor & Francis Group, an informa business

© 1989 Richard Dien Winfield

All rights reserved. No part of this book may be reprinted or reproduced or utilised in any form or by any electronic, mechanical, or other means, now known or hereafter invented, including photocopying and recording, or in any information storage or retrieval system, without permission in writing from the publishers.

Publisher's Note
The publisher has gone to great lengths to ensure the quality of this reprint but points out that some imperfections in the original copies may be apparent.

Disclaimer
The publisher has made every effort to trace copyright holders and welcomes correspondence from those they have been unable to contact.

A Library of Congress record exists under ISBN: 0813013682

ISBN: 978-1-032-87921-5 (hbk)
ISBN: 978-1-003-53546-1 (ebk)
ISBN: 978-1-032-87927-7 (pbk)

Book DOI 10.4324/9781003535461

OVERCOMING FOUNDATIONS

Studies in Systematic Philosophy

Richard Dien Winfield

 COLUMBIA UNIVERSITY PRESS   NEW YORK

COLUMBIA UNIVERSITY PRESS
NEW YORK   OXFORD

Copyright © 1989 Columbia University Press

All rights reserved

Library of Congress Cataloging-in-Publication Data

Winfield, Richard Dien, 1950–
 Overcoming foundations : studies in systematic philosophy /
Richard Dien Winfield.
     p.   cm.
  Bibliograpy: p.
  Includes index.
  ISBN 0-231-7008-X
  1. Philosophy.   2. Hegel, Georg Wilhelm Friedrich, 1770—1831.
I. Title.
B53.W53   1990
142—dc20   89-35460
                    CIP

Printed in the United States of America

Casebound editions of Columbia University Press books are Smyth-sewn
and printed on permanent and durable acid-free paper

For my daughter, Kalindi

Contents

Introduction ... 1

I: BEYOND FOUNDATIONS TO SYSTEMATIC PHILOSOPHY

1. The Route to Foundation-Free Systematic Philosophy ... 13
2. Dialectical Logic and the Conception of Truth ... 35
3. Conceiving Something Without Any Conceptual Scheme ... 55
4. Logic, Language, and the Autonomy of Reason: Reflections on the Place of Hegel's Analysis of Thinking ... 77
5. The Apotheosis of Intersubjectivity ... 91
6. Hegel Versus the New Oxthodoxy ... 99
7. Can Philosophy Have a Rational History? ... 117

II: THE FOUNDATION-FREE ETHICS OF FREEDOM

8. The Limits of Morality ... 135
9. Capital, Civil Society, and the Deformation of Politics ... 171
10. The Reason for Democracy ... 217
11. The Logic of the State ... 249
12. The Theory and Practice of the History of Freedom: The Right of History in Hegel's Philosophy of Right ... 271

Notes ... 295

Index ... 305

OVERCOMING FOUNDATIONS
Studies in Systematic Philosophy

Introduction

Overcoming foundations has become the watchword and preoccupation of contemporary thought. Under its spell, more and more thinkers repudiate the traditional appeals to some privileged given as the ground for advancing beyond opinion and convention to wisdom and right. However, if the revolt against foundations has cast well-worn strategies aside, what has it to offer in their stead? As a call for philosophy to abandon all reliance upon unjustified assumptions, antifoundationalism might seem committed to fulfilling philosophy's perennial search for the radical self-responsibility of an autonomous reason. Yet, more often, overcoming foundations represents a call to overcome philosophy as well. Whether this be seen as therapy to cure vain yearnings or as edification to make thinkers more aware of their frailties, the touted overcoming of philosophy rests on insupportable assumptions of its own.

First, it presumes that all philosophical thought is foundational, such that philosophy's topic and method are always dictated by presupposed terms. Although this supposedly entails that we forsake seeking unconditioned truths in deference to describing how theories are defined by their governing assumptions, how thought can be justifiably determined to be foundation-ridden by a thinking so characterized is never explained. When antifoundationalists describe how the particular assumptions of different philosophical systems underly what rests upon them, they still inexplicably presume that their act of deconstruction can transparently reveal the limits of our own conceptual scheme as well as make pronouncements applying to all theorizing. It matters little whether the foundational characterization of knowing be rooted in a description of consciousness, language, culture, or some other basis. In every case, the unmasking of foundations operates with its own assignment of primacy to the determining ground from which rationality is supposed to issue. Hence, the moment the overcoming of foundations is proclaimed an overcoming of philosophy, one can be sure that our would-be therapists have fallen back upon the same unqualified claims from which they seek to rescue us.

The essays that follow are intended as a remedy for the bogus cure that would overcome foundations by condemning reason to foundationalism. Although these essays cover a wide range of topics, they are united in examining how philosophy can overcome foundations without overcoming itself. Taken together, they provide an outline for doing philosophy systematically in the antifoundational sense of observing full autonomy and self-responsibility. Broadly speaking, these essays fall into two groups, one addressing how foundations can be overcome in the quest for knowledge, the other addressing how foundations can be overcome in ethics. Although authors and texts are intermittently discussed, these essays aim more at pursuing a philosophical strategy than at making interpretive points. Nevertheless, one figure cannot help but loom large throughout, whether cited by name or not. This is Hegel, who, contrary to the misinterpretations waylaying his epigones, remains the chief thinker to have pursued systematic philosophy with due recognition of the need to overcome foundations. Philosophy without foundations may still await its fulfillment, but we are thankfully too late to have to be entirely original.

"The Route to Foundation-Free Systematic Philosophy" introduces the problem with which we must begin: Namely, how can the critique of foundational thought be pursued without making foundational claims of its own? Drawing upon Hegel's *Phenomenology of Spirit*, the essay argues that an overcoming of foundations leading to a discourse free of privileged terms can be provided by a phenomenological investigation restricted to observing how foundational thought undermines itself in doing its own self-critique.

What, then, is the nature of the discourse ushered in by the self-elimination of foundational thought? "Dialectical Logic and the Conception of Truth" examines this question in light of how formal, transcendental, and dialectical logics grapple with the problem of reason's self-justification. This essay shows that logic's constitutive attempt to think valid thinking requires the very same freedom from foundations with which systematic philosophy must begin. Whereas formal and transcendental logic fail to reach this threshold by strapping reason with privileged terms and determining structures, dialectical logic escapes their difficulties by offering a self-determining conceptual development that both issues from no grounds and realizes rational autonomy. This it can succeed in doing by beginning with indeterminacy and presenting the self-exposition of self-determined determinacy. Then dialectical logic can achieve a truth residing neither in correspondence nor coherence with any givens, but in the self-determined immanence of its categories.

Although these features provide a preliminary notion of how philosophy must proceed if it is to move beyond foundations, it remains to be established how something determinate can be conceived without taking any determinacy for granted. "Conceiving Something Without Any Conceptual Scheme" addresses this challenge. The essay begins by raising the problem of accounting for determinacy. This has posed a dilemma for philosophers because failure to conceive the category of something leaves philosophy resting on an inexplicable assumption, whereas conceiving determinacy requires, paradoxical as it sounds, employing no determinate givens. Attempts to evade the issue by accepting the irreducibility of something, as in classical doctrines of substance and transcendental argument, collapse into incoherence. Examining the failure of such attempts to conceive determinacy by appeal to given terms and given determiners, the essay charts how determinacy can and must instead be conceived without presupposing anything determinate. Following the lead of Hegel's account of determinate being in his *Science of Logic,* the essay shows how the resulting theory of determinacy can offer the necessary antidote to foundationalism.

Granted that philosophy can free itself of foundations only if it begins with a theory of determinacy involving the same self-exposition of categories required by logic, how are we to understand the roles of consciousness and language in systematic thought? "Logic, Language, and the Autonomy of Reason: Reflections on the Place of Hegel's Analysis of Thinking" raises this issue by investigating why Hegel addresses thinking within his philosophy of reality as an activity presupposing nature, consciousness, and language, rather than treating thought as an unsituated, unconditioned first topic of philosophy. As the essay argues, that thinking operates on the basis of all these factors need not undermine the autonomy and foundation-free character of philosophy. Although thought has preconditions on which its exercise depends, these preconditions cannot play the role of juridical conditions that determine what counts as valid thought. If consciousness or language are given such juridical roles, one falls prey to the incoherencies of foundational epistemology. These dilemmas can be avoided by conceiving consciousness and language as real, but nonjuridical conditions of thinking that leave epistemological issues undetermined while leaving the autonomy of reason unimpeached by the necessary vehicles of thought. The essay concludes by suggesting how language allows for a nonrepresentational, foundation-free thinking, whose irrefutable autonomy renders semantic analysis a useless instrument for philosophical investigation.

Accordingly, we must avoid the popular temptation to fetishize intersubjectivity as a deciding ground of knowledge and values. As "The Apotheosis of Intersubjectivity" argues, the fact that knowledge claims and ethical norms are embedded in intersubjective contexts in no way makes either juridically relative to these surroundings. If intersubjective structures are conceived as determining conditions of reason and justice, there reappear the very problems of foundationalism that the turn to intersubjectivity was intended to overcome.

Consequently, the new orthodoxy in philosophy, which embraces naturalized epistemology and a holist coherence theory of truth and value as the outcome of antifoundationalism, is misguided in thinking that it has escaped the pitfalls that give it its guiding direction. "Hegel Versus the New Orthodoxy" exposes the untenability both of this approach and of using Hegel's critique of epistemology, dialectical logic, and philosophy of spirit in its support.

What, then, are the ramifications of overcoming foundations for the history of philosophy? "Can Philosophy Have a Rational History?" discusses this question by first showing why it cannot be coherently maintained that the history of philosophy is determined by either the history of extraphilosophical factors or an internal necessity whereby antecedent theories impose a direction on those that follow. Any claim that philosophy is determined by an external history leads to either a self-refuting relativism or an assertion of an absolute self-transparent age in which the role of extraphilosophical factors becomes superfluous. Alternately, if the internal history of philosophy be viewed as conditioning its thought, philosophy is condemned to a self-defeating foundationalism whose own affirmation is insupportable or its history becomes an autonomous development determined by the historically independent demands of reason. The essay proceeds to show that whereas this disqualifies deconstruction as the privileged tool for understanding the history of philosophy, it allows for a rational reconstruction unveiling the conceptual implications that may hold between successive theories in conformity with the self-determining character of philosophical discourse.

Not surprisingly, the epistemological issues revolving around the overcoming of foundations have their counterparts in the problems of justifying ethical norms. The remaining essays in the collection explore the parallel challenge of overcoming foundations in ethics. "The Limits of Morality" sets the stage by calling into question the prevalent assumption that ethics must choose between two incompatible alternatives: an invidiously formal morality grounded in the unembedded structure of the self and an ethic of community that leaves ethical norms historically relative. Taking Hegel's analysis of morality in his *Philosophy of Right* as a touchstone, the essay shows that morality is reconcilable with an ethic of community provided both are reconceived as structures of freedom, whose self-determined character grants them a validity free of foundations.

"Capital, Civil Society, and the Deformation of Politics" addresses the closely related problem of how to remedy the recourse to natural determinations—that is, factors given independently of freedom, that have tainted the major political ideologies and political systems of modernity. As the theory and practice of liberalism, social democracy, communism, and fascism have shown, the appeal to natural determinations as foundations of legitimacy has led to a subordination of the political domain to prepolitical factors and to an analogous reduction of social freedom to something determined by natural differences. The essay argues that an alternative to this problematic foundationalism can be found in the interaction theory of freedom introduced by Hegel's *Philosophy of Right*. By following its lead, the deformations of modern theory and practice can be overcome through a redetermination of justice as a self-ordered system of institutional freedom in which society and state are radically demarcated and legitimacy is no more rooted in nature than in convention. Focusing upon the structure of civil society, the essay concludes by analyzing how social freedom requires public intervention to eliminate social disadvantage and protect political freedom from social domination.

"The Reason for Democracy" extends the argument of the foundation-free interaction conception of justice from civil society to government. It takes as its point of departure the failure of the traditional rejections and justifications of democracy. Whereas the former fail by being unable to exclude freedom from politics, the latter collapse by appealing to teleological or social contract principles. In the face of these problems, the essay shows that democracy can only be justified if it is an end in itself, if what falls under democratic decision is not antecedently decidable by reason, and if democratic procedures are bound by constitutional limits maintained by an organic division of powers. As the essay argues, these requirements can alone be satisfied by a foundation-free theory of justice establishing the exclusive normative validity of self-determination.

If indeed the state is properly an institution of political freedom presiding over the other spheres of self-determination, it would appear that the state will exhibit the category of individuality, which best captures the self-informed character politics seems to possess. In that case, however, does political philosophy turn into a hermeneutic discipline that must address its theme much as art criticism interprets its unique objects? "The Logic of the State" examines this possibility as it is posed by Michael Foster. The essay argues that the self-determined character of the just state does not make its structure opaque to reason and accessible only to historical understanding. On the contrary, the individuality of the state involves a universal dimension inherent in constitutionality allowing for a theory of the just state that can conceive the validity of political institutions independently of history.

"The Theory and Practice of the History of Freedom: The Right of History in Hegel's Philosophy of Right" brings this same point to a head by examining how conceiving the historical genesis of justice fits within the project of an ethics free of foundations. Although Hegel does address factual history in his *Lectures On the Philosophy of History*, the discussion of history in his *Philosophy of Right* has its place as a prescriptive inquiry into what must occur for the institutions of right to come into being. To the degree that ethical institutions do not owe their legitimacy to any foundations, their genesis can play no role in their legitimation. Indeed, the very concept of their genesis depends upon a prior determination of what they are in their own right. Hence, the history of freedom in the *Philosophy of Right* properly intervenes only at the conclusion of the analysis of right. The essay investigates how the structure of right itself dictates the manner by which its institutions can arise and how this sheds light on bringing into being a system of justice free of foundations.

A Note on the Text

The above essays were written between 1979 and 1988. Those that have been published before are listed below with their publication details.

"The Route to Foundation-Free Systematic Philosophy." *The Philosophical Forum* (Spring 1984), vol. 15, no. 3.

"Dialectical Logic and the Conception of Truth." *Journal of the British Society For Phenomenology* (May 1987), vol. 18, no.2,

"Conceiving Something Without Any Conceptual Scheme." *The Owl of Minerva* (Fall 1986), vol. 18, no. 1.

"Logic, Language, and the Autonomy of Reason: Reflections on the Place of Hegel's Analysis of Thinking." *Idealistic Studies* (May 1987), vol. 17, no. 2.

"The Apotheosis of Intersubjectivity" (adapted from "Commentary on 'Hegel's Concept of *Geist*'"). In Peter G. Stillman, ed., *Hegel's Philosophy of Spirit*. Albany: State University of New York Press, 1987.

"Hegel Versus the New Orthodoxy." In William Desmond, ed., *Hegel and His Critics*. Albany: State University of New York Press, 1988.

"Can Philosophy Have a Rational History?" In Bernard P. Dauenhauer, ed., *At the Nexus of Philosophy and History*. Athens: University of Georgia Press, 1987.

"Capital, Civil Society, and the Deformation of Politics." *History of Political Thought* (Spring 1983), vol. 4, no 1.

"The Reason for Democracy." *History of Political Thought* (Winter 1984), vol. 5, no. 3.

"The Theory and Practice of the History of Freedom: The Right of History in Hegel's Philosophy of Right." In Robert L. Perkins, ed., *History and System: Hegel's Philosophy of History*. Albany: State University of New York Press, 1984.

I
BEYOND FOUNDATIONS TO SYSTEMATIC PHILOSOPHY

1
The Route to Foundation-Free Systematic Philosophy

To a degree unmatched by any other discipline, philosophy has never ceased disputing its own boundaries. Whereas elsewhere some initial consensus as to what defines the matter at issue always reigns, in philosophy not only are object and method contested, but it is even controversial whether philosophy can legitimately begin with any determinate form or content at all.

1. THE RELATIVITY OF POSITIVE SCIENCE

Such problems never arise so long as one remains on the ground of positive science. Unlike philosophy, positive science takes up a given subject matter and considers it as such, and nothing more. What positive science knows is thus not the immediate truth, but something that is an object for its investigation by virtue of being presupposed. Not only does its analysis proceed from a predetermined content, but its knowing is itself predetermined in that it takes for granted its own relation to its object.

Consequently, positive science can only result in knowledge that is relative both with regard to its form and content. What its cognition addresses is not true reality without further qualification, but rather what it relates to as given. Conversely, its knowing is not absolute, grasping things as they are in themselves, but only a comprehension of what it posits as its object, either by defining its terms, preselecting its domain from the given array of facts, or otherwise taking certain matters for granted.

So defined, positive science is by no means limited to empirical inquiry. Since its subject matter has no other restriction than that it be a given content, positive science equally includes such allegedly formal disciplines as mathematics and symbolic logic. Although neither draws directly from objects of experience, each begins its analysis from an assumed subject matter comprised of defined relations such as number and logical operator.

Thus, all debate in the positive sciences, be they empirical or not, rests on nothing more than common assumptions that can just as easily be superseded by the adoption of a different set of terms establishing a new paradigm of science. However, this predicament cannot be ascribed to discourse as a whole, as Quine and Kuhn have suggested,[1] for the relative character of the object and knowing of positive science leaves it incapable of ever establishing exclusive universality for its own standpoint.

Of course, there is nothing problematic in the knowing of positive science so long as its relative status is acknowledged.

2. THE DILEMMA OF METAPHYSICS

If, however, positive science no longer limits its claims to conclusions conditioned by a subject matter taken for granted but instead claims absolute truth for its analysis, then it falls into the pitfalls of what has in modern times been branded metaphysics. The confusion of such discourse is twofold.

On the one hand, although metaphysics begins with some given content or other, it fails to relate to its object as something determined for it in virtue of the particular assumptions and standpoint of the inquiry. Instead of regarding its subject matter as a stipulation of its own knowing with no other assured reality, metaphysics takes it to be in itself, to be true without the qualification of simply being that given content chosen to begin with.

On the other hand, although the knowledge metaphysics arrives at proceeds from some assumed content, it does not admit to being relative to that chosen starting point. Because the object is here taken to be immediately true in itself and not something conditioned by the inquiry taking it for granted, the knowledge of it purports to be true knowledge without further qualification. In other words, metaphysical discourse presumes to have an absolute knowledge that corresponds to true reality.

Nevertheless, precisely by asserting absolute knowledge of what is in itself, metaphysics commits the basic fallacy of claiming immediate truth for a determinate given content and knowing, both of whose unqualified validity are simply taken for granted.

Unfortunately, ever since antiquity, philosophers have all too often made such metaphysical knowing their own. Neither content to pursue the limited ends of positive science nor able to dispense with all assumptions, they have perenially referred to the given content of their knowledge as true reality and thereby canonized their knowing an absolute knowledge of things as they are in themselves.

Since one arbitrary assumption is as good as any other, such thinkers seized upon any number of objects of positive science and reconsidered them as truths in themselves. As a result, controversies over what was the true content inevitably arose. However, because each truth was equally asserted to be immediate and irreducible, there could be no higher court to adjudicate them. In face of this dilemma, the need was felt early on for an absolute first principle out of which the full content of what is in itself could be unambiguously derived.

This provided only further quandary, for to opt for a first principle with the resolve of ordering all else with regard to it does not solve the problem of what content it and its derivative order are to have. Once again, conflicting theories could not help but emerge, claiming primacy for a different principle of reality. Since each absolute was taken to be equally primordial, none could be refuted without introducing some higher principle of validity whose very authority could only undermine the putative primacy of the first principle under defense. At best, one could point to the various degrees of internal consistency in each of the various positions. This, however, could hardly remove the problem of arbitrariness, for consistency offers no test of truth, unless one metaphysically asserts its primacy as the criterion of true knowing.

In face of these recurring problems, the example of Socrates suggested that if philosophers were to make any unqualified truth claims, they would first have to strip their thought of all assumptions and reach the point of knowing nothing at all. Of course, this would not then remain an empty halt, but would be the point from which true knowing would somehow proceed. As Plato posed the matter in his discussion of dialectic in the section of the divided line in the *Republic*, if knowing was to be true knowing, it had to reach a first principle beyond all assumption from which all other true ideas would follow without reference to anything else.

Whatever its critical intention, the Platonic formulation clearly fails, for it leaves unanswered how one can determine what is the true first principle beyond assumption from which all else derives without already assuming all sorts of things concerning what can and cannot be presuppositionless. As a case in point, when Plato finally seizes upon the Good as that highest notion on which all others depend, he already has to assume certain truths as to what the Good is and why it has primacy.

So the circle of metaphysics remains unbroken. Whether a first principle be offered or not, the immediate reference to reality and the true knowing of it here continues to be based on the *assumption* that knowledge corresponds to reality, that thought adequately unravels what is in itself, regardless of its particular relation to the knower.

3. THE TEMPTATION AND FAILURE OF ALL TRANSCENDENTAL PHILOSOPHY

In the face of these difficulties of metaphysical knowing, it is natural to take the route of transcendental philosophy and call into question the presupposed correspondence of thought and reality and with it the possibility of making any absolute truth claims whatsoever. Indeed, since all true knowing must fall within knowing itself, it does appear reasonable to suspend all knowing of reality and instead make knowing the object of investigation before examining what is accessible through it.

Once this transcendental turn is taken, however, it becomes questionable whether it in any way avoids the problem of metaphysics.

To begin with, the entire move to transcendental argument seems to be based upon certain assumptions concerning the character of knowing itself. To the degree that any such assumptions are not themselves criticized, they are naturally subject to the same objection against immediate truth claims that transcendental philosophy rightly aims at metaphysics.

Any transcendental inquiry takes for granted that the conditions of knowing can be examined prior to any particular knowing. This implies that knowing, whether based in the structure of consciousness, the context of ordinary language, or an ideal speech situation, is determined in its own right, apart from what it knows.[2] On this basis, knowing is variously preconceived as an instrument that brings its object into our reach, as a medium in which the knowable appears, or as a general structure of signifying that constitutes what it refers to.

Although transcendental philosophy here attempts to determine the full character and limits of true knowing, it is readily apparent that the alternate paradigms underlying its line of questioning can lead to no real knowledge at all.

As Hegel has pointed out,[3] if knowing is an instrument or a medium, then it alone cannot reveal the object as it is in itself, but only as it is transmitted by the instrument or medium that knowing putatively is. Of course, if one then attempts to subtract the distorting effects of such an instrument or medium, one is only left where one began prior to knowing's intervention—namely, with no knowing at all.

The outcome is no better when, on the other hand, all reference to real objects of knowledge is rejected as metaphysical and the transcendental structure is alternately conceived to constitute what it refers to independently of any thing in itself. In that case, what one has cannot be true knowledge without further qualification; it is merely what results *when* the stipulated transcendental structure is itself taken for granted. If one nevertheless claims that that structure is irreducible or the only form of knowing or the special shape of rigorous science, it must be recognized that any such assertion is not itself transcendentally constituted, but metaphysically presupposed.[4]

Compounding these dilemmas is the no less vexing problem of legitimating the knowing of the transcendental philosopher whose discourse has as its object the transcendental structure itself.

At first glance, it would appear that the very doing of transcendental philosophy ineluctibly contradicts its own project. Namely, if the constitutive aim of transcendental philosophy be to bracket out all immediate truth claims and instead investigate the structure of true knowing prior to any actual true knowing itself, then one has the paradoxical situation of an inquiry attempting to determine correctly the conditions of knowledge without providing any specific knowledge at all. In other words, one faces the problem, diagnosed early on by Hegel, of attempting to know before knowing.

Since the specific knowing tacitly pursued by transcendental discourse is that of the critique of knowing in general, the problem here confronting transcendental philosophy resolves itself into the following question: How can the critique of knowing be self-critical and avoid stipulating the character of the transcendental structure, be it consciousness, language, or whatever, in a metaphysical fashion?

The answer that suggests itself would seem to involve but one thing: eliminating the distinction between the critique of knowing and the knowing under critique. To avoid falling back into metaphysics, transcendental philosophy must somehow proceed so that knowing does its own critique, transcendentally constituting not just objects of experience but every relation of the transcendental structure itself.

Starting with Fichte and Schelling and continuing into our century most notably with Husserl,[5] thinkers have pursued this task in hope of eliminating the uncriticized standpoint of transcendental argument. Recognizing the anomaly of Kant's metaphysical deductions of the categorial content for the critique of pure reason, they have attempted to radicalize the transcendental problematic to the point of having the entire critical apparatus be self-referring from the very start.

Although a truly consistent transcendental philosophy must tackle just such an enterprise, the required solution turns out to have a structure that eliminates the whole framework of transcendental argument. This becomes evident when one considers what occurs when the critique of knowing and the knowing under critique become indistinguishable, as is required if the transcendental structure is not to be metaphysically stipulated.

To begin with, the knowledge under critique is to be true knowledge—that is, knowing whose knowledge corresponds to its object and knows itself as such. The transcendental structure, which comprises the worked-out critique of knowing, is thus itself a knowing of true knowing.

On the other hand, the critical standpoint that has the transcendental structure as its object must have the same determination if it is to be true knowing and not just metaphysical dogma. In other words, the knowing of true knowing (the activity of the transcendental philosopher) must have true knowing as its object in the same way that true knowing has its own object. This can only be if true knowing *is* a knowing of true knowing. In that case, the transcendental knowing of true knowing has the same relation to its object as does true knowing itself, for what both have knowledge of is true knowing.

However, once this somehow occurs, not only is the difference between the critique of knowing and the knowing under critique eliminated, but so is the basic distinction between knowing and its object. For if knowing is a knowing of true knowing, then the object of its knowledge is indistinguishable from its knowing of it.

The consequence of this result should be clear. As pointed out above, the basis of transcendental discourse is nothing other than the contrast and difference between knowing and its object, a distinction that first allows any consideration of the conditions of knowing in general separate from knowledge of a specific object. Consequently, when transcendental philosophy becomes self-referring, with the knowing under critique assuming the same structure as the critique itself, then the very framework of its epistemology goes under. Since one can no longer speak of knowing in distinction from its object, one can hardly speak of knowing at all. What one is left with, as Hegel has suggested in his discussion of Absolute Knowing in the *Phenomenology of Spirit*, is really the self-elimination of transcendental argument, where the underlying differentiation of knowing and its object collapses, leaving nothing but an undifferentiated unity in which there is neither anything in itself nor any relation of reference.

For all its emptiness, this utterly indeterminate result of a consistently pursued transcendental philosophy is not without its lesson. It shows that whereas metaphysics can arrive at no absolute truth, transcendental philosophy can arrive at no determinate absolute knowing either.

4. PHENOMENOLOGY AS INTRODUCTION TO SYSTEMATIC PHILOSOPHY

How then can philosophy begin at all?

In face of the relative character of positive science and the failures of metaphysics and transcendental philosophy, there seems to be nothing to go on but a purely negative proscription. This sole apparent lesson from the experience of metaphysical and transcendental inquiries is that one cannot begin with any immediate truth claims, either about reality or about knowing.

This might suggest that one must begin with nothing at all, casting all assumptions aside and resolving to think with neither determinations *in res* nor transcendental structures. Such a resolve would, however, itself be a mere subjective postulate if it be immediately offered as a starting point. It would tacitly assume both the primacy of indeterminacy and the primacy of that nonmetaphysical, nontranscendental knowing that here reputedly begins without determinate knowledge. In other words, the immediate resolve to think without assumption would effectively assume prior to philosophical investigation that the concept of philosophy is presuppositionless knowing.

On the other hand, the temptation to begin with a heuristic principle would be equally inadequate, for whatever might follow from it would remain conditioned by the positing of that principle.

It thus might seem that the only way out of this impasse is the route of holism, which seeks to cure philosophy of its longing for truth by restricting it to the edifying task of bringing us to an awareness of how all questions of justification rest on pragmatic agreements rather than on any mirroring of nature or transcendental constitutions. Advanced most forcefully by Hans-Georg Gadamer and Richard Rorty,[6] the holist position claims to avoid the pitfalls of past philosophy by openly admitting that the pragmatic underpinnings of all argument leave discourse an open-ended conversation where no terms have any privilege beyond what agreed practice gives them. Nevertheless, in asserting this, holists effectively make the very kind of juridical claims they properly criticize. Not only do they here metaphysically assume that their pragmatic description of discourse accurately mirrors the reality of conversation, but they elevate it to a transcendental ground by asserting that all justification is constituted through the pragmatic agreement of conversational practice. Consequently, the holist reduction of philosophy to edification only reinstates the dilemma of foundational arguments it wishes to overcome.

To avoid such recursions to metaphysical and transcendental discourse, a radically novel path suggests itself.

This alternative is provided by phenomenology, here generically conceived as an explicitly positive science of knowing bent on observing whether a threshhold of indeterminacy can be reached that is neither metaphysically referred to nor transcendentally constituted. If such an indeterminacy can be obtained, so the strategy goes, then phenomenology will have secured a starting point for a new form of philosophical discourse that takes nothing for granted.

Phenomenology, taken in this sense, proceeds in recognition of the fundamental dilemma of metaphysics and transcendental philosophy. As their examples have indicated, no immediate truth can be legitimately claimed by any knowing that is determinate with regard to either its object or knowledge. What phenomenology suggests is that, instead of making truth claims, one can stipulate knowing that claims truth for its knowledge and observe, in the manner of positive science, how it develops itself by making and testing its own truth claims.

On this basis, one has a phenomenological inquiry that is radically nontranscendental as well as nonmetaphysical in the traditional sense. Because one here simply observes a structure of knowing that is openly taken for granted as a given content, phenomenology escapes the metaphysical dilemma by making no claims concerning either the unqualified reality of its subject matter or the truth of the claims made by the subject matter itself. If phenomenology did and claimed either that it comprises the doctrine of knowing or that the truth claims made by the subject matter were those constitutive of knowing per se, then it would be a transcendental phenomenology like Husserl's, making the indefensibly metaphysical claim that it was itself rigorous science laying bare the true underlying structure of all discourse.

Instead, phenomenology here embraces the limits of positive science, stipulating the content it observes and accordingly recognizing that what claims do emerge are not truths in themselves but only determinations generated by the assumed subject matter itself.

Nevertheless, phenomenology stands unique among positive sciences in that its given object makes its own truth claims and also tests them by itself. In so doing, the stipulated structure of knowing gives itself successive shapes of knowing, each with a different knowledge and a different standard of truth. Since the subject matter thereby determines its own development, the method of this positive science has the peculiar character of being a pure observation, since the phenomenological investigator need not interfere with the self-examination of the subject matter. As a consequence, although phenomenology is only a positive science, it has a singularly nonarbitrary character whereby whatever content comes into view does so by being generated from nothing but the bare structure of knowing taken up at the start.

These generic features all follow from the character of the structure that comprises the given starting point of phenomenology's positive science.

This structure is knowing that claims truth for its knowledge. All this involves, according to the stipulation of phenomenology, is knowing that refers to what it knows as something both in relation to it and determined in itself independently of that relation. As such, the knowing under consideration is always a knowledge of what is putatively determined in its own right. Knowing's relation to its object is its knowledge, whereas the truth of that knowledge is the known object taken by itself as that to which the knowledge refers.

At first glance, it might appear nonsensical for knowing to refer to what is not merely in relation to it but in itself. However, the mere fact that knowing involves the distinction of knowledge and truth, of what is *for* it and what is *to* it, means that what is in itself falls no less within knowing as one of its constitutive contrast terms.

Consequently, the problem of judging the truth of knowing's knowledge does not involve any introduction by the phenomenologist of some criterion of validity. Of course, if that were necessary, the phenomenological investigation could not help reverting to metaphysical assertions about what is the criterion of truth. This can here be avoided simply because the given structure of knowing not only makes its own truth claims but contains within itself the criterion by which its own knowledge can be verified. This criterion is, needless to say, the pole of in itselfness, or, otherwise put, that which it knows. Thus, as much as knowledge is knowing's relation to this content, the truth of this knowledge is simultaneously and inseparable for knowing as its referent.

If this solution relieves the phenomenologist of having to supply a criterion of truth, it also relieves him or her of having to apply the criterion and thereby lay claim to certain methodological procedures.

The latter can also be avoided in that knowing not only refers to what it knows but knows *both* what it refers to and what its own knowledge is. Since knowledge and its referent are linked together for knowing as contrast terms of its own relation, knowing does not simply supply the truth criterion of its knowledge but equally comprises a comparison of its knowledge with its truth or referent.

However, given its constitutive structure, the comparison cannot sustain itself. The obvious reason for this is that as soon as knowing has its two aspects before it, its truth is not just in itself but something *for it*. Accordingly, knowing discovers that what is for it is not simply what it took to be the truth but rather this truth *in* its relation to knowing.

Knowing thus finds itself before a new referent, consisting in the givenness for knowing of the former criterion of its knowledge. However, since its knowledge is but its relation to its referent, once the referent changes, the determination of knowledge must also alter itself.

In this fashion, the stipulated structure of knowing successively generates a whole new shape for itself, with completely altered contrast terms of truth and knowledge. On the one hand, the referent of knowing has changed from what was putatively in itself into the determination of this truth *as* it fell within knowing. On the other hand, the opposing pole of knowledge has changed from being knowing's relation to what was formerly in itself into its relation to the transformed object.

Nevertheless, insofar as these new correlative contents *are* distinguished and related to one another as the constitutive truth and knowledge of a new shape of knowing, the same inversion cannot help but proceed anew. Since the knowledge of the new object stands as such in contrast to its truth, the referent once again falls within knowing for knowing itself and accordingly changes from what is in itself to what appears to be in itself within and for knowing.

As should be apparent by now, this process of successive inversions continues unabated so long as knowing continues to claim the truth of its knowledge, distinguishing what it knows from its relation to it.

For this reason, the structure of knowing taken up by phenomenology distinguishes itself from other objects of positive science not only by making truth claims and testing its knowledge but further by comprising a self-determining content that continually generates a new shape of knowing by virtue of its basic structure. Since knowing's self-examination produces its own development, the phenomenologist need not introduce any criterion of truth to verify the knowledge of knowing, nor any other content beyond the basic structure itself. Instead, the phenomenologist has simply to observe the subject matter at hand and allow it to develop by itself without any outside interference. In this respect, phenomenology exhibits its own nonarbitrary, scientific character to the degree that all its determinations emerge through the inversions of knowing that automatically follow from the bipolar structure taken for granted at the start.

Phenomenology's point of departure can therefore be nothing more than the shape of knowing where what is known to be true has no further determination than that it *is* in itself, while the corresponding knowledge has no further determination than that it *is* a relation to what *is*. In other words, phenomenology must begin with that shape of knowing whose criterion of truth is being and nothing more and whose knowledge is itself utterly immediate.

All further truth criteria must derive from the inversions of knowing resulting from this rudimentary shape of immediate knowledge of what is. Although this proscription leaves utterly undetermined what will be the actual succession of shapes, it can already be anticipated how the succession must come to an end, if it does at all.

The basic structure of knowing itself indicates that the generation of new shapes of knowing can reach a conclusion only when what is for knowing as its referent becomes identical in structure to knowing's relation to it. At that point, the truth of knowledge cannot become something else by virtue of being referred to as something for knowing. Since what is in itself here bears the very same structure as knowing's relation to it, grasping it in its relation to knowing *is* grasping it as it is in itself. In other words, here what is truth is indistinguishable from what knowledge is.

If such a point is reached, then the entire process of inversion comes to an end. Since, furthermore, the process is unique and nonarbitrary, the emergence of a shape of knowing whereby truth and knowledge become indistinguishable would signal the completed development of the totality of shapes of knowing. As such, phenomenology would here address its own last content.

However, due to the character of this one possible terminus of phenomenology, much more lies at issue.

To begin with, if the stipulated structure of knowing does develop into a shape such that the distinction between truth and knowledge falls away, then it must be observed that the very structure of truth-claiming knowing has eliminated itself through its own development. When truth and knowledge can no longer be differentiated, there is neither anything for knowing to distinguish from itself nor any relation to be had to a referent. Without something in itself to which knowing can relate and contrast itself, there is simply nothing to be known, nor any knowledge to be exercised. Thus, once knowing and what it knows are indistinguishable, all remnants of truth and knowledge are eliminated.

Given nothing to refer to nor any referring to perform, knowing that claims truth for its knowledge here effectively collapses into literally nothing at all.

With all contrast removed and no determinate truth claims remaining, the one possible terminus of phenomenology immediately presents an unprecedented beginning beyond the pale of either metaphysical or phenomenological discourse.

Because the stipulated structure of truth-claiming knowing has here eliminated itself, phenomenology loses the object of its pure observation. Accordingly, the very stance of phenomenology is annulled. Since nothing determinate remains, there is equally no given subject matter by which any new positive science could proceed. Furthermore, because there are no truth claims left concerning either the objects of knowledge or knowing itself, there is no opportunity for metaphysical discourse, whether traditional or transcendental in approach.

What there is is a collapse of all truth and knowledge into a wholly indeterminate unity that is neither something in itself nor in relation to some shape of knowing. It is simply indeterminacy, freed of all transcendental conditions and all claims to immediate truth. It is not being *in res* nor a concept of reason; it is utterly unqualified indeterminacy.

Since this result of the possible self-elimination of phenomenology has no distinction within it, it cannot refer back to any preceding ground or derivation. As such, it is really no result at all but a pure beginning taking nothing for granted.

If now determinations of any sort were to emerge from this starting point alone, they would be immune from the dilemmas of metaphysics and the relativity of positive science. They would rather form the content of a discourse presupposing neither method nor subject matter. Such a nonmetaphysical, thoroughly nonpositive science could then warrant the name of systematic philosophy in virtue of two corollary features entailed in its unprecedented starting point.

On the one hand, this prospective discourse would be systematic in the basic sense of proceeding without any foundations whatsoever. By beginning with no primitive terms of any sort nor the assumption of some determinate absolute knowledge, it could claim the presuppositionlessness that eludes all other forms of discourse.

On the other hand, this foundation-free discourse could avoid reverting to metaphysical and transcendental arguments only if it generated both its subject matter and method solely through what groundlessly emerges from the indeterminacy with which it begins. Instead of relying upon external reflections upon what is assumed to be given to provide it with a content and an order of consideration, its discourse would have to be self-determining. Thereby it would exhibit a concrete systematicity consisting in a total immanence where everything within it, including the order of its own development, is endogenously determined. Accordingly, the discourse at hand would be self-grounding precisely by proceeding without foundations. As a result, this systematic science would achieve what philosophy has always aspired to—namely a self-grounding development of determinacy where no category is accepted that has not already been legitimated within philosophy itself.

5. HEGEL AND SYSTEMATIC PHILOSOPHY

The first thinker to have raised the possibility of such nonmetaphysical, nonphenomenological systematic philosophy is Hegel. In his *Phenomenology of Spirit,* he has attempted to demonstrate how phenomenology does in fact complete itself with the self-elimination of knowing as it appears, thereby providing the starting point for a presuppositionless systematic philosophy.[7]

Hegel begins his *Phenomenology* by taking up the structure of knowing that claims truth for its knowledge, which he terms "consciousness" (*PS* 52f.), and then appropriately observes its most basic shape, where knowing immediately knows what is. Calling this starting point "Sense-Certainty" (*PS* 58f.), Hegel then proceeds to show how a succession of different shapes of knowing arises through inversions of consciousness until one is finally reached whose truth and knowledge are indistinguishable. Although Hegel christens this shape "Absolute Knowing" (*PS* 479f.), he readily observes that it is no sooner reached, then it shows itself to be no knowing at all but rather the very elimination of all knowledge of an in itself.

Nevertheless, Hegel's systematic claims regarding absolute knowing have all but been ignored by subsequent critics, starting with Marx and Kierkegaard and extending into our own time. Instead of properly regarding absolute knowing as the collapse of the posited structure of consciousness, they have commonly interpreted it as a determinate congnition that somehow unites subject and object such that its knowing both comprehends and constitutes things as they are in themselves. In this form, absolute knowing is considered to be the privileged standpoint from which Hegelian science purportedly proceeds to conceive the absolute. Accordingly, Hegel becomes labeled an objective idealist, a philosopher of subject-object identity, a thinker of self-revealing totality, and the consummator of metaphysics for whom thought and being are one.[8]

Admittedly, it is not hard to find certain remarks of Hegel which, taken in isolation, do tend to suggest just such interpretations.

In the introduction to the *Phenomenology*, for example, Hegel announces that what follows can be considered a representation of the path of natural consciousness to the true knowing of what it is in itself (*PS* 49), or alternately, as the complete history of the self-education of consciousness to science (*PS* 50). Since absolute knowing is the stated goal where consciousness reputedly grasps its true essence (*PS* 57) and becomes the genuine knowing comprising the very element of science (*PS* 15), it would indeed seem that absolute knowing is determinate twice over—once by comprehending the particular essence of consciousness, and twice by being the true standpoint of the special discourse of science.

This conclusion would appear further bolstered by prominent statements in the *Science of Logic*. There Hegel analogously notes that the *Phenomenology* results in the concept of science[9] once consciousness arrives at absolute knowing and attains its innermost truth (*SL* 71).

Certainly it is tempting to follow the critical tradition and conclude from these remarks that absolute knowing is a definite standpoint. However, to do so would be to ignore Hegel's accompanying refutation of all attempts to do philosophy from the vantage point of a determinate absolute knowing.

As he argues in the introduction to the *Phenomenology*, when philosophy begins, any claim it makes to an absolute knowing can have no more weight than the immediate assertion of any other standpoint. At its start, philosophy has yet to establish its own principles. Taking nothing for granted, it can no more immediately advance a particular form of knowing than accept standards from outside itself (*PS* 49). For this reason, to assert absolute knowing as the privileged cognition from which science begins is to fall into the general fallacy of metaphysics, the fallacy of setting out to conceive the unqualified truth upon the basis of a presupposition.

In the *Science of Logic*, Hegel makes this point unambiguously clear by taking to task the very position with which he has subsequently been so often identified. This occurs when Hegel turns his general critique of metaphysics upon those metaphysicians of his day, most notably Fichte and Schelling, who began their inquiry with intellectual intuition, that determinate absolute knowing of subject-object identity.

As Hegel argues, because these thinkers have advanced intellectual intuition as the irreducible prius of all determination, they have placed it prior to science, effectively leaving it no more than their own subjective postulate (*SL* 76). Furthermore, by immediately advancing this absolute knowing with a determinate content of subject-object identity, they have left unaccounted for the very relations of subject, object, and identity for which they claim absolute primacy (*SL* 78).

It might be answered that a description of the elevation of natural consciousness to intellectual intuition could resolve these problems. However, as Hegel is quick to point out, all that would contribute would be a denial of the immediate truth of absolute knowing for every subject (*SL* 76). The subject-object identity would still remain a metaphysical assumption whose origin might be phenomenologically described but not presuppositionlessly developed within science proper.

Although all these arguments make it relatively evident that absolute knowing cannot be a determinate standpoint from which philosophy proceeds, what is not so obvious is how absolute knowing can fulfill its stated function of concluding phenomenological discourse and ushering in presuppositionless science.

At first glance, Hegel's own formulation of the problem seems hopelessly paradoxical.

On the one hand, as much as absolute knowing can be no determinate cognition, Hegel nevertheless advances it as a prerequisite for the unfolding of systematic philosophy.

His reasoning is simple enough. The entire project of phenomenology is mandated, he argues, in that pure science presupposes overcoming the opposition of consciousness (*PS* 49; *SL* 49, 51, 69). This must first be accomplished because conscious knowing's generic reference to an *in itself* embodies the perennial metaphysical procedure of seeking to know without qualification on the basis of an immediate truth claim. Thus, only when the structure of consciousness can be eliminated as the underlying principle of determination can there be an escape from the illegitimate assumptions of metaphysics.

According to Hegel, the phenomenological development of consciousness to absolute knowing performs precisely this service insofar as absolute knowing dissolves the contrast between knowing and its object, which is constitutive of consciousness (SL 49). Therefore, absolute knowing must be presupposed by systematic philosophy if that science is to start with no immediate truth claims.

In this sense, absolute knowing reveals the truth of consciousness, the truth that conscious knowing can neither give itself an absolute grounding nor hold fast to any determinate knowledge nor finally stand as the irreducible framework of science. And in this same sense, absolute knowing further delivers the concept of science, if that concept denotes in the first instance nothing but the elimination of all metaphysical reference to an *in itself*.

On the other hand, however, this entire propadeutic function of absolute knowing appears immediately contradicted by the putative character of its result: Namely, whereas systematic philosophy is said to require the prior achievement of absolute knowing, that same systematic philosophy is no less purported to be presuppositionless.

In this regard, Hegel's argument is unambiguous.

Although the *positive* science of phenomenology can begin with its predetermined subject matter of consciousness, philosophy proper must proceed without any given content or else fall into the arbitrary postulating of metaphysics. Not even a notion of method or of philosophy itself can be originally presumed, for both must rather belong to the very content of science if it is to rise above *ad hoc* argumentation (SL 43, 53). At its start, philosophy can only be an empty word, claiming nothing and referring to no determinate cognition nor any determinate ground.

How then, we must ask, can systematic philosophy be presuppositionless and yet be mediated (SL 68) by a phenomenology terminating in absolute knowing? How can absolute knowing provide access to science (SL 49) when science is to take nothing for granted?

As paradoxical as it may sound, what alone resolves this problem is nothing other than the indeterminacy of absolute knowing. It removes the seeming aporia in phenomenology's prodadeutic relation to systematic philosophy by affording a solution so simple as to be perennially overlooked and ignored.

If, as the termination of phenomenology requires (see section 4), absolute knowing is no determinate cognition, but rather the collapse into indeterminacy of all reference to an *in itself*, it then signifies the elimination of the constitutive structure of consciousness whose development phenomenology has as its business to observe. With the emergence of absolute knowing, phenomenology accordingly loses the very subject matter without which its own observational stance collapses.

Consequently, indeterminate absolute knowing not only overcomes the opposition of consciousness but also eliminates the very standpoint of phenomenology itself. Since, however, absolute knowing is nothing but the immanent result of phenomenology, phenomenology here shows itself to be a self-eliminating discourse that leaves no determinate remain.

Therefore phenomenology can introduce foundation-free systematic philosophy without posing any abiding mediation to undermine the latter's presuppositionlessness.

In short, because phenomenology resolves itself into absolute knowing, which is nothing at all, it can legitimately serve as a propadeutic to the nonmetaphysical science that takes nothing for granted.

If Hegel's refutation of a determinate absolute knowing does not already indicate this, one has only to turn to his own description of what absolute knowing is. Whether one looks to the numerous observations in the *Phenomenology* or to the scattered recollections in the *Science of Logic,* the basic characterization is always the same: In absolute knowing, the opposition of knowing and its object fully dissolves itself such that the moment of *for itselfness,* certainty, and the moment of *in itselfness,* truth, become indistinguishable (*PS* 21, 51; *SL* 49).

As would be expected, this dissolution of the contrast of certainty and truth here accomplishes itself in a twofold manner. On the one hand, certainty overcomes its opposition to objectlikeness by so externalizing itself that it knows its own act to be the very form of *in itselfness* (*PS* 479). On the other hand, truth ceases to be the subjectless referent of certainty by taking on in its own objectlikeness the very structure of certainty. Insofar as absolute knowing holds these aspects together, it immediately presents the mutual cancellation of truth and certainty in their constitutive difference to one another (*PS* 479–80, 485–86, 487; *SL* 69).

So purged of all distinguishable dimensions of *for itselfness* and *in itselfness,* absolute knowing is left with neither knowledge for which truth can be claimed nor any object to which to refer. Because all *in itselfness* is here nothing but the positing of consciousness, it can no longer carry on its constitutive distinguishing of its knowledge from its object and judge its truth. As Hegel points out, truth-claiming knowing has in effect disappeared into the undifferentiated unity to which absolute knowing has reduced truth and certainty (*SL* 73).

Consequently, absolute knowing is not only no determinate cognition, but no knowing at all. Its pure unity has eliminated all relation to other and thus all mediation as well. By Hegel's own account, absolute knowing has here resolved itself into pure undifferentiatedness, and, as such, it ceases to be cognition. As he observes, what is left is only simple immediacy, which he sees fit to call "being" (*SL* 69, 72).

With this most meager remainder, the problem of passing from phenomenology to science proper falls by the wayside. The *Science of Logic* spells this out plainly enough in its introductory sections. As Hegel there explains, because the final result of absolute knowing is utterly unmediated indeterminacy, it stands as no result at all. Its simple immediacy precludes all reference to any preceding factor and instead comprises a pure beginning without further qualification. For this reason, the entire development of phenomenology from sense-certainty to the indeterminacy of absolute knowing can now be seen as a mediation that eliminates itself as soon as its result is reached.

Thus, Hegel notes, although being has indeed emerged, it has here done so through a completely self-sublating process (*SL* 69). Accordingly, what being reveals is nothing but its own indeterminacy. As introduced by absolute knowing, being is neither an ontological relation of the Absolute, a category thought by an unqualified standpoint, nor God before creation. It is simply the uncontrasted, unanalyzable indeterminate from which philosophy can proceed without foundations (*SL* 73).

With it and nothing more, Hegel purports to inaugurate systematic philosophy. In his *Science of Logic*, he starts with being as offered up by the self-annulling conclusion of the *Phenomenology of Spirit*—that is, being that is no ground nor primitive term nor totality revealing itself to *Dasein* but sheer indeterminacy. Since being has no distinctions that could refer back to any derivation, let alone to any preconceived notion of what it might be a beginning of, Hegel recognizes that being properly becomes a beginning only after determinations of some sort have developed out of it. Since such a development cannot proceed by reference to reality or by grace of some predetermined methodological standpoint, what follows from being can only do so in terms of a wholly immanent development. Thus, whereas phenomenology presents the self-development of a given content, whatever might follow from being would comprise self-determination per se. Insofar as the latter development would begin from indeterminacy, *what* determines itself could only be revealed at the end of the process, for only then would the full subject be manifest. Conversely, only at this concluding point would being itself stand revealed as the beginning of what finally results as a whole (*SL* 71f.).

All this might appear to be wishful thinking, for how could anything follow from being if there are no other resources available than indeterminacy? Hegel's answer to this problem is simple, if elusive. Indeed, there can be no reason for any further advance from being, for that would turn being into a ground, a cause, or a determiner, instead of mere indeterminacy. Nothing determinate can emerge from being either, for anything that has its own character in contrast to something else determinate would require more than being as its correlate. Consequently, Hegel notes, what alone can occur is that nothing groundlessly emerges from being, which is to say that another indistinguishable indeterminacy follows from being without any reason at all (*SL* 82f.).

Hegel recognizes that this by no means establishes new determinacy, since nothing is immediately the same as being, just as being is immediately nothing. Nevertheless, this direct passage into one another does comprise something irreducible to being—namely, the process of becoming, which is determinate in virtue of containing the two components of being and nothing that continually resolve themselves into one another (*SL* 82, 105 f.). This emergence of becoming is of capital importance, for it builds a development of determinacy that takes no given determinacy for granted. As such, it can be considered the first positive deed of a foundation-free, nonmetaphysical science of determinacy.

As for what would finally result from the development from being, this much can be anticipated from the immanent character of the advance: If the development from being is to have any conclusion, this cannot be certified by any external reflection upon the succession of preceding determinations. The last determination must itself be so structured as to relate all the preceding ones together as constitutive elements of the whole that is both their result and underlying unity. In this way, the self-determination from being can close with itself and come to a conclusion all its own.

In the *Science of Logic,* Hegel attempts to show that being does give rise to a self-determining succession of categories that comes to conclude itself in just such a final determination. Terming the latter the "Absolute Idea," Hegel appropriately describes how it comprises a retrospective ordering of all the preceding categories in terms of the whole in which they result (*SL* 829, 838). As such, it is itself their totality, the ultimate subject of the development that has being for its pure beginning. Since the Absolute Idea here builds the ordering principle of its own unfolded content of determination, it comprises the method by which the discourse has proceeded. Consequently, if Hegel's effort be taken in earnest and there be granted a presuppositionless development from being, both its method and subject matter can only be said to emerge at the very conclusion. This feature is precisely what distinguishes systematic philosophy from all other types of discourse. Because in it, both method and subject matter get established as a *result* of its own development, instead of being presupposed, systematic philosophy can overcome the dilemmas of foundationalism and achieve self-grounding legitimacy.

Of course, in abeyance of a fully worked-out phenomenology, the very possibility of such a discourse must remain an open question. Furthermore, even if the starting point of being were thus secured, only a completed development from it could indicate what new science would result.

Certainly, it has yet to be shown whether Hegel or any one else has actually fulfilled the task of phenomenology or that of the systematic philosophy that might follow. Nevertheless, the unexpired tradition of metaphysics perenially leaves its challenges before us, together with the old adage that philosophy at its start is but an empty word.

2
Dialectical Logic and the Conception of Truth

If philosophy is to legitimate its own quest for truth, it must somehow establish the authority of reason. To this end, logic must bear special consideration.

LOGIC AND RATIONAL ARGUMENT

All logic is either descriptive or prescriptive. Descriptive logic describes how given arguments and given conventions of reasoning are ordered. Since descriptive logic is limited to analyzing the factual operations of reasoning, it is a positive science whose results can offer nothing of juridical importance for the philosophical task of determining how reason should operate to transform opinion into truth. All descriptive logic can provide are judgments concerning how arguments have been made—judgments relative to the honesty, interpretive perspicacity, and observational accuracy of the descriptive logician, as well as to the representative character of the data selected for analysis. Not only do these judgments of fact have no relevance to the normative evaluation of how thought should operate, but they cannot pretend to offer any definitive account of the reality of argument, given the relative character of factual knowledge.

Prescriptive logic, on the other hand, does not describe how reasoning operates, but rather prescribes how it should proceed to think the truth. Although one may very well question whether prescriptive logic has in fact been properly developed, it makes no sense to argue that there can be no prescriptive, but only descriptive logic. If one takes such a position, advocated by Quine[1] and many others, one effectively asserts that thinking has no juridical standards that are objectively valid, but only opined standards, based upon subjective assumptions, linguistic usage, cultural tradition, pragmatic agreement, or some other unjustified factor. If thought is so limited, there is no choice but to do no more than describe its operations and deconstruct its operative canons in terms of the factors conditioning them. As much as this position has found wide acclaim, it is as totally absurd as any form of absolute skepticism. Those who wish to universalize descriptive logic to the exclusion of prescriptive logic patently contradict themselves by denying the possibility of objectively true reasoning while at the same time making putatively objective arguments concerning the structure of all rationality. If they were to be consistent, these thinkers would have to admit that their characterization of reasoning is itself a mere opinion with no more argumentative weight than opposing views.

Nevertheless, even if no rational argument can be given to deny the possibility of prescriptive logic, any attempt to develop prescriptive logic seems to involve a hopelessly paradoxical dilemma: Namely, if prescriptive logic provides the canon of thought that makes argument rational and able to supply justification, then how can prescriptive logic be properly determined without presupposing the standard of rationality it should supply? Does it make sense at all to speak of a prescriptive logic as a canon of thought if the very principles of prescriptive logic cannot be rationally justified without already being taken for granted?

This vicious circularity seems to open the door to skepticism, even if skepticism is paradoxical on its own terms. For, if no prescriptive logic can be defended without presupposing itself, rational argument seems to be impossible. Or, conversely stated, insofar as all argument must conform to the canons of prescriptive logic to be certified as rational, there is no way to decide between competing candidates for prescriptive logic since each one will satisfy the requirement of conforming to the principles of prescriptive logic by conforming to itself.

Somehow this problem must be surmounted if prescriptive logic is to be possible and philosophical reason is to achieve self-justification.

Historically, philosophers have offered three fundamentally different candidates for prescriptive logic that indeed appear to exhaust the possible structures of reason. These alternatives are formal, transcendental, and dialectical logic.

FORMAL LOGIC AND THE QUEST FOR TRUTH

Not illogically, the candidate for prescriptive logic to have been first developed is formal logic. Both its motivation and character are defined by the recourse to given determination that underlies its approach to the conception of rational argument. Formal logic as a normative canon of thought rests upon the understanding, so forcefully propounded by Aristotle,[2] that reasons can be supplied to justify opinions only if there is some antecedently apprehended given principle upon which justification can rest. If, on the contrary, justification must be pursued without a given principle to serve as an accepted ultimate reason for all others, then it would appear that no justified reason can ever be supplied, since the reasons needed to provide justification would ever be wanting justification for themselves, due to the infinite regress of legitimating reasons requiring others to back them up. Consequently, it would seem that rational argument must proceed from some given determinacy whose authority need not be based on any other and proceed according to some given method whose procedure is similarly unmediated by any other. Only then will the move from the given determinacy supporting all further reasons have a form that can be legitimate instead of being undermined by the same sort of infinite regress whose avoidance seemed to necessitate some given content at the base of all argument. What this suggests is that the reason supplying reasons transforming opinion into truth will have a structure characterizable by a formal logic where both the primitive terms of reasoning and the form of reasoning are given. It follows that thinking can then be characterized in abstraction from what is thought insofar as reasoning will invariably have certain given premises and functions underlying all its applications.

All the other basic features of formal logic as a canon of reason are directly entailed from the recourse to given determinacy it employs to rescue justification. Since reason is here held to have primitive terms or premises from which it proceeds, together with given operations that underlie its reasoning, the formal logic of thought is a deductive logic whose results are purely analytic in character. Insofar as thought has a formal structure, whose primitive terms and functions are not determined by thinking but given prior to its exercise, all further content of thought must derive from an external source, be it intuition, imagination, the given wealth of language, or something else. As a consequence, thought does not generate new content but only arrives at what is in conformity with its primitive terms and invariable functions. What results from the deductive reasoning of formal logic are thus purely analytic conclusions contained in the premises and externally supplied propositions, as modified by the given operations of thought. In effect, the ensuing reasoning is entirely tautological and, as such, is governed by the principle of contradiction that ordains that justification is achieved provided the justified opinion does not contradict any of the premises and given content from which they are derived.

This leads to a conception of truth that is entirely formal. If reasoning must operate with given terms and functions and come to analytic conclusions in conformity with the principle of contradiction, the truth it justifies possesses no other distinction from unjustified opinion than that the thinking of it is self-consistent. What such reason contributes to the quest for truth is knowledge of one thing and one alone, the correspondence of thought with itself. As a whole, then, logic can here be understood to be nothing but reason's self-understanding of how it can stand in conformity with itself. Consequently, if formal logic be taken as the exclusive arbiter of rationality, then reasoning provides only the formal criterion of truth entailed in the coherence, or self-consistency, of argument.

As common as this characterization of reason may be, its adoption has been plagued by conceptual difficulties.

The more trivial of these are the dilemmas that arise when formal logic is given ontological status by being treated not just as a canon but as an organon of reason, prescribing not simply how reason can conform to itself but how it can correspond to, and so truly conceive, reality. This confused position is pursued by dialectical materialism as it is classically formulated by Engels, canonized by Lenin, and ritualized by his successors. Although dialectical materialism pretends to offer a dialectical logic, it actually characterizes reason in terms of a formal logic of contradiction consisting in an assortment of logical operators and functions that are just as given prior to all and every exercise of reasoning as the analogous terms in the deductive logic of Aristotle.[3] In offering these givens, dialectical materialism does not just stipulate the laws of reason without subjecting them to critique; it further presupposes the correspondence of thought and reality, treating its formal logic of contradiction as a metaphysical principle ordering reality as well as thought. Indeed, even if its logic of contradiction were common to reality and thought, that logic could not specify the relation of identity *and* difference that correspondence involves. As a result, dialectical materialism would have to provide some other principle or principles of unity to guarantee the ontological role of dialectics—something it cannot do without abandoning the postulated primacy of its formal logic of contradiction.

This problem, however, is of secondary importance to the basic dilemma dialectical materialism faces in justifying either the logic it stipulates for reason or the application of that logic to being and the correspondence of thought and reality it is intended to secure. Because dialectical materialism conceives thought to have a given structure defined by a variety of operators and laws, there is no way it can possibly escape the vicious circularity of having to employ those rules in any reasoned attempt to justify them.

It is this problem that ultimately undermines the whole enterprise of advancing formal logic as a canon, let alone an organon, of reason. The example of logical positivism exhibits this particularly clearly, for unlike dialectical materialism, logical positivism resolutely accepts the formal consequences of characterizing reason in terms of given structures and avoids the fallacies entailed in applying formal logic to reality. Identifying reason and rational argument with deductive reasoning, logical positivism consistently concludes that all a *priori* knowledge is analytic, consisting in tautologies governed by the principle of contradiction. By contrast, all synthetic knowledge is judged to be empirical and subject to all the uncertainties endemic to empirical knowing. Logical positivism recognizes that the presumed analyticity of *a priori* knowledge, codified in formal logic, has by itself no relation to objective truth and rejects as analytically indemonstrable and empirically unverifiable any assumption of the correspondence of thought and reality. Further, in the strict form advanced by Ayer,[4] logical positivism refrains from claiming that the relations of analyticity expressed in formal logic comprise the essential form of meaningful speech, or the universally valid form of reason's correspondence with itself. If logical positivism were to make these claims, it would immediately fall victim to the dilemma of having to justify its candidate for the canon of reason and of being unable to do so without taking it for granted.

To avoid this problem, logical positivists like Ayer take the analyticity of reason to be ultimately a matter of convention, reflecting the meanings of terms as they are pragmatically accepted in linguistic usage. This, of course, sets the stage for challenging the whole analytic-synthetic distinction, as Quine and his followers have done,[5] for it reduces analyticity to something that can only be descriptively, rather than prescriptively, determined through observing the conventions of discourse. The result is that logical positivism adopts the skeptical view that philosophy must be analytic in the sense of limiting itself to pointing out the consistency or inconsistency of the linguistic usage of the terms employed in articulating the synthetic knowledge obtained from experience. Although this might make it seem that logical positivism gives up altogether the enterprise of prescriptive logic, this is not the case for the fundamental reason that logical positivism does not offer its reduction of reason to deductive reasoning as a matter of convention and empirical happenstance but as the irreducible fate of thought, excluding all theories to the contrary.

By giving its blanket characterization of reasoning this juridical role, logical positivism puts itself in the self-annulling position of affirming a doctrine of reason whose own validity can neither be empirically verified nor analytically established.

What the plight of logical positivism underlines is the ultimate absurdity of claiming that all *a priori* knowledge is analytic and that deductive reasoning can be the principle of rationality. It is absurd to claim that all *a priori* knowledge is analytic because that very claim is itself synthetic, depending upon an antecedent acceptance of entailment that first makes it possible to count on any analysis whatsoever. Similarly, deductive reasoning cannot be the model of philosophical argument, for, as Plato and Aristotle pointed out,[6] all deduction ultimately rests upon nondeducible premises and canons of deduction that would have to be justified by some other form of cognition. In each respect, the conclusion is the same: Formal logic cannot provide reason with a canon, for reliance upon any given determinacy leaves reason ruled by dogmatically accepted principles for which no justification can be coherently offered. Not even the introduction of an intuitive intelligence to apprehend immediately the indemonstrable premises and procedures of formal logic can salvage the latter's prescriptive role. Plato's and Aristotle's recourse to intuition of first principles in order to ground deductive reasoning may testify to awareness of a serious problem, but it only resurrects the same dilemma of rooting justification in something given that is, as such, beyond justification. Just as formal logic cannot account for the legitimacy of its own rules of thought, so intelligence cannot justify its intuitions without introducing reasons that undermine the foundational primacy of what it intuits as first principle.

THE IMPASSE OF TRANSCENDENTAL LOGIC

Transcendental logic is explicitly designed to resolve the difficulties that come to the fore when formal logic is offered as a prescriptive doctrine of reason. Recognizing the incoherence of restricting *a priori* knowledge to analytic conclusions and the uncritical dogmatism of conceiving reason to be ordered by given terms and functions, the proponents of transcendental philosophy tie the self-legitimation of philosophical thought to the acquisition of synthetic *a priori* knowledge consisting in a logic specifying the conditions whereby knowing can have knowledge that is in conformity with the object of cognition. This transcendental logic was first developed by Kant in a confusedly incomplete manner in which the conditions of objective knowledge applied only to objects of experience—with the result that the rules of the understanding were relegated to formal logic, while knowledge of the structure of experience was left to a standpoint whose authority was never critically established. Subsequent thinkers, such as Fichte and Husserl, were well aware of the fact that if transcendental logic was developed only with regard to the knowing of objects of experience, then both the rules of the understanding and the reasoning of the transcendental philosopher would be accepted without having their own objectivity established. For the latter to be accomplished, the scope of transcendental logic would have to be radically extended to incorporate the determination of the conditions of the possibility for knowing not only objects of experience but objects of thought in general, including transcendental logic itself.

The project of transcendental logic is accordingly best understood by leaving aside the peculiarities of Kantian philosophy and considering instead the general endeavor of the transcendental turn in relation to the basic problems of prescriptive logic.

Confronting the failure of previous attempts to base truth in some privileged givenness, transcendental logic seeks to salvage justification by conceiving rational validity to lie in what is determined by some privileged determiner. This determiner is the transcendental condition that plays the same role whether it be characterized as noumenal subjectivity, intentionality, *Dasein,* communicative competence, language games, or the hermeneutic situation. Whatever its guise, the transcendental condition provides for objective knowledge, meaningful speech, or, if one will, just the ongoing conversation of mankind by comprising a structure determining the object of knowing in its relation to knowing so as to permit knowledge to conform to its object, whether that object be an actual thing or a conceptual or linguistic content.

Transcendental logic turns to develop objective validity in these terms of determined determinacy in light of the basic objectivity problem of knowledge. So long as what is knowable is available to knowing only as knowledge and the object of knowing has a given determinacy to which knowledge must conform to be true, there seems to be no way to certify any correspondence of knowledge and its object, since knowing must always refer to what it knows to evaluate its knowledge claims. If, however, the structure of knowing, or reference, if one adopts a linguistic perspective, determines the object so that its very givenness is a content constituted by that structure, then the correspondence between that object and the reference to it can be secured, since the object would conform to the structure of knowing, and knowing would be in a position to know what it had put into the object. Synthetic *a priori* knowledge would then be possible, for the determined determinacy of the object of knowing would be a new content, rather than an analytic given, and yet be determined by a structure underlying and therefore prior to all particular acts of reference of "experience."

On this basis, objectivity would consist in contents, be they of concepts, meanings, or things, that are conditioned rather than unconditioned and self-determined. If, following Kant, one were to acknowledge that a universal that determines its own particulars and an individual that is a law unto itself are both unconditioned, then one would have to grant that the particulars of objectivity would here be subject to given laws, just as valid universals would apply to independently given particulars. Significantly, this would hold just as much for corporeal things as for thinking, for if reason is to be an object of knowledge, it would have to fulfill the same conditions.

When transcendental logic proceeds to specify the conditions of knowing in their determining role, entailing all the above mentioned features, it must somehow avoid making immediate reference to givenness, be it of the object of knowing or of knowing itself, while equally avoiding falling into solipsism whereby the object of knowledge and all standards of truth are mere postulates. These troubles arise the moment transcendental logic launches its explication of the conditions of objective knowing as something that must be performed before any actual knowledge claims can be justified. In the absence of such preliminary inquiry, all putative knowledge would seem to assume that certainty guarantees truth—which is to say that knowing conforms to real and conceptual objectivity. Transcendental logic, however, itself presumes a certain knowledge of its own; namely, that knowing or reference can be examined independently of actual knowledge and its particular objects. In this respect, transcendental logic effectively follows formal logic in viewing reason to have a formal character underlying all its operations.

At the same time, though, transcendental logic does seek to show how all that is objective in thought and reality is determined without reliance upon any dogmatically accepted givens. If this striving is taken seriously, then transcendental logic cannot legitimately refer to the immediate givenness of a thing-in-itself or to any other content given independently of transcendental constitution. Conversely, if transcendental logic is to succeed in distinguishing objective knowledge from opinion, then it must somehow determine the object of knowledge without reducing it to an arbitrary stipulation of knowing. In other words, what is an object of thought must be immanent to knowing, as something constituted in terms of its structure, and transcendent, as something that is nonetheless more than a subjective representation. This must be true whether the object of thought is a real thing or a concept, for in either case, the absence of distinguishable aspects of immanence and transcendence, or of reference and referent, removes the possibility of establishing its objective validity.

Although Kant undermines his own transcendental logic by retaining reference to a thing-in-itself and limiting transcendental constitution to objects of experience, his transcendental deduction of the categories presents a strategy that transcendental logic must follow if it is to secure objectivity of knowledge. What Kant indicates there is that solipsism can be avoided and objectivity retained only if the conditions of knowledge are one and the same as the conditions of the givenness of the object of knowledge. Then transcendental logic could specify the principles of objective truth since what would make knowledge or reference possible would also supply the independent givenness of the referent of knowing, and do so such that knowledge could correspond to it. The possibility of synthetic *a priori* knowledge would thus be secured for thought would be able to know in a justifiable manner objects that are neither stipulations of thought nor conclusions analytically deduced from such assumptions. If this possibility extended beyond objects of experience to the concepts and procedures of reason itself, then transcendental logic would be in a position to supply the self-justification of thought philosophy requires.

Try as it may, however, transcendental logic cannot possibly succeed in this endeavor due to the inexpungable element of givenness that underlies its argument. This element is none other than the content of the transcendental condition. Because it is the determining condition of objective knowledge, it cannot possibly possess the character of being transcendentally constituted, which is what is supposed to insure that an object of thought can have validity. The logical reason for this is that a determiner determines what is other than itself and thus has a character of its own antecedent to its act of determination. Indeed, it is precisely this unconditioned givenness of its own content that allows it to be the condition of what it determines. If, however, objectivity lies in being determined by the conditions of true knowledge, then these conditions cannot themselves enjoy objective validity. Simply by investigating the conditions of knowing as a necessary prelude to the attainment of objective knowledge, transcendental logic places itself in an insoluble situation. Although it rightly criticizes the dogmatic acceptance of givenness in prescriptive formal logic, transcendental logic cannot remove its own dependence upon givenness without forsaking its explication of the transcendental conditions of knowledge. As much as transcendental logic might seek to redeem the autonomy of reason from dogmatism, it reduces that autonomy to a formal liberty in which the spontaneity of reason operates within a given framework that it can never justify or criticize.

It might appear that transcendental logic could escape this bind if the standpoint of the transcendental logician could be equalized with the knowing it examines so that the knowing of transcendental logic would be constituted with the same objectivity that it mandates for valid knowledge. Then reference to the transcendental conditions of knowledge would no longer be a dogmatic assertion of a given, unconstituted foundation. If this could be accomplished, allowing the critique of knowing to become identical to the knowing under critique, then the element of givenness in the transcendental condition would be eliminated. Instead of determining something else, the transcendental condition would now determine itself, so that rather than being something given, it would be determined in accord with the transcendental logic whose substance it is. In effect, transcendental logic would become a self-determining logic of objectivity, whose explication of the possibility of true knowledge would satisfy the same requirements it establishes for valid objects of thought.

Although the problems of transcendental logic certainly point to such a solution, the latter's attainment would actually cancel the entire transcendental enterprise. This is because the whole of transcendental logic rests upon the premise that the conditions of knowing can be antecedently investigated without introducing actual knowledge claims about particular objects of thought. Only then does it make sense to speak of transcendental conditions of knowing, insofar as these can be juridical conditions of knowing rather than conditioned objects of knowledge, only if the object of knowing can be distinguished from the structure of knowing. If, on the contrary, transcendental logic were to become self-determining, so that the knowledge it examines were the same knowing exercised by the transcendental logician, then the distinction between knowledge and its object would disappear, making impossible any investigation of knowing that is prior to that of its object. This leaves transcendental logic at an impasse: either it accepts the given character of the transcendental condition and succumbs to the reliance upon givenness it seeks to repudiate, or it eliminates that element and annuls itself. However it proceeds, transcendental logic cannot supply the self-legitimation of reason philosophy demands.

DIALECTICAL LOGIC AND SELF-DETERMINATION

Although the problems of transcendental logic bring it to the verge of self-elimination, this outcome does not signal the hopelessness of reason's quest for self-justification. Taken together with the failure of prescriptive formal logic, it teaches instead that philosophy cannot be presuppositionless and self-grounding if it relies on either given or determined determinacy to supply reason with its order and validity. So long as reasoning is stamped with any residue of givenness, it remains shackled to an assumed content that deprives it of the unconditioned universality it needs to provide justification and transform opinion into truth. In demonstrating this through its own demise, transcendental logic nevertheless points beyond itself to an alternative prescriptive logic that does not succumb to such problems.

This is dialectical logic, whose mandate follows directly from the central dilemma of the transcendental turn. As we have seen, in order for transcendental logic to avoid dogmatically asserting the conditions of knowing, it had to become self-determining—something it could not do without canceling itself by eliminating the givenness of the transcendental conditions, which alone allows them to be what they are, the antecedent determiners of objectivity. This suggests that prescriptive logic must indeed conceive reason as self-determined determinacy to escape dogmatism, but that this solution can be achieved only when reason has neither any privileged givenness nor determiner at its root.

Dialectical logic takes up this challenge and attempts to work out a logic with no primitive terms or principles. In undertaking this unparalleled endeavor, dialectical logic testifies that presuppositionlessness, self-grounding, and unconditioned universality all consist in self-determination. As novel as this may sound, the plausibility of developing self-determined determinacy or self-determination as a candidate for prescriptive logic is apparent the moment it is examined in light of these qualities that reason must possess to justify its own privileged role in seeking truth.

First of all, self-determination enjoys or, indeed, *is* identical with presuppositionlessness to the extent that what is neither given nor determined but self-determined rests on nothing antecedent to itself. Although self-determination gives itself determinacy, it has no element of givenness whatsoever, for, unlike a determiner such as the choosing will, self-determination does not have any content or form until it has determined itself. Consequently, self-determination exhibits a freedom from givenness so radical that it can only be conceived to issue from nothing at all. Self-determination must, in other words, begin from sheer indeterminacy, for otherwise it would rest on a foundation that it has not determined, leaving it dependent rather than free.

Similarly, self-determined determinacy is totally self-grounding insofar as whatever form or content it has is a product of itself. Because self-determination proceeds from nothing and generates its own order and substance without reference to anything else, all its aspects and relations rest upon what it has determined itself to be, which is nothing other than self-determined determinacy. Accordingly, what self-determination *is* can only be determined at the conclusion of its own process of determination, since until then, the "content" of self-determined determinacy is not yet at hand. Conversely, the "form" or, if one will, the "logic" of its determining is also available no sooner than the conclusion of self-determination, for the reason that the ordering principle of its content is none other than what has here given itself its own determination. Indeed, to speak of a "form" and "content" of self-determination is inappropriate since neither can be distinguished from the other. The content of self-determination is nothing other than its own self-ordering, just as its form is this same content that orders itself.

All of this presuppositionless, self-grounding interpenetration of form and content signifies that self-determination is unconditionally universal or, to put it more precisely, that self-determination is unconditioned universality itself. Because self-determined determinacy owes its entire character to itself, nothing conditions it. Thus, even though it has a determinate content, what is particular about it is neither limited with regard to any given circumstance nor relative to anything other than itself. The determinacy of self-determination instantiates only itself, and it is this independence that gives it a universality free of all conditions.

In this respect, the unity of self-determination has a very special relation to the particular content of which it is the "self." It is universal with regard to its own determinacy because the latter is nothing but its instantiation. At the same time, however, the self-identity of the subject of self-determination is a universality indistinguishable from its particular content, for it is the latter's unity by being the very same self-determined determinacy in which that content consists. As such, its universality in respect to its particular determinacy is a concrete universality, containing its particularization within its unity, just as its particularization is a universal particular, containing the very process of self-determination that it instantiates. If individuality consists in a unification of universal and particular, where the uniqueness of its particular content comprises the general identity of the individual, then self-determination can be said to exhibit the structure of individuality, or, rather, self-determination is the determinacy of individuality.

Of course, it might be suspected that self-determined determinacy can be ascribed the requisite features of presuppositionlessness, self-grounding, and unconditioned universality only insofar as one presupposes what self-determination is as well as what philosophy must be to think the truth. It turns out, however, that if one simply follows out what results from totally excluding assumptions, from eliminating all given determinacies and determiners, from dispensing with all formal and transcendental logic, one arrives at self-determination and with it, at everything that self-justification seems to require.

To begin without any assumptions is to begin with nothing at all—that is, with indeterminacy. If anything were to follow from nothing without illicit introduction of any independently given content or given process of determination, it would have to arise out of indeterminacy in a totally self-generated way. Since nothing else would be available to provide it with character, what it is would have to be self-determined. However, because it would not be the self-determination of any given substrate but a self-determination issuing from indeterminacy, incorporating nothing to start with, it would have to be self-determination per se. Then, it would possess the radically self-grounding, unconditionally universal, and individual character already indicated.

Clearly, even if it were true that the only thing that could arise from indeterminacy were self-determination, this would not guarantee that anything can follow from it. Indeed, it can well be objected that any attempt to begin from a presuppositionless starting point invites theoretical anarchy and that without given premises and arbitrary stipulations, nothing at all could ever possibly result.

In answer to this objection, it should first be noted that proceeding from indeterminacy by developing self-determination does not amount to conceptual chaos. To forego reliance upon all given methodological principles and all assumptions regarding subject matter is not equivalent to giving free reign to the arbitrariness of the theorist. To allow both method and content to issue from the unguided caprice of the latter would hardly be congruent with presuppositionless science and the development of self-determination. It would rather comprise a science issuing from a privileged determiner, the theoretical anarchist, and would therefore consist not in self-determined determinacy but in a determined subject matter owing its form and content to the arbitrary stipulating performed by that theorizer.

If, then, presuppositionlessness and self-determination are not synonymous with conceptual anarchy, it is nonetheless true that there can be no *positive* criteria with which to judge whether a particular candidate for dialectical logic has properly developed its putatively presuppositionless, self-grounding subject matter. Any application of positive criteria must be precluded because it would involve reference to standards of method and content that would not be generated within what is to be judged but externally given. Consequently, such criteria could have no validity, for they would have to be or rest upon assumptions insofar as they are not elements of the self-determination from indeterminacy that presuppositionlessness could alone entail.

That there can be no positive criteria for judging dialectical logic does not, however, rob it of necessity and leave it unsusceptible to critical validation. On the contrary, it is just the absence of prior criteria that allows for theoretical necessity in the first place. After all, what leaves all criterialogical knowing victim to skeptical challenge is precisely the very dilemma of evaluating truth on the basis of given criteria, which, as such, must lie outside the purvey of truth itself. The scientific rigor of a candidate for dialectical logic can be evaluated instead in a purely negative fashion by making sure that none of its determinations owe their character or order of presentation to introductions of extraneously given material or the positing of an extraneous determiner.

Although these points may suggest how dialectical logic could develop self-determined determinacy presuppositionlessly without succumbing to theoretical anarchy, they do not themselves indicate how any move can be made beyond indeterminacy to something determinate. In other words, the question of why there should be determinacy is not yet answered. That question can nevertheless only be asked by dialectical logic, since any theorizing that operates with given determinacy takes determinacy for granted and so cannot account for this most common and basic of assumptions, which, so long as it is assumed, seals the dogmatism of the discourse in which it figures.

A plausible answer to this question is provided by Hegel in the opening sections of his *Science of Logic*, a work that today still represents the only comprehensive attempt to conceive a presuppositionless, self-grounding dialectical logic consisting in the presentation of self-determined determinacy. What Hegel offers in his discussion of being, nothing, and becoming is an account of determinacy that takes no determinacy for granted.[7] The solution he points to can be understood in an admittedly anticipatory way along the following lines.

To begin with, an advance from indeterminacy to something determinate cannot be caused or grounded or have any reason behind it at all. To search for any would entail imputing to indeterminacy a definite character—namely, that of being a determining principle. This, however, would violate the constitutive nothingness of indeterminacy and reintroduce an element of givenness precluding presuppositionlessness. Accordingly, if anything were to follow from indeterminacy, it would have to arise utterly immediately without any grounds for doing so simply because there would literally be nothing determinate underlying it to serve as a mediating reason.

One could thus say that the proper answer to the question "Why is there determinacy?" is that there is and can be no reason, for any attempt to assign one presupposes determinacy by treating indeterminacy as if it were a definite determiner. All that can be offered in answer is an account of *how* indeterminacy gives rise to something else. What is clear from the start is that what follows from indeterminacy must do so immediately, which is to say, without reason, and without being determined by anything.

Analogously, what follows from indeterminacy must not only be uncaused, ungrounded, and undetermined in any way, but it must be whatever it is without involving contrast to anything determinate and without containing any element of givenness, which, not having any ground in indeterminacy, could only be present by virtue of some inadmissible introduction.

This means that the only thing that could follow from indeterminacy without recourse to givenness or a given determiner is *nothing* and that nothing could only arise immediately from indeterminacy. When Hegel moves from "being" to "nothing" in his *Science of Logic*, he is suggesting just this groundless passage from indeterminacy to an indistinguishable nothingness.

Admittedly, the groundless "presence" of nothing hardly signifies an emergence of determinacy. It does, however, entail something more than itself and the sheer indeterminacy from which it cannot be differentiated. With nothing one has a "second" category that, because it cannot be differentiated from indeterminacy (or "being" as Hegel calls it), immediately passes over into indeterminacy or, to be more precise, is at once indeterminacy without any passage at all. Similarly, indeterminate being no less passes over into nothing, for it is utterly identical to what alone can immediately follow from it without further support. As a whole, then, the groundless succession of nothing from being involves at one and the same time the immediate transitions of being into nothing and nothing into being. Although this process has nothing determinate within it among its component elements, it comprises something that as a whole is distinguishable from them, the twin indeterminacies figuring within it. Consequently, it can be appropriately named "becoming" and designate something distinguishable from being and nothing. In this regard, it is determinate, and, more significantly, it comprises a determinacy that issues from nothing determinate at all. Consequently, the move from being to nothing to becoming that Hegel describes can be understood to provide an account of how there is determinacy without taking any determinacy for granted.

If this at least suggests how dialectical logic might get off the ground in presenting determinacies through which self-determination constitutes itself presuppositionlessly, it still leaves unclear what relation the ensuing dialectical logic has to the self-justification of reason and the quest for truth.

Certainly, if dialectical logic could be said to present any argument at all, it would not be in the manner of the deductive reasoning of formal logic or the constitution of transcendental logic. Although it would be improper to say that dialectical logic is predetermined by any antecedent motivation, what does provide the historical motive for taking it seriously is the recognition that philosophical argument cannot consist in either deductive reasoning or transcendental constitution insofar as each relies upon unjustifiable premises. Dialectical logic may indeed make use of propositions in explicating self-determination, but what it presents cannot be guided or legitimated by any propositional calculus, rules of syllogism, or logic of discovery.

In this regard, the argument of dialectical logic would be neither analytic nor synthetic in the customary sense in which these terms are used. Dialectical logic would no more analyze what is already present in a given subject matter than judge synthetically how given concepts are connected to one another in virtue of something external to them. As Hegel suggests,[8] dialectical logic would rather proceed analytically and synthetically at once, insofar as everything it conceives would be both contained in the ultimate determinacy that is determining itself and not yet given in the preceding determinacies that are stages in the self-determination proceeding through and incorporating them.

All this signifies that the "argument" of dialectical logic would reside in the completely self-grounded character of what it presents. The justification of the ordering and content of this subject matter would have to lie in nothing other than the fact that both owe their determinacy entirely to themselves. If they do, their presentation achieves the perennial aim of all philosophical discourse, the aim of accounting within itself for every aspect of its own inquiry. Since, furthermore, what is offered is self-determination, one could even say that dialectical logic succeeds in attaining self-justification by presenting the very logic or determinacy of self-justification itself.

Be this as it may, it still cannot be claimed that dialectical logic is a logic of thinking or a logic of reality. Because dialectical logic presents self-determination per se rather than the self-determination of a given content, its categories are not categories of reality anymore than of thought. They are instead categories of determinacy without further qualification. Possessing this unprecedented formality, dialectical logic is therefore neither an ontology of true being nor an epistemology of true knowledge. How then can dialectical logic contribute at all to reason's self-justification and the attainment of truth? Even if dialectical logic does uncover in self-determination the structure of presuppositionlessness, unconditioned universality, and self-grounding, how does this solve philosophy's preeminent dilemma?

By itself, dialectical logic provides but a partial and seemingly paradoxical answer to these questions. Through its deed of developing self-determination as presuppositionless, self-grounding determinacy, dialectical logic indicates that the whole enterprise of prescriptive logic is misguided so long as it seeks the self-justification of reason's determinacy without first investigating determinacy per se. Failing this most elementary investigation, any theory of reason or reality succumbs to the dogmatism of taking determinacy for granted. Dialectical logic avoids this error by taking the problem of presuppositionlessness and self-justification to its radical extreme and providing a theory of determinacy in which no givenness is assumed. In so doing, dialectical logic does not prescribe rules of thought nor principles of reality, but instead conceives the true categories of determinacy. Their truth resides not in any correspondence to reality or thought but in the presuppositionlessness and unconditioned universality they possess as elements of self-determined determinacy. Only with them at hand is it possible to advance to a conception of reason and reality free from the hold of opinion. That conception, however, lies beyond the reach of dialectical logic insofar as reality in general and thinking in particular incorporate determinacy with further qualification.[9] For this reason, dialectical logic is only a first, yet necessary step in philosophy's quest for truth and self-justification. Until this step is taken, philosophy will have no other choice but to seek refuge in the cul-de-sacs of deductive reasoning and transcendental argument, languishing in bewildered retreat from the absurd appeals of skepticism.

3
Conceiving Something Without Any Conceptual Scheme

THE SELF-EVIDENCE OF THE CATEGORY OF SOMETHING

What it is to be determinate, to have quality, to be something hardly appears to be a problem worthy of thought. How could anything be more self-evident or familiar or resistant to questioning? It seems virtually impossible to be unacquainted with the category of something, whether in reality or in thought or speech. To encounter anything real at all is to encounter something, whereas to think or speak any intelligible content is already to refer to something thought or spoken. Indeed, it is unimaginable how one could fail to understand something, since if one did lack all notion of something, there would be nothing determinate to understand or encounter.

Yet despite the ubiquitous self-evidence of categories of determinate being, of quality, of something, philosophers have unremittingly asked, "What is something?" and offered manifold discordant answers. To some extent, the divergence of response has been due to the varied way in which the question has been formulated. Some have posed the problem in a narrowly ontological form, where what is at issue is how something can be in reality. Others have treated the question in a narrowly epistemological manner, focusing their concern upon what something is as an object of knowledge. Still others have limited their inquiry to the semantic or psychological problems of how something can be meant in speech or represented in thought. Each of these formulations comprises a different question calling for a different answer, to the extent that meaning, representation, knowledge, and reality can be distinguished. For just this reason, no such formulation inquires into what something is per se, as a category. All these formulations instead consider the category of something as it is further qualified by being meant, represented, realized, or known. However, since these further qualifications involve an application of the category of something, the controversies specific to their formulations can hardly be addressed without accounting for the category itself. It is here, in this account, which all ontological, epistemological, psychological, and semantic considerations take for granted when they apply the category, that the philosophical controversy surrounding something is rooted.

Admittedly, much if not most philosophical debate concerning what something is has committed the category mistake of confusing ontological, epistemological, psychological, or semantic explanations with the account of something per se. This has occurred even though all such efforts automatically neglect and presuppose the categorial exposition by addressing something from the outset with added qualifications. Eliminating this confusion, however, does not augur any easy resolution to the philosophical problem that something presents. For the moment something is itself called into question rather than treated as an unproblematic given, analyzable straight away in its relation to reality, knowing, or meaning, the possibility of a categorial account seems as paradoxical as it is indispensable.

Since things, representations, meanings, reasons, and knowledge are all something to the extent that they are determinate, a philosophical account of something finds itself in the peculiar position of being unable to employ any of these other terms as categorial elements of its exposition. If any were employed not just as means of expression but as components of the category of something, terms incorporating something would be used to determine it, causing the whole enterprise to collapse in a vicious circularity. For as soon as the category of something is specified by means of elements that are already something themselves, the question is begged.

This does not mean that an account of something must be precluded simply because all inquiry involves living individuals inhabiting a historical world using a given language to express their thoughts. None of these determinate conditions need interfere so long as no claim is made that any one of them enters in determining what is and what is not entailed in the category of something. Provided they are treated not as transcendental principles juridically determining what counts as knowledge but as conditions of all inquiry, which, as such, permit right as well as wrong theories to be thought and expressed, their contribution is a matter of indifference to the truth of what they allow to be expressed.

The real problem concerns instead how the category of something can be accounted for without being taken for granted. To explicate something without begging the question, what it is must somehow be determined without employing anything that is already determinate. In regard to qualitative determinacy in general, this signifies that an account of quality must avoid using any antecedently given qualitative terms in specifying its subject. Yet how can something be explicated if its account cannot rely upon any determinate givens?

Calling the category of something into question seems to present an insoluble dilemma. To provide a noncircular answer would appear to require accounting for determinacy with no other resource than indeterminacy. That, however, seems prima facie impossible. After all, how can the category of something be explicated in terms of nothing? Yet, if that cannot be done, all inquiry will be left resting on a dogmatic foundation consisting in the assumption of something, an assumption that is always present the moment a determinate subject matter is considered, but that can never be fully warranted if the very category of something defies analysis.

THE LURE OF THE IRREDUCIBILITY OF DETERMINACY

If this impasse does not reinstate the self-evidence of something, it provides ample incentive to evade radically questioning what it is to be determinate by acknowledging the irreducibility of something. Instead of attempting to construct something from nothing, why not take the opposite route, admit that something underlies all account of what is determinate, and attempt to conceive how every determinacy is founded on a determinate given? Logically speaking, there are two ways of pursuing this endeavor. One is to show how anything determinate is irreducibly explicable in terms of some privileged given. Alternately, one can argue that something has its determinacy in virtue of being determined by some privileged determiner.

These parallel strategies have frequently been pursued in narrowly ontological and epistemological or semantic terms, respectively. The appeal to an irreducible given has often taken the form of an identification of some real substrate as the foundation of all other determinate content, whereas the appeal to a privileged determiner has ever more commonly taken the form of a turn to the structure of consciousness, language, or culture as the ultimate arbiter of all definite meaning and knowledge. Nevertheless, both strategies involve an approach that applies as much to something as such as to how something is meant, thought, known, or realized. Only when these options are examined in their full generality can the root of their problems be exposed and remedied.

Dilemmas of the Theory of Substance

The approach that acknowledges the irreducibility of something by conceiving a given foundation for all determinacy has classically been pursued as a theory of substance. Its argumentative strategy has consisted in showing that no account can be made of any determinacy that is meant, known, or real without appeal to a given substrate on which all determinate qualities and relations are based and which all determinate things exemplify. Although the advocates of the theory of substance have disputed whether there are one or many substances, whether all or any of the qualities and relations rooted in substance are necessary or contingent, and which can be objects of different sorts of knowledge, their disputes have all rested on the acceptance of this common argumentation on behalf of substance itself.

The Justifications of Substance

Classically formulated by Aristotle, but recast and reenacted by countless others, this argument has an undeniable force in all three of its aspects.

The justification of substance in regard to meaning can be said to come first, for if substance is a precondition for meaning anything determinate, all discourse depends upon its semantic foundation. Naturally, the problem of determinacy is crucial to speech, for if words lack some specific meaning, they become meaningless, annihilating all conversation whether in the inner dialogue of thought or in discourse among individuals.[1] Yet for meaning to be determinate, what is meant must have definite attributes, and these must not all be accidental. They cannot be solely accidental, both because the accidental attributes of something would seem to be infinite and hence beyond enumeration,[2] and because there would be no fixed point of reference to which the accidents could be predicated.[3] However, for there to be attributes, either accidental or not, there must be something to which they are attributed—namely, the given subject of their predication. Although this subject must have attributes to be something definite, it must still have its own determinate character in order to be a subject of predication, in distinction from its attributes. Hence, meaning requires not only that what is meant have necessary attributes but that what is meant involve an already determinate subject of which these are predicates. In other words, for anything determinate to be meant there must be given substance—that is, a determinate substrate providing a subject of predication.

If this is the case for meaning, it must also hold true for knowledge. Knowledge is empty unless it is determinate. However, in order for anything determinate to be known, the minimal requirements of meaning must be met. For if knowledge is justified opinion and an opinion is meaningless unless it expresses something determinate, there can be no determinate knowledge unless there is a given subject of predication to provide determinacy for knowledge's warranted belief. Hence, determinate knowledge rests on substance to the extent that meaning does.

Further, if anything determinate is to be known, it cannot consist entirely in accidental attributes, since this would deprive all knowledge claims of any specific relation to their object, just as it would render what is known utterly meaningless. Hence, knowledge of anything determinate must be knowledge of something that involves a given substrate with a necessary, determinate relation to some specific qualities inhering in it. This will be true just as much of knowledge of determinate concepts as of determinate things. In each case, substance seems to enter in as an irreducible factor of knowledge.

In regard to reality, the arguments for the irreducibility of substance are fully analogous. In order for anything to have a determinate existence, how can there not be some underlying given substrate, bearing certain attributes rather than others? Although attributes may already have determinate meaning by being subjects of a predication defining their specific quality, they cannot exist by themselves without contradicting their character as commonly attributable qualities, as "third man" arguments can testify. Hence, the existence of something determinate requires a real substrate in which quality can actually inhere, a substrate that must already have its own character in distinction from its qualities simply in order to be their bearer. Further, since something becomes indistinguishable from everything else if all its qualities are accidental, the given substance can underlie a determinate being only insofar as it has a determinate relation to its attributes, where at least some are essentially its own. In these respects, the reality of something determinate depends upon presence of substance, comprising a given substrate, determined in some essential way through its attributes but without being reducible to them.

The Fatal Enigma of Substance

All of these arguments stand or fall upon the resolution of a problem vital to the irreducibility of substance. The moment one grants that something meant, known, or real has its determinacy in virtue of a given substrate in which all quality inheres and to which all relation refers, the question naturally arises as to how that given substrate can have its own determinate character independently of all the meanings, knowledge, and things that owe their determinacy to it. If everything is either substance or a quality or relation of substance, substance itself would have to be intelligible without reference to any particular substances or to any qualities or relations. Yet how can the given substrate of all qualities and relations have any definite character of its own without them?

An easy answer seems to be that substance has its own specific nature by virtue of being a composite of distinct elements—namely, form and matter, or some such contrast of essentially inhering attributes and the substrate that becomes further determined by bearing them. After all, although a given substrate of determinacy might have no specific character without some quality, it cannot just be quality. In order to be the determinate basis of quality and relation, substance must add to qualities something else that allows them to inhere in a determinate fashion and comprise an identifiable something. However, if substance is to be accounted for as the unity of such components, while maintaining its primacy as the basis of all determinacy, how can these components be something determinate in their own right prior to the formation of substance that arises from their combination?

Attributes cannot have any meaning nor be known or realized without referring to some given substance that is itself distinguished by qualities of its own. Similarly, the substrate awaiting attribution is utterly indeterminate and hence meaningless, unknowable, and nothing at all, unless it already has determinacy as something given—that is, according to the theory of substance, as a composite bearer of some quality. In either regard, the components of substance cannot provide an account of its character without taking it for granted or repudiating its constitutive role as the basis of each and every determinate something.

However, if substance cannot be determined in virtue of given definite components without falling into vicious circularity, substance will have to be determinate in virtue of what it is itself. Yet, if substance is to be determined by itself, it must lose its constitutive character as the irreducibly given something on which all determinacy rests. For if it has any irreducibly given character, it has qualities that it does not give itself but simply bears from the outset.

Hence the appeal to substance not only begs the question, but undermines itself through the vitiating circularity of allowing what makes something determinate to be already determinate.

The Dilemma of Rooting Determinacy in a Privileged Determiner

The collapse of the theory of substance teaches that the account of something cannot lie in any given substrate—that is, in any prior something. In face of the inscrutable difficulty of conjuring something from nothing, this lesson has led more and more philosophers to refrain from claiming irreducible immediacy for any given content and to consider the category of something and all other determinations to be constituted in terms of epistemological or semantic conditions. Instead of advancing some meant or known term as the basis of all determinate being, these thinkers have taken the structures of knowing and meaning as irreducible foundations underlying the specification of each and every category, opinion, knowledge claim, and thing.

The argument on behalf of the irreducibility of such determining conditions has the same ring whether these conditions be characterized as the opposition of consciousness, the structure of language, the historical practices of culture, or a given conceptual scheme. In each case, some undeniable feature of the reality of discourse is picked out and given the privileged role of being the prior condition of all other terms.

For thinkers such as Kant and Husserl, the opposition of consciousness is unavoidably fundamental, due to the fact that all categories, meanings, knowledge, and objects of knowledge can be considered by us only as they are given in our conscious awareness. According to them, this signifies that all determinacy is mediated and determined by the structure of consciousness. Hence, as Kant suggests, the notion of an object of consciousness in general precedes the concepts of something and nothing,[4] just as the notion of a representation is indefinable and ultimately unanalyzable insofar as all terms that could be employed to account for it would already be representations themselves. By the same token, Kant admits, the pure categories are equally irreducible and indefinable, since definition is itself a judgment and hence already contains these categories insofar as they are logical functions of judgment.[5]

Similarly, thinkers such as Wittgenstein argue that insofar as all discourse operates in terms of linguistic practice, every meaning, be it qualified as a category, an opinion, a knowledge claim, or an object, is irreducibly constituted by the structure of language that is operative in its expression. What it is to mean, know, or be something can thus only be accounted for by pointing to the way language allows these terms to be signified and communicated.

Alternately, those who follow Heidegger and Gadamer in emphasizing how consciousness and discourse are imbedded in historical, practical engagements argue that these cultural practices, not just intentionality or grammar, are the basis on which all discourse rests. Hence, no matter what terms might be employed to account for the category of something, each and every one will already be determined by the practices underlying the formation of frames of reference.

In each case, all inquiry is irreducibly situated with some encompassing conceptual scheme, which plays the same foundational role whether it be rooted in the pure categories of the understanding, ideal, or ordinary language or, most concretely, in the historical practices of a given culture.

Although the appeal of these arguments cannot be denied, they all rest upon a critical maneuver whose justification is far from self-evident. In each case, conditions of discourse are identified and then elevated to determining structures that not only make possible the thought and expression of subjects of inquiry but juridically constitute what they allow to be presented. It may be true that any account of the category of something will be undertaken by conscious individuals employing the language of a particular culture in accord with a certain conceptual scheme, but this does not mean that any of these enabling conditions can determine which account of something has validity. Indeed, the very fact that all of these conditions are operative in true as well as false discourse should suggest that it makes little sense to appeal to them in resolving questions of knowledge.

Although each version of this approach confidently presumes that it offers an encompassing account for every topic imaginable, what sets in relief their common dilemma are the difficulties that arise when the category of determinacy is itself at stake. For if it is argued that what accounts for something being determinate is its constitution by some irreducible epistemic or semantic condition of discourse, the question naturally arises as to how that condition can have its own determinate character. It must not be what it is by virtue of other terms that it itself constitutes, since that would involve the circularity of taking its own specific character for granted. Yet, if the condition has a definite nature allowing it to be identified as intentionality, language games, some conceptual scheme, or whatever, how can it have this identity without involving given terms with their own qualities? If the epistemic or semantic condition in question is still to maintain its privileged position as the determining ground of all contents of discourse, how can these constitutive terms have their own character without already being mediated by the condition they determine?

If the privileged condition be identified, for instance, as the structure of consciousness, its own determination will already involve a whole slew of categories, (such as subject, object, unity, relation, self-relation, and so on), whose own meanings should derive from intentionality. The same difficulty applies to every other case. If language games be given primacy, everything making linguistic practice what it is must somehow be at hand, just as, if conceptual schemes or cultural contexts be made privileged conditions, what gives them their characteristic identity must already be determinate. Yet, none of these constitutive factors can have any prior determinacy of their own if the conditions they characterize are to be irreducible foundations of all discourse.

To escape this self-destructive question-begging, the privileged determiner of all content must somehow account for its own determinacy —that is, constitute itself as the constitutive condition of all discourse without relying upon any independently given terms. In other words, if all categories are to be dependent upon a conceptual scheme for their character, that scheme must be the source of its own specifications. If that is the case, the categorial scheme by which all terms are specified will determine the categories that give it its own identity. Then the basis of determinacy will be self-determined.

Although the appeal to the irreducibility of conceptual schemes requires such a denouement, the conditions of discourse can no more be self-determining than can be substance. In order to play its defining role as the irreducible condition of discourse, an epistemic and/or semantic structure must have its privileged givenness prior to every term it grounds. Otherwise, it loses its irreducible primacy. To be self-determined, however, a conceptual scheme could not have any given character, for if it did, it would already be something prior to its act of constitution.

For this reason, the category of something cannot be accounted for by appealing to any privileged conditions of discourse. The moment this strategy is adopted, the whole question is begged simply because something, be it a determinate category or a determinate thing, cannot owe its character as something to an independently given something, which is, after all, what any determinate condition of discourse already represents.

CONCEIVING SOMETHING WITHOUT PRIVILEGED GIVENS OR CONCEPTUAL SCHEMES

Despite its seeming self-evidence, the irreducibility of something cannot be maintained, neither in terms of some privileged given underlying all quality and relation nor in terms of some privileged determiner of contents of discourse. This signifies that any philosophy that bases its argument upon something determinate condemns itself to self-vitiating circularity and dogmatism. It also means that philosophy must account for the category of something if it is to free its argument from a dependence upon factors it cannot make intelligible. Since every definite term or principle involves determinacy, only when philosophy establishes what determinacy is can it possibly achieve a thoroughgoing clarity free of unexamined and inexplicable assumptions. Yet how can the category of something be explicated?

Clearly, its exposition cannot rely upon any given terms that are already determinate in their own right. Quality cannot be accounted for by appealing to anything qualitative, nor can something be determined in reference to factors that are independently something. Yet, if all question-begging is to be avoided, are there any viable options left?

Only two routes seem available, routes that may ultimately be no more distinct than feasible. One consists in determining determinacy by means of indeterminacy. This approach would escape the problem of circularity by appealing to the one and only resource that is not already determinate. But is indeterminacy any resource at all, let alone one from which something determinate can be categorized?

Another possibility consists in conceiving something in terms of contrastive relations among factors such that neither the relations nor the factors involved have any determinate character prior to the constitution of something in which they figure. If such a conception is possible, it would also avoid question-begging by accounting for something without employing any terms that have an independently given character. Yet can there be any such development of a contrast with no predetermination?

Perhaps the only thinker to have attempted to carry through either of these options is Hegel, who does so in his *Science of Logic* by combining both in one and the same developmental argument. In the analysis that follows, his arguments will be drawn upon to show how something can be conceived without any conceptual schemes—that is, without an appeal to independently determinate categories such as would cast the whole enterprise into a viciously circular impasse.

From Indeterminacy to Determinate Being

As we have seen, an exposition of the categories of determinacy cannot begin with any conceptual resources that already have quality and determinate being. Hence, if there is to be any categorial starting point from which something can be determined, it will have to be the category of indeterminacy, from which all quality, relation, and any other determinacy is excluded. It makes no difference whether this category be conceived as being or nothing. For if indeterminacy be thought as being that has no relation to anything else nor any distinctions within itself nor any undivided quality, it is equally nothing, signifying the utter absence of all determinacy.[6]

By itself, indeterminacy hardly provides a conceptual resource for categorizing anything other than itself. It cannot be the reason or determiner of any additional category, for then it would be ascribed the very determinate character of being a cause or principle. Furthermore, it cannot provide the means for categorizing any category whose own character rests on a contrastive relation to something determinate. Hence, if determinacy has its definite character only in distinction from the qualitative being of another determinacy, nothing determinate can possibly follow upon the category of indeterminacy. This signifies quite literally that nothing can proceed from indeterminacy in an exposition of categories, which is to say that only another indistinguishable indeterminacy can follow upon the indeterminacy with which we are forced to begin. Whether we call the former "being" and the latter "nothing" or the former "nothing" and the latter "being" makes no difference, since each lacks all distinguishing marks in order to be indeterminate. The key point is that once an account of determinacy begins as it seemingly must with the category of indeterminacy, it has nowhere to go but to another category just as indeterminate as the first.

This peculiar predicament immediately raises two questions. First, why should there be any such development from one indeterminacy to another? Second, how can such a move comprise any development at all?

The first question asks for reasons where there cannot possibly be any. Any move from indeterminacy to another category cannot possibly have a cause, a ground, or any explanatory principle at all simply because the moment any reason is offered either indeterminacy gets treated as a determiner of some sort, which violates its constitutive lack of all qualification, or some extraneous third term is surreptitiously introduced. Hence, indeterminacy can stand as a starting point of further categorial explication only insofar as what follows, follows immediately, without any ground or reason at all. To ask for any explanation is tantamount to asking for indeterminacy to be replaced by a definite determining principle, which necessarily subverts any attempt at conceiving determinacy per se.

However, even if no reason be sought for why the category of indeterminacy be followed by another category of indeterminacy, it is difficult to see how such a groundless succession involves any development. If the only successor to the category of indeterminacy can be an equally indeterminate category, which follows without any mediating principle or connection, is there any basis for claiming that an advance has been made? The moment the second category is offered, it ceases to be an advance insofar as its own indeterminacy leaves it without any mark by which it can be distinguished from the first category. If the first indeterminacy be called "being" and the second "nothing," then nothing is being, which seems to signify that a move from being to nothing is no move at all, since it just as immediately reiterates the point of departure. By the same token, the first indeterminacy, call it "being," is immediately what the second one is, nothing. Either way, the would-be succession of categories seems to vanish by itself into the selfsame indeterminacy, which neither becomes something else nor ever ceases to be at hand. If this is so, no categorial development can possibly emerge from indeterminacy, and, by extension, no account can be given of determinacy.[7]

Yet does the groundless succession of one indeterminacy by another offer no more than an undivided exposition of the same category of indeterminacy, empty and immobile? Admittedly, since the two categories are indistinguishable and their succession involves no mediating terms, it makes no sense to say that being and nothing stand in any determinate relation of which it can be unambiguously affirmed that an advance has been made from one category to another. Nevertheless, the immediate collapse of the differentiation of one indeterminacy from another, where being is nothing and nothing is being, where the second term is no sooner advanced than it is indistinguishable from the first, presents a movement that only operates insofar as there are two indeterminacies, at once different and indistinguishable. What contains them in their difference and identity is this movement itself, whose sequence of being and nothing is equally a ceasing to be, where being is followed immediately by nothing, and a coming to be, where nothing is being (*SL* 93).

Although Hegel names this movement "becoming," he is quick to admit that it does not involve the coming to be of anything determinate nor the transformation of some given something into something other (*SL* 83, 84, 87). Since its constitutive terms are equally indeterminate, there are no specific givens at hand that are available either to cease to be or to become something else. However, what is at hand is the movement of this becoming itself, which, although its terms are merely being and nothing, is distinguishable from both. Minimal as it may be, the differentiation of two indeterminacies that immediately collapses, in which being has passed over into nothing and nothing has passed over into being without any intermediate term or reason, is a category distinct from the dual categories of indeterminacy it contains. Nevertheless, it obtains its irreducibility without relying on any other means than them.

Does this category of becoming then provide something determinate in contrast to the indeterminacies of which it is composed, something determinate whose constitution from the categories of being and nothing could offer an account of determinacy that involves no determinate givens?

Hegel himself refrains from identifying the category of becoming with the category of determinate being. However, he does suggest that the category of becoming provides all the resources necessary for conceiving what it is to be determinate. According to his argument, becoming provides this service insofar as its own constitutive aspects, coming-to-be and ceasing-to-be—that is, the succession of being and nothing and of nothing and being—collapse of themselves, leaving a unity in which being and nothing are contained not sequentially but in an abiding relation to one another. The movement of becoming comes to a halt because the being that follows from nothing is indistinguishable from the latter just as the nothing that follows from being is indistinguishable from it. Hence, not only are coming-to-be and ceasing-to-be indistinguishable, but each immediately cancels itself as a sequence, leaving being and nothing as the only abiding elements of the whole that becoming comprises. Having lost its dual sequential movements, this whole now simply consists in a unity of being and nothing that contains them as component terms mediated by their identity. According to Hegel, this provides the minimal categorial structure of determinate being, by which something can begin to be categorized (*SL* 106).

How this is so is far from transparent, even if one grants that the category of becoming involves more than a restatement of the category of indeterminacy and that the coming-to-be and ceasing-to-be of becoming collapses, leaving behind no more than a unity of being and nothing. For how could any resulting unity of being and nothing constitute a threshold of determinate being? With both components utterly indeterminate and no third term available, where are the resources for specifying something rather than nothing?

Apogogically speaking, Hegel's recourse to such a unity of being and nothing has a certain inevitability. After all, if what it is to be determinate must be categorized without employing categories of determinacy, the only elements with which to build are being and nothing, which are no sooner given than they pass over into one another, thereby eliminating the very becoming in which they figure as distinguished yet identical terms. But how is determinate being thematizable in terms of being and nothing?

Being, Nonbeing, and Being Determinate

Despite the paucity of the material, the option at hand has an immediate plausibility. Since what it is to be determinate cannot be categorized by means of qualities, definite relations, or definite entities, what else can provide its minimal categorization than a unity of being and nonbeing,[8] where the contrast of the two provides the definiteness underlying all quality and relation? Without referring to any other properties, determinacy seems to be defined simply by what it is and what it is not, just as the indeterminacy common to being and nothing seems to be overcome when being is joined with nonbeing so that each delimits the other.

Admittedly, it is difficult to visualize any constitution of determinacy from being and nonbeing without referring to the presence or absence of definite qualities, relations, and entities, which all have their definite character by possessing certain features and not others. However, when determinacy itself is at stake, the contrast of being and nonbeing is not a contrast between the presence and absence of any independently given factors. Being determinate without further qualification must instead involve no more than a coterminous being and nonbeing, where being and nothing no longer figure as alternating unrelated categories but as the sole coeval desiderata of what obtains definition as sheer definiteness by being their unity.

Indeed, if all definite qualities, relations, and entities are what they are only by virtue of being something and not being something else, this only testifies to how the unity of being and nonbeing underlies all further determinacies as a prior category they inevitably incorporate. For if they all depend upon the presence and absence of different features for their own character and these features themselves similarly depend upon being and nonbeing for their respective definition, an infinite regress will only be escaped if being and nonbeing per se provide determinacy in general.

What does remain perplexing is how a unity of being and nonbeing can provide a basis for categorizing quality or something. Namely, how can the combination of being and non-being supplant their indistinguishable indeterminacy with what it is to be determinate? In what sense can nonbeing make being determinate when nonbeing itself has no specific character independent of its contrastive unity with being? How can nonbeing render being determinate when nonbeing is not already the absence of something definite? Or, if being and nonbeing have no determinate character apart from their contrast with one another, in what does their own difference consist?

Quality, Otherness, and Relation

Naturally, if the unity of being and nonbeing first comprises determinacy, the contrast terms of being and nonbeing could only be determinate themselves if each contains the same component structure. In that case, however, the nonbeing incorporated in determinacy would no longer be nonbeing without further qualification. Not only would it comprise a determinate being in its own right, but it would be one involving more than just its own being and nonbeing. Since it would also be distinct from that of which it is the nonbeing, it would have the additional feature of standing in contrast to that determinate being, which, for its part, would contain being and nonbeing while figuring in the same contrastive relation to its correlatively determinate nonbeing.

Although this indicates why being and nonbeing cannot be determinate themselves when they first unite to form determinate being, it sheds light on how the category of determinate being provides a means for characterizing something determinate whose own component contrast terms are determinate themselves. What makes this utilization especially pertinent is that it is entailed in the category of determinate being itself. Seeing how this is so makes comprehensible in what way being and nonbeing can render determinate their own unity.

To begin with, let it be granted that what it is to be determinate minimally consists in being a unity of being and nonbeing. Being and nonbeing here can have no further character than being the aspects of what determinate being is and is not, since otherwise determinacy is taken for granted. Consequently, their unity has a character distinct from each of them, the character of being determinate. It is appropriate to call this the category of quality, as Hegel does (*SL* 111), since, categorically speaking, quality cannot be explicated by means of any qualitative features. Thus, there is little alternative to categorizing it as what the unity of being and nonbeing is per se. As such, quality is not a particular property differentiated from others in terms of certain features. Nor can quality be something inhering in a given determinate substrate. As the unity of being and nonbeing in contrast to each of these terms, quality does not have a determinate basis. Rather, it itself is what being determinate minimally comprises, relying not on determinate givens for its own character but solely on the indeterminate contrast terms of being and nonbeing. As a result, nothing more can be said about quality, except to refer to these its own components or to its being as their unity (*SL* 111).

Nevertheless, insofar as the unity of being and nonbeing is qualitative, determinate, what it is, its being, is itself determinate, just as what it is not, its nonbeing, is. Although quality can be defined as a unity of being and nonbeing, wherein each is without quality, quality itself has a being and nonbeing that are determinate by virtue of being quality's presence and absence, as opposed to being and nonbeing per se. To avoid confusion, it is worth following Hegel's example, itself foreshadowed in previous philosophical tradition, by giving distinct names to the being and nonbeing of quality, identifying them respectively as reality and negation (*SL* 111).

Calling the coordinate being and nonbeing of what is determinate "reality" and "negation" might suggest a narrowly ontological interpretation of these categories. However, as Hegel himself makes clear in his remark on quality and negation, the reality at stake is applicable as much to definite feelings, imaginings, thoughts, numbers, and falsehoods as to determinate things (*SL* 112). What "reality" here designates is not "real" being in contrast to fiction, the nonempirical, or whatever, but simply the affirmative being of quality in contrast to the coordinate nonbeing that joins in rendering it determinate. In other words, what it is for quality in general to be is, categorically speaking, reality, whereas what quality in general is not is negation.

As determinate, quality is both reality and negation to the extent that qualitative determinacy both is and is not in determinate fashion. By the same token, negation is as much a determinate being as is reality (*SL* 115). For whereas reality is quality insofar as it is, negation is the nonbeing of quality. Hence, negation is not just nonbeing without further qualification, but nonbeing in relation to qualitative determinacy, or what can be categorized as otherness.[9] Since negation is determinate in virtue of being nondeterminate being, the otherness it comprises is not something extrinsic to quality. Rather, quality can be said to be otherness itself, for the reality and negation of quality are inextricable aspects in its specification.

This leaves a dual relation. On the one hand, otherness, in contrast to which quality has its own reality, is immediately distinct from quality as its negation. Their distinction is immediate in the sense that there is no additional third term in which their difference resides. Otherness is simply what quality is not. On the other hand, otherness is equivalent to quality, for even though it comprises non-(determinate being), it is a determinate being in its own right, with its own reality and negation. Hence, otherness has the same structure as quality and yet has quality as its otherness.

Something and Other

This contrast of quality and otherness, where each is immediately different yet identical, provides the conceptual resources for categorizing something. With quality constitutively standing in relation to otherness and otherness constitutively opposing quality as its negation while being just what quality is, it becomes possible and, indeed, necessary to speak of *a* qualitative being distinct from another qualitative being. Thus, whereas the unity of being and nonbeing provided for quality in general, the identity and difference of quality and otherness establishes the framework for conceiving something. It does so by providing for a determinate being that is distinguishable by virtue of its contrastive relation to another determinate being, whose own integral character rests on its involvement in the same relation. In this way, no independently given qualitative entity enters in to make something what it is. That, after all, could not possibly be the case, since it would involve taking for granted precisely what must be categorized.

Since each of the contrasted terms has no character beyond being a determinate being distinct from another, these terms present something without further qualification. Accordingly, they comprise categorial components of anything bearing additional qualities or relations.

What allows this categorization of something to avoid the pitfall of circularly relying upon any prior specific qualities or any other given determinate beings, be they substrates or privileged determiners, is simply that all it involves are quality and otherness per se in their relation to one another. Something, without further qualification, is a qualitative being whose otherness is another qualitative being standing in the same relation. Because the determinate reality of something depends on its contrast to its determinate negation, something constitutively has an other (*SL* 116). That is, something is what it is, bearing its own quality, by being in relation to another qualitative being. This is all that is available to define something, since no further specific features, principles, or connections can be introduced without taking the category of something for granted.

For this reason, the other, in reference to which something has its determinate being, cannot be distinguished through any possession of certain characteristics that the latter lacks. It can only have its own contrasting character as something different simply by being in relation to the former as its other—that is, as what the former is not without further qualification. This means that the other of something has the latter as its other. Hence, what is other is something in just the same way as is the something it opposes (*SL* 118). Each maintains its own distinct character by standing in relation to the other as the latter's other, even though, in so doing, each is both something and other in precisely the same fashion. As a result, just as quality and otherness are at one and the same time identical and different, so something is and is not identical to what is its other.

These concomitant relations of something and other cast in doubt Kant's argument that the most abstract concept is that which has nothing in common with what is different from it and that this is the concept of something, from which only nothing is distinct.[10] What the preceding discussion suggests is that, contrary to Kant, the category of something already involves the categorial succession of being, nothing, becoming, quality, and otherness, whereas being and nothing involve no prior terms. If this is the case, then what is most abstract are being and nothing, which are each identical to what is minimally differentiated from them—namely, being versus nothing and nothing versus being. As for the concept of something, it is distinct not just from nothing but from other as well.

Nevertheless, the identity accompanying the difference between something and other appears to destroy the determinate being of something very much as the indistinguishability of being and nothing seemed to call into question any development of categories from indeterminacy. For if something and other are identical, does this not eliminate all distinction between them and with it, the contrast by which one qualitative determinacy as distinct from another can first be categorized? Does it not collapse the distinction of something and other into an empty reiteration of quality per se? The identity of something and other would entail these results if it were the sole relation at stake. However, this identity itself involves the immediate difference of something and other. For only insofar as what is other has something as its immediately different nonbeing is something also an other and what is other also a something. Hence, the equivalence of something and other does not eliminate the contrast by which each has its own character. Rather, their own respective identities consist in their identity and difference.

In this respect, something has a dual character, consisting on the one hand in its relation to other, wherein both are immediately different and identical, and on the other hand in what something is apart in relation to itself. These two aspects, which Hegel calls being-for-other and being-in-itself (*SL* 119), are intertwined with one another, for something is in relation to other only insofar as it has being-in-itself— that is, a character of its own allowing it to be something different from its other and so stand in relation to it. By the same token, what something is in itself is not independent of its relation to other insofar as the only resource available to give something its own character is its contrast to something other (*SL* 120).

Although this leaves something with a most minimal characterization, nothing could be more fitting given the poverty of material with which its categorization must proceed. Indeed, if there is to be any test for judging this account of something, it can only lie in certifying its utter abstraction. To the extent the account passes muster, it provides a platform for further concretizations free of reliance upon inexplicable substrates and determining conditions. In that case, the categorization of something in its relation to other can testify to how something determinate can be accounted for, as it must be, without appeal to any conceptual scheme with its irreducibly determinate givens. What must not be forgotten is that no matter how much the account of something may employ a language rich in conceptual terms to achieve expression, what counts in regard to categorial constitution are which terms enter in as component elements of the category at issue. It is in this respect and this respect alone that the account of something warrants critical examination.

4
Logic, Language, and the Autonomy of Reason: Reflections on the Place of Hegel's Analysis of Thinking

There is hardly any feature of Hegel's philosophy whose current significance is greater, nor more neglected than the unique place given the analysis of thought. Unlike any other thinker before or after, Hegel begins his philosophical system with a logic conceiving categories without regard for their reference to reality or how a given knower might think them. He allows thinking itself to figure first as an object of investigation only within the subsequent theory of reality comprising the philosophies of nature and spirit. There Hegel treats thinking as a real activity of living individuals, inhabiting a common world of which they are conscious and able to speak. Consequently, thought becomes something properly analyzable only after not just categories but nature and such worldly features of mind as consciousness, representation, and language have been determined. As unsurprising as this ordering may appear, it represents a fundamental break from ordinary philosophical practice, a break bearing crucial importance for the nonmetaphysical, antifoundational character of Hegel's philosophy as well as signaling the genuine alternative he provides to the dilemmas plaguing so much contemporary thought.

To understand how this is so, one must consider Hegel's systematic placement of thought in light of four issues: the relation between logic and thinking, the preconditions of consciousness, the connection between language and thought, and the autonomy of reason.

LOGIC AND THINKING

The relation between logic and thought might not seem much of an issue, given the traditional view that logic provides the rules of thought.

Yet, however thinking be conceived, insoluble problems arise the moment it be held subject to laws underlying the thinking of any content and thus comprising a formal logic.

If one resigns oneself to describing such laws as an inescapable fate of thought, governing thinking so that all unconditioned, autonomous inquiry is impossible, one falls into the predicament of being unable to justify that very description. Were thinking subject to a given logic that no questioning could ever avoid employing, all thought would be hopelessly relative to rules whose own validity could never be established.

If, on the other hand, one treats the given laws of thinking as a prescriptive logic ordaining how correct thinking should proceed, it becomes impossible to argue for these laws without having to take them for granted. Any argument in their favor that does not conform to them would not qualify as correct thinking and would therefore immediately refute itself. Conversely, any attempt to justify these laws by following their strictures would be arguing in circles. Thus, there could be no way to decide among competing candidates for the prescriptive rules of thought, since no argument could be made on behalf of any rules without dogmatically accepting their authority in advance.

Recourse to apogogic proof provides no remedy either, even when pursued to the radical lengths to which Aristotle goes in seeking justification for the principle of contradiction. It might seem that this principle is one about which it is impossible to be mistaken, insofar as nothing determinate can either be or be meant if everything can be true and not true in the same fashion.[1] Yet to be certain of this outcome would require previous knowledge of the nature of being and meaning, as well as some prior understanding of why indeterminacy would be an unsatisfactory starting point for philosophical investigation.

In light of these problems, Hegel recognized that it makes no more sense to conceive of thought as a rule-governed activity than to begin philosophy's quest for truth with assumptions concerning either subject matter or method. If philosophy is to cast aside all reliance upon opinion—as it must do to obtain justified knowledge—it has to legitimate all its terms within its own investigation. For this to be accomplished, philosophy must free itself of all foundations and instead become completely self-grounding. The great insight of Hegel, which accounts for the unique starting point of his philosophical system, lies in his awareness that philosophy can be radically self-grounding only if it begins without any content whatsoever and yet comes to present a content that could somehow develop from such indeterminacy without any introduction of extraneous terms. What Hegel seeks to show in his *Logic* is that the only content that avoids the pitfalls entailed in issuing from some given foundation is self-determined determinacy.

Comprising the entire subject matter of a genuinely presuppositionless logic, this active, self-developing content cannot be the self-determination of a given structure, such as intellect, will, or reality as a whole, if foundationalism is to be avoided. If, for instance, the content of this logic were understood to be categories as they are thought, thought would be taken for granted as the given foundation of categorial development, leaving thinking a dogmatic assumption of philosophy. To escape this familiar trap of philosophies that begin straight away with the topic of thought, the self-developing content of logic must rather be self-determination per se. Only the development of self-determination per se preserves the presuppositionlessness self-grounding requires, for self-determination is literally nothing before it has commenced to determine itself, just as it is subject to no ordering principle distinct from itself. For this very reason, a logic consisting in the self-presentation of the categories through which self-determination constitutes itself must precede the analysis of thinking as well as the analysis of any other specific subject matter.

Significantly, Hegel conceives the category of individuality, often termed the "concrete universal," as the elementary structure of self-determination, and he determines the category of the concept in terms of individuality. Although in *Logic* Hegel presents the concept in its own right, without considering how the concept figures as an object of thought, the logical determinacy ascribed to the concept has immense significance for thinking, granted that the latter comprises a conceptual cognition. For even if philosophy must begin not with an analysis of thought but with a development of self-determination per se, thinking must eventually be shown to have a character permitting it to think such a development, if thought is to be the proper vehicle for knowing the truth and the philosophy of logic is to be accounted for.

It thus should come as no surprise that when Hegel turns to thought itself, after having analyzed its preconditions, the conceptual character of thinking bears a telling connection to freedom. If indeed the concept is self-determined determinacy, the object of thought is rendered a self-ordering content. In that case, thinking is perfectly suited to conceive the self-grounding categorial development of logic. Furthermore, thinking thereby obtains the autonomy to which philosophical thought has always aspired. With freedom generically within the object of thought, one has precisely what could be hoped for, if what is conceived is to be thought as it is in its own right, rather than as it is ordered through the veil of a determining mind. By the same token, the thinking of such concepts would in no way be conditioned by any independently given factors, for conceiving self-developing concepts would mean presenting concepts whose presentation is conditioned by nothing save the self-ordering of the concepts themselves.

Consequently, if thinking is the cognitive activity in which conceptual determination is comprehended, thought would neither be subject to any rule system nor realize any given structure. Those who interpret Hegel as conceiving thinking to be subject to the same rule system as reality ignore the fundamental Hegelian insight that for reason to grasp the self-determined content of concepts, thinking would have to be free of all given laws and principles. That would have to be the case in any event if thinking is to conceive truth without being burdened by assumptions. Otherwise, thought would be defined by given terms, stripping it of the unconditioned, presuppositionless autonomy required for any move beyond opinion to truth.

For the same reasons, it would make little sense to speak of the self-determination of concrete universality as a metaphysical foundation whose realization comprises the whole universe, allowing conceptual thought to correspond to reality. Ever since Marx and Kierkegaard, Hegel has been charged with just this impropriety of moving beyond the limits of reason by means of an ontology that metaphysically asserts that concrete universality is the substance of the world. If, however, concrete universality is self-realizing, nothing distinct from itself can be its realization. Therefore, the logic of the concrete universal is not a logic of the world or, for that matter, a logic of thinking, but just a logic of self-determined determinacy.

In this sense, Hegel's *Logic* does indeed replace ontology, not by providing another variation on metaphysics, but by supplanting it entirely with a theory of determinacy making no immediate reference to reality or knowing. Rather than upholding a metaphysics of concrete universality, Hegel rejects the metaphysics of ontology altogether by attempting to free the conception of determinacy from reference to some given in itself, a reference that is the defining characteristic and fatal bane of any representational knowing seeking to mirror reality. This, once again, is why Hegel begins his philosophical system by considering categories in their own right before conceiving reality and thinking in his subsequent *Realphilosophie*. When he does proceed to consider the realities of nature and mind, it is not as realizations of a given logical foundation but as irreducible entities that may indeed incorporate categories as component features of their concepts, but not as principles determining their specific character. After all, if the concepts of nature and mind are self-developing, they could not be determined by any prior term without destroying the immanent character of their unfolding.

In this light, it is quite understandable why Hegel characterizes the self-determination of thought and conceptual contents as a movement beginning not with a given totality but rather with the least determinate component of the whole, which is last to be thought as the self-determining subject of the preceding development. Since that subject matter is self-determined, what it is can only become manifest at the conclusion of its own self-determination. If the order were reversed, thought would be arbitrarily asserting its subject matter prior to the very thinking that is supposed to determine its proper content.

This is why, contrary to appearances, Hegel's systematic philosophy does not entail a coherence theory of truth. Certainly, he does continually speak of the truth of a content lying not in a corresponding object or concept but in a subsequently developed content incorporating the former. So the categorial domain of the concept is the truth of that of being and essence,[2] just as spirit is the truth of soul and consciousness,[3] and the state is the truth of family and civil society.[4] If this signified that truth resided in coherence, Hegel's philosophy would fall victim to the basic incoherence undermining all coherence theories of truth. They inevitably get trapped in self-referential inconsistency due to the impossibility of obtaining through coherence either the knowledge that truth lies in coherence or knowledge of the total context in coherence with which truth is reputedly located.

If one were to rely on coherence to establish that truth lies in coherence, one would obviously be begging the question, using precisely what must be proved as the bulwark of the proof. Consequently, the principle of the coherence theory of truth would be either lacking justification or based on knowledge obtained by other means, contradicting its very claim that all knowledge is rooted in coherence.

Similarly, the ultimate context in coherence with which knowledge supposedly has its truth could not be known through anything other than an immediate reference violating the coherence principle. For if that context were known in virtue of being coherent with something else, it would no longer be the ultimate context it purportedly is, while that in terms of which it is knowable would equally be unknowable through coherence unless it too were not ultimate. As a result, there would be either an infinite regress wherein the framework of coherence remains ever unattainable or an ultimate framework that is known not in terms of anything else but through precisely the direct metaphysical reference against which coherence theory properly rebels.

Hegel avoids these problems by refraining from developing any content in terms of a given framework. What allows him to escape this variety of foundationalism is nothing other than following the advance of self-determined concepts, an advance that always results in, rather than presupposes, what it is that forms the whole at issue. Nevertheless, this resulting whole can be considered the truth of its previously determined components, since only when they stand incorporated within the whole of which they are constitutive elements is their complete character at hand.

This relation is especially significant for understanding both how thinking should proceed and how it stands in relation to its preconditions. As Hegel has shown, the requirements of self-grounding discourse demand that thinking not be the first topic of philosophy. On the other hand, since no topic can be properly conceived without first addressing whatever may underlie or be incorporated within it, thought cannot be analyzed prior to the determination of its preconditions. Yet, if thought has preconditions, how can it have the autonomy that would permit thinking to grasp truth? This question takes on particular acuteness in Hegel's case, for at the same time that he attempts to develop presuppositionless thought in the most uncompromising way, he equally seeks to take full account of how thinking must be conceived as an activity concretely located within the world.

THE PRECONDITIONS OF CONSCIOUSNESS AND FREEDOM OF THOUGHT

Among the most prominent of the constitutive elements of thinking Hegel addresses are, not surprisingly, consciousness and language. For indeed, what could be less controversial than recognizing that thinking is a conscious activity employing language? What is not so uncontroversial is whether the validity of thinking is in any way determined by the respective structures of consciousness and language.

Needless to say, much of modern philosophy has fallen into two camps distinguished according to whether they investigate the validity of thought in terms of the structure of consciousness or language. By contrast, Hegel refrains from giving either structure any juridical role, even while admitting that no thinking can occur that is not conscious and does not employ language as the medium of its expression.

With regard to the structure of consciousness, Hegel even goes so far as to claim that philosophical thought is impossible unless it can free itself from the opposition of consciousness.[5] This opposition consists in conscious knowing's perennial distinguishing and comparing of its representations and the putative independently given objects to which they should correspond. In view of the foundational problems of any cognition that seeks to justify its knowledge claims by referring to some privileged given, it is evident that conscious knowing's reference to something in itself as its given standard of truth leaves it unable to carry through the self-grounding thinking to which philosophy aspires.

By the same token, any philosophy that gave the structure of consciousness the foundational role of being the irreducible given in terms of which all objects of knowledge are determined would find itself unable to justify either the primacy it ascribes consciousness or the features with which it describes it. In both cases, argument would fall into the same circularity that vitiates all foundational thought. If consciousness were to have primacy, it would have to be taken for granted by any attempt to justify its privileged status. This would equally apply to any attempt to describe consciousness, for if nothing can be known objectively without prior access to the structure of consciousness, objective knowledge of what consciousness itself comprises remains ever beyond the limits of knowing.

Needless to say, Hegel considers Kant to be a thinker who pursues just such foundational epistemology, where consciousness figures as the determining ground of objectivity. Although Hegel never tires of pointing out the internal inconsistency of transcendental philosophy's attempt to know before knowing, his own analysis of consciousness within *Realphilosophie* indicates the full extent of Hegel's rejection of the Kantian approach.

That the analysis of consciousness follows well after the science of logic alone indicates Hegel's total break with foundational epistemology. It suggests both that Hegel sees fit to develop categories without determining them in terms of any given structure of knowing and that he views any examination of consciousness to require philosophically justified categories of determinacy without which no aspect of consciousness could be legitimately described in the first place.

Yet what really seals Hegel's rejection of Kantian foundational epistemology is the *Philosophy of Spirit's* characterization of consciousness as an actual entity, whose being in the world presupposes both a preexisting nature and the corporeal and emotive reality of the living individual to which it is constitutively tied. In many respects, Hegel's theory of consciousness is in direct response to the dilemmas that arise from Kant's doctrine of the analogies of experience. In that doctrine, Kant argued that it would be impossible to distinguish whether representations were objective or mere imaginings unless certain categorially specified rules determined the connection between them. Although Kant properly recognized that a representational knowing can never have direct access to the objects to which its representations putatively refer but can only compare one representation to another when seeking verification, he still sought to restrict the domain of objective knowledge to the representational cognition of consciousness. As a result, he had little choice but to locate the objectivity of representations in their interconnections.

When, however, Kant attempted to secure objective knowledge in that manner, he was compelled to introduce principles that undermine the foundational primacy of consciousness and lead to precisely the concrete conception of consciousness Hegel introduces. Kant's Third Analogy, that "All substances, in so far as they can be perceived to coexist in space, are in thoroughgoing reciprocity,"[6] proves to be his undoing. In arguing for the principle of this analogy, Kant points out that whereas the order of representations putatively conveying an objective event must be a necessary one to insure that their sequence is not just a product of imagination, the order of representations putatively conveying coexisting objects must be a matter of indifference. Otherwise, there would be no way of knowing whether successive perceptions represent coexisting or successive states of affairs. Kant seeks to secure knowledge of objective coexistence by requiring that the order-indifferent representations of putatively coexistent objects represent things that could not be without the simultaneous presence of the others. However, the whole notion of order-indifference rests on the presumption that the knower has a particular vantage on the world of coexisting things, a vantage whose view can be changed at will, producing a subjectively determined sequence of perceptions whose order is a matter of indifference to the abiding coexistence of what is perceived from this or that perspective.

Clearly, if this be so, the knower can no longer be characterized as a pure consciousness with no footing of its own in the world it experiences. Rather, consciousness would have to be spatially and temporally located and aware of its own position so as to be able to judge when its change of view is precisely that, rather than a perception of a changing situation. This requires that consciousness possess a corporeal reality with which it can empirically identify. However, if consciousness must be able to perceive its own presence in the world as a precondition of its knowledge of coexisting objects, then Kant's Second Analogy of Experience, that "All alterations take place in conformity with the law of the connection of cause and effect,"[7] must be revised. Since that analogy renders all objects of experience conditioned things, precluding the experience of anything possessing the autonomy a conscious individual exhibits, the being in the world of consciousness would necessitate that alterations take place in conformity with freedom as well. In other words, the domain of objects of experience would have to be extended so as to admit the presence of corporeally individuated conscious selves as legitimately perceivable entities. Only then would self-consciousness actually be possible, for finally the knower would be able and indeed be compelled to be conscious not just of other objects and other selves but of the empirical reality of him- or herself. The reason for this "compulsion" is that empirical self-consciousness would now be a coeval feature of any knowledge of objects, eliminating the great lacuna of Kantian philosophy, which rests so much importance upon the unity of self-consciousness without ever being able to account for it.

Hegel takes all of this into note in his discussion of consciousness. Instead of giving consciousness a transcendental primacy, where everything objective is determined in terms of its cognitive structure, he conceives it within reality, as a form of mind presupposing nature and the living body it inhabits.[8] Further, Hegel explicitly extends the range of the objects of consciousness to include not just conditioned things subject to causal determination but also living organisms, other conscious individuals, and, last but not least, consciousness itself.[9]

Yet if all this undercuts the foundational epistemology of those who present consciousness as the irreducible framework of discourse, it does not show how thinking can transcend the limits of representational knowing that still define the standpoint of consciousness, no matter how extended be the range of its given objects. Although thinking may be performed by a conscious individual, the act of thought must somehow be nonrepresentational in character if reason is to ground itself without illicit appeal to the privileged givenness of what is putatively in itself.

That Hegel treats thinking not within his theory of consciousness but in his subsequent theory of what he calls "psychology" indicates how he is not only aware of this problem but intent on solving it. The solution he offers is what would be expected in view of how the science of logic links self-determination to the determinacy of the concept. What Hegel suggests is that thinking can avoid the immediate reference to givenness defining representational knowing provided that what the thinker is conscious of in thinking are thoughts whose truth lies not in mirroring anything in itself but solely in exhibiting the immanence of self-determination. To the degree that concepts present a self-determined content, thinking them would provide precisely the abstention from foundational reference that is required for thought to be a vehicle of truth.

Nevertheless, the question still remains as to how a concept can be an object of thought, especially if thinking is a conscious activity, whose contents always remain representations of some sort or other. It would seem that the thinking of concepts would require a very special type of representation whose content is not restricted to what is given to consciousness in experience but freely determinable. Significantly, Hegel turns to language to provide this sort of representation and accordingly treats language as a precondition of thought, whose analysis must precede that of thinking.

LANGUAGE AND THINKING

What language offers is the sign, a representation whose meaning lies not in the given content of the sign itself but in another representation connected to it by the mind. As such, the sign liberates representation from the bond of having to refer to some given object of consciousness. Rather, the sign allows for reference to contents that are themselves products of mind. This makes possible the free generation of objects of thought, as is needed for any thinking that is to ground itself. Accordingly, language here apparently allows for the expression of concepts and the thinking of conceptual development.

Naturally, if language makes thinking possible and the sign is itself a product of mind, then the production of signs must be ascribed to a representational intelligence—that is, a productive verbal imagination, which, although not engaged in thinking, still manages to create signs at will by establishing the connections between representations that give signs their meaning. This avoids the circularity of having thinking be the source of the very words that are required to make thoughts manifest to others as well as to the consciousness of the thinker. In addition, it makes intelligible how the semiotic material of thought need not limit what conceptual content can be expressed by its means. If, indeed, the meaning of signs and words is a creation of mind that relates them only to whatever representation the mind itself determines, their meaning is no more limited by the given intuitions of the signs and words themselves than by any other given intuition. With this the case, meaning is freed of the burden of mirroring represented givens, making it possible for thought to have no other bounds than those it imposes upon itself.

Further, if the meanings of signs are to be retained and reproduced so as to allow for communication, some account must be given of a reproductive verbal memory to preserve the products of the above mentioned productive verbal imagination. Hegel attempts to conceive all of these activities of mind in the sections on imagination and memory immediately preceding his treatment of thought.[10] Whether or not his explanation is adequate, the relation between language and thinking it suggests provides a viable way out of the fundamental dilemmas undermining the alternative approach that has gained so great a contemporary following.

This approach, which has fueled the linguistic turn of analytic philosophy, does for language what Kant did for consciousness. Its defining move is not without appeal. Indeed, if language is, as Hegel himself admits, the medium in which thought necessarily expresses itself, it is tempting to conclude that language is not only a precondition of thought but a determining foundation that constitutively determines both what range of contents can be thought and what counts as true versus false thinking.

As plausible as this view might appear, it is just as incoherent as any coherence theory of truth. After all, if the content and validity of thought is conditioned by language, how can the advocates of this position claim truth for their view without violating the limits language imposes upon thinking? Are they not laying claim to a standpoint having unqualified access to the reality of language and thought? If knowledge were conditioned by language, there could be no cognition of the presumed primacy of language that was not relative to its structure. Whether that structure allowed for true as opposed to false thinking would therefore be just as utterly unknowable as the truth or falsity of any other matter, including the supposedly privileged role of language. In effect, these advocates of linguistic analysis fall into the same self-referential inconsistency that is the fatal flaw of all transcendental argument, whether the conditions of knowing be located in language, consciousness, intersubjectivity, relations of production, hermeneutic circularity, or any other prior ground.

Although Hegel would be the last to deny that thinking has preconditions, including nature, consciousness, and language, he does not commit the error of transcendental thinkers and treat these preconditions as principles that determine the limits of knowing and the standards of truth. He is well aware of the inconsistency of that view and appropriately recognizes that the various preconditions of thought have no bearing on what makes knowledge valid precisely because they make possible all thinking, whether true or not. With regard to the relation between language and thinking, this signifies that the structure of language can no more prescribe what is correct thinking than it can be known to mandate how thinking in general must operate.

Consequently, semantic considerations are irrelevant to questions of truth. As much as semantic investigation may uncover how language functions, this leaves utterly undecided not only whether what language expresses is true or false knowledge but whether the discourse of semantic theory is valid in its own right. As a result, language analysis is a useless instrument for philosophical investigation. At best it may provide a descriptive account of linguistic practice worthy of a positive science, but not a prescriptive theory mandating proper resolutions to problems of reason.

Therefore, there is no other alternative but this: either the validity of thought is conditioned by language, consciousness, or some other factor, in which case neither this nor anything else could be known with any authority, or the truth of thinking is utterly unlimited by the preconditions of thought and the medium in which it expresses itself. If philosophy is not a hopeless enterprise and thinking operates through words, then language would have to be a medium that in no way juridically determines what gets expressed by its means. Language might indeed be governed by grammar and current usage, but these would still have to permit the free creation of meanings and expressions whose validity is unlimited by as well as irreducible to the very vocabulary and syntax providing the given material from which novel terms could be created.

Only if language lets thought free can words express "concrete universals" and enable philosophy to exercise the autonomy it has always required. In so doing, philosophical thought would not be manipulating symbols according to the given rules of a formal logic nor contemplating given universals nor representing appearances. Instead, thinking would engage in an activity using language to present an unconditioned, self-determined conceptual development.

By so conceiving thinking within reality, as something conditioned by nature, consciousness, and language, yet free of all transcendental foundations, Hegel thus makes intelligible his own exercise of the autonomous reason that can alone pursue the presuppositionless, self-grounding discourse required by the quest for truth. His deed is no less our gain, for by situating the analysis of thinking in this way, Hegel offers us the one strategy for rendering true Aristotle's auspicious claim that philosophy is the freest of sciences.

5
The Apotheosis of Intersubjectivity

In recent years, philosophers have been at pains to find something to replace the subject as a foundation of knowledge and value. While direct appeals to the "given" have long been repudiated for ignoring how "objectivity" is itself mediated by the structure of the self, the Kantian and Husserlian appeals to subjectivity have equally come under fire for treating consciousness both as a privileged foundation and as a pure unworldly structure. In response, the clamor has risen for philosophy to abandon its traditional claim to an eternally valid, autonomous reason. Instead, philosophers are urged to heed the concrete situation of philosophical investigation, where thought allegedly lies bound to given terms and conceptual schemes embedded in actual human practice.

These developments have all precipitated a turn towards intersubjectivity. For many, this turn has meant conceiving intersubjectivity as the ground of consciousness, supplanting the unity of apperception as the foundation of knowledge. Some, like Habermas and Apel, consider intersubjectivity to provide an ideal, universal structure of non-distorting communication within which truth and value can still be known once and for all. Others understand intersubjectivity to be a historically developing reality, conditioning discourse and ethics and stamping both with historicity. One version of this latter view, inspired by Heidegger and Wittgenstein, and further developed by Gadamer, Rorty,

---

This essay integrates comments on Robert R. Williams, "Hegel's Concept of *Geist*," (in Peter G. Stillman, ed. *Hegel's Philosophy of Spirit* [Albany: State University of New York Press, 1987]), given at the 1986 Hegel Society of America meeting, and comments on Vincent M. Calopietro's "Moral Agency: The Habits of Our Being," given at the 1987 Metaphysical Society of America meeting.

and MacIntyre, imposes limits upon philosophy that either elude discursive analysis or invite abandoning the quest for truth and the good in favor of edifying histories of the intersubjective conditions underlying given theories. Another variety, heralded by Marx and Lukács, considers the historical character of intersubjectivity to pose no limits upon knowledge and justice in that history arrives at intersubjective structures with a privileged universal character (in their case, the proletariat as revolutionary subject), grounding an absolute standpoint (realized, for Lukács, in the leadership of the vanguard party) from which the true nature of reality can be conceived.

However differently these positions conceive intersubjectivity, whether rooting it in language, culture, or economic relations, they all agree that intersubjectivity is the fundamental structure from which subjectivity is derived and that it is an epistemological and normative foundation, juridically conditioning all knowledge and values.

Hegel might well appear to be the progenitor of the contemporary turn to intersubjectivity. If one follows the influential interpretation of Alexandre Kojève and conceives intersubjectivity to be the fundamental structure of spirit,[1] it is tempting to conclude that Hegel subscribes to the two theses defining that turn: the theses that subjectivity is derivative of intersubjectivity and that intersubjectivity is the ultimate ground of knowledge and value, providing the medium of access to being and the good. Yet can these be true and does Hegel's analysis of spirit really lend support to either one?

IS INTERSUBJECTIVITY THE GROUND OF KNOWLEDGE?

It makes sense to examine first whether intersubjectivity can be the ground of knowledge. This question does not figure within Hegel's *Philosophy of Spirit*, for he already treats it in his *Phenomenology of Spirit*. There Hegel provides no doctrine of spirit, but rather seeks to show how all attempts to ground knowing in any structure, egological or intersubjective, are doomed to failure. If one were to give intersubjectivity the foundational privilege of being the ground of knowledge, one would commit the familiar transcendental fallacy of seeking to know before knowing; one would make immediate knowledge claims concerning the character and epistemological primacy of intersubjectivity, even though the whole turn to intersubjectivity as a ground of knowledge is motivated by the need to bracket out all truth claims until the conditions for knowing have been determined. Taken to its logical conclusion, this difficulty implies that philosophy cannot begin with any foundation but must rather undertake an investigation whose categories derive from no given content and whose development follows no given method. Only after that investigation, historically initiated by Hegel in his *Science of Logic,* can one proceed to conceive real structures such as consciousness and intersubjectivity not as epistemological foundations but as topics of the philosophy of reality.

IS SUBJECTIVITY DERIVATIVE OF INTERSUBJECTIVITY?

Hegel's *Philosophy of Spirit* does directly bear upon whether subjectivity is derivative of intersubjectivity because this is a question for the philosophy of reality and not an epistemological issue. Certainly, Hegel understands consciousness to be a very concrete structure that can only be conceived as the embodied awareness of a living individual inhabiting a world of nature common to others. Further, he does link various features of mind to intersubjective relations. Most notably, he argues that thinking requires language for its expression and that certain forms of self-consciousness depend upon practical involvements with other subjects. In addition, when he turns to justice, he argues that all roles in which individuals bear rights and duties are dependent upon the interactions in which those roles are constituted.

These commitments might seem to imply that theoretical and practical agencies owe their entire character to relations between selves, in support of a foundational role for intersubjectivity. Yet how could such an encompassing claim be defended?

Two strategies of justification have commonly been offered in support of such a theory of agency. One emphasizes how the genesis of agency depends upon the interventions of others and interaction with them. The second justification stresses how the agent never exists independently of others but is always embedded in a context of intersubjective relations underlying all activity.

The first argument, which observes how every agent first attains responsibility and autonomy through upbringing by other agents, commits the genetic fallacy of presuming that what holds true of the genesis of something also holds true of its actuality. Each individual may first become an independent agent thanks to the interventions of others. However, this of itself hardly entails that once agency is acquired, its exercise need consist, either in whole or in part, in a similar intersubjective immersement.

Hence, what must decide the issue is the second argument, the argument that in agency's actual existence, agency is always embedded in a network of interaction and that, therefore, agency is intersubjective in character. Once again, the argument proceeds from an observation difficult to ignore: that the subject is always immersed in a given historical, cultural framework carrying with it a vast network of concrete relations. Nevertheless, it still bears asking whether the fact that agents may always exist in community with others signifies that the essence of agency resides in this embeddedness. A stronger argument seems required.

What kind of an argument could this be? One option might consist in a logical or perhaps ontological argument, to the effect that individuality depends upon a contrastive differentiation of one individual from another. As Strawson has shown,[2] this point can be applied to persons by arguing that the identity of individuals rests on their spatiotemporal contrast to others. Analogously, such reasoning could be extended to agency by arguing that agency is individual and that its individuality must rest upon contrastive relations among a plurality of agents. However, even if this argument could be sustained, it would not guarantee that agency must always involve action codetermined by the action of others, nor that ethics is defined intersubjectively. Other essential aspects of agency might still be given independently of the logic of individuality.

This possibility could conceivably be eliminated by focusing on the key features of agency and following a strategy akin to Kant's argument in his "Refutation of Idealism."[3] There Kant attempts to show that self-consciousness is not possible independently of consciousness of something other than the self, insofar as the temporality of mental experience depends upon awareness of something enduring standing in contrast to the succession of representations. Analogously, it might be argued that self-consciousness not only rests on consciousness of a nonself, but also upon awareness of another self, as some have taken Hegel's master-slave dialectic to suggest. Similarly, one could appeal to Wittgenstein's private language argument and maintain that insofar as rational agency depends upon thought, thought depends upon language, and language is something intersubjective, that agency must be intersubjective as well.

Although these strategies might succeed in demonstrating how certain preconditions and elements of agency are intersubjective, they fail to establish the exclusive intersubjective character of agency so long as what defines agency involves more than the above aspects. Thus, even though rational agency and ethics in particular might depend upon language and other intersubjective factors, this dependence does not mean that what is specific to agency and its different modes cannot involve features that have no reference to others.

Generally speaking, it is not enough to establish that intersubjective factors are preconditions of agency, since preconditions may not define the essence of what they make possible. What must further be shown is that intersubjectivity provides not just preconditions but the determining principle of agency, constitutively exhausting its nature. Hence, in order to establish that agency as a whole or some aspect of agency is intersubjective, it must be shown that relations among selves do determine what defines the reality at issue.

In this regard, it is not enough to portray agency as a mode of response to the actions of others. That still leaves entirely open to what extent the response is a function of the self or a function of interaction. If the intersubjective element consists solely of acting on a representation of the actions of others, then the ensuing act may be no different in character than a purely technical one proceeding upon the representation of natural things. Moreover, although the occasion of conduct may lie outside the self, the response it elicits could still rest upon powers that are traits within the agent. Hence, to claim that moral agency is defined by an openness to being persuaded or by an openness to being determined in light of ideals in no way transcends the monological framework of a Kantian ethic, where the essence of moral autonomy lies in an egological capacity to be persuaded by reason to act on principle, irrespective of what others may do or not do.

Yet even if openness to persuasion and openness to ideals did involve an intersubjective determination of agency, what makes these features constitutive of moral agency? Neither being persuaded how to act nor acting to realize an ideal is sufficient to differentiate moral from immoral or amoral behavior. After all, one can be persuaded to perform technical actions that are ethically neutral, just as one can pursue ideals that have no ethical character. And regarding agency in general, is it really impossible for an agent to act without either being persuaded or coerced by others?

These difficulties suggest two lessons. First, there is a dimension of agency that is not intersubjectively determined: namely, the faculty of choice that is a function of the self. Because it underlies all voluntary actions, whether or not they are specific to modes of community, this faculty can be called the natural will, given as it is independently of convention. However, although this faculty of choice may be an enabling condition for all voluntary interactions, it does not provide a principle determining what is essential to the nonnatural, artificial modes of agency whose exercise both requires and constitutes conventional institutions. Only when we regard specific types of conduct that are institutionally specific are we in a position to conceive forms of agency that are essentially intersubjective. In those cases, where we address such artificial agencies as property ownership, family membership, market participation, and citizenship, we do confront forms of agency whose defining activity can only be undertaken within a specific institutional framework that determines the role and corresponding conduct at home within it.

How such interaction could be constitutive of ethics becomes apparent once rights, rather than virtues, habits, and teleological ends, become recognized as the loci of normative validity. Since rights are not privileges but prerogatives of action to which all bearers of rights are entitled, their exercise is automatically embedded in an intersubjective framework of right and duty in which all agents exercise their rights only through mutually limiting their acts in function of their obligation to honor the entitled actions of others. Thus, to take the simple case of property rights, determining oneself as a property owner involves embodying one's will in a suitably recognizable domain corroborating the correlative objectifications of other owners. Similarly, exercising political rights is equally bound up with honoring those of others, without which the very institutions of self-government allowing for political rights cease to function.

Admittedly, moral agency might appear to be endemically indifferent to such institutional practices, since the appeal to conscience enters in when the enforcement of right depends upon the agent independently determining what ought be done. Yet moral agency too could be understood to be intersubjectively determined to the degree that acting out of conscience involves an entitled mode of conduct directed upon the right and welfare of other moral agents. On these terms, morality's status as a sphere of right would equally depend upon the concomitant moral activity of others, both in comprising the type of agency to which moral conduct is directed and in respecting the exercise of moral autonomy by holding the individual morally accountable.

Accordingly, in morality, as in every other sphere of right, a particular agency would be realized, owing its character not to any natural essence, antecedent dispositions, homage to a transcendent being, or functions of the self, but rather to the enacted structure of interaction in which its entitled freedom can be exercised. Although the formation of habits might give individuals a set of inclinations conforming to the rights and duties specific to each sphere, the structure of rights always involves interrelated acts of will that are never bound by given inclinations and a correspondingly defined character. Habits may warrant consideration in leading us to the threshold of right. But once we have entered that domain, we engage in conduct for its own sake, acting with or against our inclinations and in or out of character, as the case may be. This does not mean that in this realm of institutionalized freedom our ethical agency looses all specific form and content. On the contrary, we here play definite roles in activities determined not by our habits but by the structures of interaction in which we freely participate.

THE LIMITS OF INTERSUBJECTIVITY

Although Hegel's *Philosophy of Right* provides the prime example of an ethics that takes seriously this intersubjective dimension of rights, Hegel's recognition of the pivotal role of interaction in this domain involves neither deriving subjectivity as such from intersubjectivity nor treating intersubjectivity as an epistemological or normative foundation. Unlike those who seek to dissolve the subject into structures among selves, Hegel makes quite clear that many of the most important features of subjectivity are not dependent upon intersubjective relations and that, on the contrary, intersubjectivity is inconceivable without independently given subjective endowments.

Language may make conceptual thought possible, but linguistic acts are themselves impossible without a prior representative intelligence.[4] It must already be at hand, endowed with both a productive verbal imagination to create signs and a reproductive verbal imagination to retain the connection between representations in which the established semiotic meaning consists.

Similarly, a struggle for recognition may be required to generate the type of self-awareness that is reflected in the acts and understanding of another. Yet, Hegel is clearly aware that any such struggle presupposes individual selves already possessing the self-consciousness of desire, as well as the theoretical and practical capabilities needed to perceive and act towards others.[5]

The same holds true of all relations of justice. Individuals may be able to exercise the artificial agencies of property owner, moral subject, family member, civilian, and citizen only by participating in the interactions in which each role is at home. Yet, no exercise of rights and duties can occur unless one enjoys the body, mind, and choosing will needed to recognize the acts of others, perform one's obligations, and take the acts of freedom to which one is entitled.

These examples, all prominently supported by Hegel's text, indicate how the self has important faculties that are presupposed by rather than derived from intersubjective relations. They also show that Hegel does not identify spirit with intersubjectivity, but instead conceives intersubjective relations as features figuring in only some forms of spirit. Further, since Hegel understands intersubjectivity to comprise such nonsocial realities as language, property relations, morality, the family, and politics, it would be a category mistake to equate intersubjectivity with social community. Moreover, since the intersubjective structures of right are ends in themselves, comprising ethical reality itself, they cannot figure as foundations from which other normatively valid relations are to be derived.

To conceive intersubjectivity in its proper place is not to deny that philosophy is necessarily practiced by living individuals with bodies and minds, employing language in a community whose institutions and culture are products of history. There is no harm in granting that all these factors, as generally defined, are conditions of discourse and action. But it must not be forgotten that, as such, they are conditions of true as well as false discourse, no less than of ethical as well as unethical conduct. Therefore, none can play the role of an epistemological or ethical principle determining what makes knowledge and conduct valid rather than invalid. Similarly, the nonderivative features of subjectivity do not entail solipsism. Because they are no more foundations of knowledge and morals than are any other factors, their presence does not undermine objectivity in theory or practice. Hegel is well aware of this, and we would do well to follow him in regarding intersubjectivity for the limited reality it is, instead of fetishizing it as a social divinity.

6
Hegel Versus the New Orthodoxy

THE NEW ORTHODOXY IN PHILOSOPHY

A new orthodoxy has taken hold of contemporary philosophy,[1] straddling the stylistic divide between analytic and Continental thought and penetrating the ideological barrier between East and West. This new orthodoxy is defined by three commitments, each increasingly acclaimed as a fixture of the conceptual scheme from which we cannot escape. Of these commitments, two involve abandonments of traditional modes of philosophizing. One lies in a repudiation of "Cartesianism," decrying the strategy of turning to self-reflection as a privileged abode of certainty in order to ground philosophy upon indubitable principles. The second consists in a repudiation of foundationalism, condemning all attempts to conceive the truth by appealing to privileged givens as grounds of argument.

In rejecting these two traditional approaches, the new orthodoxy advances a pair of claims from which its own principle emerges. In repudiating "Cartesianism," it holds that self-reflection always operates within an historical linguistic and cultural context whose epistemic role must not be abstracted away. In repudiating foundationalism, it holds that all philosophical reasoning operates with foundations that can never be justified because no argument can proceed unless there is already an accepted conceptual scheme providing shared parameters of rationality.

Together, these two affirmations commit the new orthodoxy to a theoretical and practical holism. It maintains that all knowledge claims and principles of right are contextually grounded in coherence with conceptual schemes rooted in historically given practices. With this verdict, the new orthodoxy embraces a naturalized epistemology and ethics, relegating the distinctions between *a priori* and *a posteriori*, subjectivity and objectivity, norm and behavior, and theory and practice to constructs of empirical contingent conventions. In place of the Cartesian, foundationalist image of "philosophy as a mirror of nature,"[2] representing what world, consciousness, and language are in themselves from some timeless "view from nowhere,"[3] the new orthodoxy offers the picture of a corrigible, historical reason operating within pragmatically adopted frames of reference. Whether it be called "hermeneutics," "deconstruction," "internal realism," or simply "post-analytic philosophy," the new orthodoxy condemns reason to impotence, stripping it of its long-sought autonomy and self-responsibility and reducing it to doxology. With its triumph over the mistaken aspirations of tradition, the new orthodoxy leaves philosophers with little to do but chronicle the practices and conceptual schemes underlying historical philosophical positions, unmask how the former condition the latter, foster an edifying awareness of how our own theories are laden with assumptions, and engage in a reflective equilibrium determining the coherence of given theories inhabiting the same philosophical paradigm.

Not surprisingly, those who speak for the new orthodoxy have turned to Hegel for much of their inspiration. His phenomenological critique of the claims of consciousness offers them a source for radical anti-Cartesianism. His relentless attack on all appeal to givens provides the cutting edge for their radical antifoundationalism. His development of categories as elements of a logical totality, whose truth resides in categorial immanence, gives their holism its basis. And lastly, his concrete conception of spirit, wherein consciousness figures as an embodied subject, embedded in interaction with others, requiring language for the expression of thought, and participating in institutions of right arising in history, serves to support the historicized holism of their "naturalization" of epistemology and ethics.

While appropriating these Hegelian achievements, the new orthodoxy has jettisoned Hegel's pursuit of a presuppositionless science, whose autonomous reason can retrieve the incorrigible truth of categories, nature, mind, and justice from within the sweep of history. This it rejects as a vestige of foundationalism from which Hegel never successfully escapes. In the eyes of the new orthodoxy, Hegel fails to reconcile himself to the proper limits of the theoretical and practical holism his own work so strongly supports. Instead of relinquishing the impossible quests of past philosophy, Hegel absolutizes logical totality and the reason that conceives it, absolutizes his own philosophical standpoint, absolutizes the practice of the modern age, absolutizes the history of nations leading to modernity, and absolutizes the history of Western philosophy. All this, the new orthodoxy asserts, must be purged to retrieve the rational kernel within the mystical shell.

Yet can the truncated Hegelianism of the new orthodoxy pass muster? Can anti-Cartesian antifoundationalism stop short at theoretical and practical holism? And if it cannot, but must accept the challenge of developing a presuppositionless science, how can Hegel's embrace of categorial immanence and the concreteness of spirit be reconciled with his pursuit of a foundation-free yet systematic philosophy?

The answer to these questions can be found by examining how the new orthodoxy supports its own position through a use and abuse of Hegel rooted in interpretations of the *Phenomenology of Spirit*, the *Science of Logic,* and the doctrines of subjective, objective, and absolute spirit.

CAN THE CRITIQUE OF EPISTEMOLOGY RESULT IN A NATURALIZED EPISTEMOLOGY?

It makes sense to begin with the new orthodoxy's use of the critique of epistemology it finds in the *Phenomenology of Spirit*. Hegel describes this work as an attempt to free discourse of the opposition of consciousness, where knowing remains captive to a structure of reference in which some putative given always provides the standard for truth.[4] The new orthodoxy, however, views the *Phenomenology*'s critique of consciousness as testimony to the ultimate captivity of thought to historically given standpoints and conceptual schemes.

Admittedly, the path of doubt that consciousness traverses in the *Phenomenology* can easily be viewed in this light. The incessant inversions of consciousness do show how the epistemological project of consciousness can never succeed. Insofar as whatever consciousness appeals to as its standard of truth is accessible only as something for consciousness' own structure of awareness, there is nothing to test knowledge claims against other than representations of an equally subjective character. This, of course, is the oft-cited Achilles heel of the representational model of knowledge. As Hegel is well aware, the pitfall of representational knowing is equivalent to the dilemma of foundationalism to the extent that foundational arguments always appeal to some privileged given as the standard of knowledge.

What the new orthodoxy finds so noteworthy in Hegel's account is its exhaustive character. To the new orthodoxy, the completeness of the *Phenomenology*'s gallery of different foundational projects suggests that there can be no shape of knowing that does not operate in terms of a self-defeating appeal to givens. Hegel may claim to have reached a final shape of consciousness whose knowing is absolute. Nonetheless, so long as such knowing measures its knowledge against any putative given, as it must do to retain the reference constitutive of consciousness, the new orthodoxy has good reason to regard "absolute knowing" as a misnomer, designating but one more shape of corrigible cognition.

Besides being exhaustive, the progress of shapes from self-consciousness through spirit has an unprecedented concreteness documenting how the foundational knowing of consciousness involves intersubjective practices approximating the institutions of different historical epochs. For the new orthodoxy, this signifies something as fundamental as the corrigible nature of self-reflection. It provides the key insight leading the critique of epistemology to naturalized epistemology—the revelation that the frameworks of reference characterizing shapes of knowing are not *a priori* schemes rooted in some timeless structure of consciousness but transient paradigms embedded in historical practices.

On this account, Hegel has little choice but to redeem the incorrigibility of absolute knowing by arguing for the absolute character of the historical epoch through whose practices his own standpoint is constituted. If, however, as the new orthodoxy claims, the phenomenological analysis of spirit shows how historical practices frame the givens and modes of reference by which knowledge claims are adjudicated, it is impossible for any historical formation to engender an absolute standpoint in which knowing is freed of the limits of representation. So long as given practices provide knowing with foundations determining what it accepts as valid, every historical epoch and every frame of reference are equally tainted. Hence, Hegel's critique of epistemology undermines his own claims of wisdom, leaving behind the naturalized epistemology that transforms philosophy into edifying deconstruction.

Bracketing out whether Hegel's *Phenomenology* actually has this as its outcome, it bears asking whether the critique of epistemology can stop short at the naturalized epistemology with which the new orthodoxy aborts philosophy. In upholding the naturalization of epistemology, the new orthodoxy makes three claims. First, in acknowledgment of the critique of epistemology, it maintains that representational or foundational knowing can never succeed in justifying its knowledge claims. Second, it maintains that knowing is embedded in historical practices. Third, it affirms that all knowing is foundational in character, reflected in the fact that knowing's immersion in historical practices straps it with frames of reference predetermining its standards of truth.

There is nothing incoherent about the first two theses. Significantly, they do not imply the third. In order to arrive at the last thesis, they must be supplemented by arguments establishing that all knowing is foundational and that the historical practices in which knowing is embedded not only make knowing possible but juridically determine what counts as knowledge. Without these additional arguments, the critique of epistemology does not result in naturalized epistemology.

Although it can be debated whether the new orthodoxy seriously attempts to supply these further arguments, what cannot be denied is the utter absurdity of the third thesis, on which its whole position is anchored. In advancing the third thesis, the new orthodoxy offers a suprahistorical, incorrigible claim concerning the character of knowing. Yet, to do so, the new orthodoxy must somehow occupy a standpoint free of the historically conditioned, foundational character its own position ascribes to cognition. If it seeks to escape this contradiction by regarding its own theoretical claims as burdened by foundational assumptions rooted in the practices of its time, it must admit that its naturalized epistemology has no more authority than any other competing picture. For it must confess that the corrigible character it ascribes to knowing precludes any objective knowledge about the practices of this or any other time or, for that matter, about the new orthodoxy's own conceptual framework or that of any other standpoint.

For these reasons, it makes no sense to claim either that all knowing is representational—that is, foundational—or that the historical practices underlying knowing determine what counts as true or false. Accordingly, if any coherent argument is to follow from the critique of epistemology, it will have to be that there is a knowing free of foundations and that the historical practices that make knowing possible leave undetermined all juridical questions of knowledge.

Can the *Phenomenology* concur with these conclusions, or does it result in the incoherent naturalized epistemology that the new orthodoxy finds nascent in Hegel's critique of epistemology? If we return to the three theses that underly the turn to a naturalized epistemology and examine whether the *Phenomenology* is really committed to them, it becomes evident that Hegel does not condemn himself to the dilemmas of his latter day followers.

Admittedly, the new orthodoxy is correct in maintaining that the *Phenomenology* testifies to the truth of the first thesis, that representational knowing can never ground its knowledge claims. Further, the shapes of consciousness observed under the heading of "Spirit" may stand as evidence for the second thesis, that knowing is embedded in historical practices, provided two propositions hold true. First, all the prior shapes of consciousness must be incorporated within and grounded by those of "Spirit," since otherwise, not all, but only some modes of knowing will be historically embedded. Second, the *Phenomenology* must comprise a systematic doctrine of consciousness rather than a positive science addressing a given subject matter whose own status is taken for granted. The second proviso is particularly suspect, since the *Phenomenology* can serve its propadeutic role as introduction to science only if it refrains from making truth claims in its own right and restricts itself to observing how the stipulated structure of consciousness makes and tests its own truth claims en route to exhibiting the futility of its own epistemological project (see chapter 1).[5]

However, what decides the issue is whether the third thesis, that all knowing is foundational and historically conditioned, is embraced by the *Phenomenology*. To some extent, this question depends upon whether the *Phenomenology* is a scientific doctrine of knowing. If the *Phenomenology* is only the observation of how a certain stipulated structure of knowing fails in its quest for knowledge, no conclusions can be drawn from the *Phenomenology*'s outcome about knowing per se. In any event, Hegel repeatedly maintains that the problems besetting consciousness' search for truth are not representative of knowledge in general, precisely insofar as the *Phenomenology* carries out its introductory service of freeing discourse from the opposition of consciousness by which foundational knowing is defined. As has been noted, the new orthodoxy dismisses all talk of such liberation by interpreting "Absolute Knowing" as just another shape of consciousness, carrying within itself the same representational opposition of knowledge and what is given in itself. However, Hegel emphasizes that "Absolute Knowing" is not a privileged standpoint from which knowing conceives what is in itself, in the fashion of the contemplative intelligence of precritical metaphysics. It rather comprises a self-dissolution of representational knowing, where the quest to ground knowledge in something in itself is beset by an inability to distinguish representing from what is given, eliminating the foundational project altogether (PS 21, 51; SL 49). Hence, Hegel characterizes the outcome of his phenomenological critique of epistemology as a collapse of representational—that is, foundational—knowing (PS 479–80, 485–86, 487; SL 69). Far from rendering the foundational dilemma an inescapable fate, this collapse results in an indeterminacy from which Hegel launches a philosophical cognition that refrains from conceiving its categories either in reference to what is given or as representations of some underlying structure of knowing (SL 73). Whether or not such a philosophical cognition can function remains to be seen. What is already clear is that the *Phenomenology* is not committed to the third thesis, on which the naturalization of epistemology rests.

IS HOLISM THE ANSWER TO THE LOGICAL REQUIREMENT OF CATEGORIAL IMMANENCE?

By exhibiting the internal collapse of the foundational project of representational knowing, the *Phenomenology of Spirit* confirms how the critique of epistemology need not and, indeed, cannot result in a naturalized epistemology. Nevertheless, Hegel's own sequel to the *Phenomenology*, the *Science of Logic*, still offers much to recommend it as a harbinger of the new orthodoxy's theoretical holism.

Since the *Science of Logic* comprises Hegel's positive alternative to the dilemmas of representational knowing, the categories whose development it presents can no longer have their truth in correspondence with some putative given that they are supposed to mirror. Because logic consists in thought thinking itself, Hegel recognizes that a proper science of logic must involve a self-exposition of categories that refer to nothing but themselves. Their content will have to be at one with their presentation, allowing what is first for thought to be first in thinking (*SL* 43ff., 68). Only then can logical science avoid taking for granted the categorial method it is supposed to establish. Further, such a self-exposition of categories will satisfy the requirements of rational autonomy and presuppositionless by both avoiding any references to extraneous givens and relying on its categories to determine themselves. In so doing, it will provide philosophy with a new beginning, leaving behind foundationalism and the correspondence theory of truth entailed by any appeal to privileged givens.

Granted these basic features of Hegel's *Science of Logic,* it is not hard to see how it could be used to buttress a coherence theory of truth in which all categories of thought are holistically determined. Since logic can escape reliance upon given foundations only if its categories are their own exposition, determined exclusively through themselves and one another, it would appear that each one will be what it is through its place in the whole immanent development of categories. On these terms, every category will stand defined by incorporating the categories preceding its development and by being a component element of those that follow. Furthermore, because the development of categories will have to be self-determined, what it is that determines itself will be at hand only at the conclusion of the development as a final category incorporating all other logical categories as features of its self-determination (*SL* 72, 829, 838). Although this categorial whole can be thematized only at the conclusion of the development, after all its elements are explicated, its component categories are fully intelligible only in terms of their incorporation within it. This seems to signify that the truth of putative categories will reside in their coherence with logical development, a coherence consisting in their integration into the conceptual totality with which logic concludes.

Although Hegel maintains that this categorial immanence is the mark of a foundation-free, presuppositionless science, the new orthodoxy understands it as testimony to the holistic character of reason. Far from signaling a break from foundations, it rather reflects how rational thought always operates in terms of a conceptual framework in coherence with which concepts have their true meaning. By showing how categories are fully intelligible only as moments of a categorial totality, Hegel's logic demonstrates the impossibility of his own vestigial yearning to exercise an incorrigible thinking that takes nothing for granted. Although Hegel may maintain that science must begin with an indeterminacy independent of any conceptual framework, the integration of all categories within the Absolute Idea signifies that the logical whole must be assumed from the outset. So, in any event, concludes the new orthodoxy, enlisting the *Science of Logic* in support of the two theses of its theoretical holism: 1) that truth resides in coherence, rather than correspondence and 2) that all thought operates in terms of a given conceptual scheme.

Yet can truth reside in coherence, as the new orthodoxy affirms? The turn to the coherence theory of truth is motivated by the inability of correspondence theory to establish how there can be any access to what is in itself, which knowledge should mirror. The coherence theory of truth is intended to overcome this problem by avoiding all immediate reference to a standard of truth, the defining pitfall of representational knowing. However, in asserting that truth lies in coherence, the new orthodoxy falls into a dual dilemma. According to theoretical holism, all objects of knowledge have their intelligibility in coherence with some encompassing theoretical context. Yet, if this is so, what is the status of the coherence theorists' reference to the theoretical context in coherence with which knowledge claims have their truth? If knowledge of this context and its privileged role is obtained by referring directly to it, irrespective of some encompassing context, this knowledge violates the coherence theory of truth. If, however, reference to what knowledge is in coherence with is obtained in accord with the coherence principle, then the context it knows cannot be the ultimate context but must instead be known through another in terms of which it is intelligible. But then, knowledge of the latter context presents the same difficulty, leading either to an infinite regress in which no context can be known as that in coherence with which knowledge is true or else to an admission that the ultimate context must be accessible through a direct reference, placing coherence dependent upon an ultimate truth known through correspondence. Either way, the coherence theory of truth self-destructs, demonstrating the impossibility of knowing through coherence what the context is in coherence with which knowledge lies or, for that matter, of knowing that truth lies in coherence.

This incoherence of the coherence theory of truth has fatal implications for the holist idea of a conceptual scheme. Through the critical work of Davidson, the new orthodoxy has come to recognize the absurdities of maintaining the incommensurability of conceptual schemes.[6] However, in doing so, the new orthodoxy has not abandoned the idea of a conceptual scheme. Instead, it has accepted what it takes to be the Hegelian notion of our having one all-encompassing conceptual scheme circumscribing everything that can be intelligible to us. In embracing this idea, the new orthodoxy falls into the same trap besetting its advocacy of the coherence theory of truth.

Logically speaking, this trap is a very common one, reflecting the foundationalism of any transcendental argument. It consists in the incoherence of grounding all intelligibility in some given cognitive condition. Although such grounding should preclude any immediate cognition, it rests on prior knowledge of the condition of intelligibility and its privileged role. Transcendental knowledge is therefore impossible because it involves the incoherence of what Hegel diagnosed as attempting to know before knowing.

The idea of a conceptual scheme involves just this fallacy. By affirming that all intelligibility lies grounded in a given conceptual scheme, the new orthodoxy presumes to have transcendental knowledge both of what that conceptual scheme is, at least in some minimal sense, and how it serves as the condition of all meaning and knowledge. Yet how can the conceptual scheme be known? To be consistent with its grounding role, it must be known in terms of its own scheme. That is, it must be determined by itself as an object of knowledge. Yet, if it lies at the root of all intelligibility, how can one be certain that the idea of a conceptual scheme that it presents to us is equivalent to the conceptual scheme itself as it underlies intelligibility? To be certain would seem to require access to what the conceptual scheme is in itself, prior to what it makes intelligible to us. Direct access of that sort must be precluded, however, since it would contradict the grounding role of the conceptual scheme. Hence, the very idea of a conceptual scheme precludes any knowledge of what it is or that it has the grounding role ascribed to it. All that can be done is assume that our conceptual scheme grounds intelligibility such that what we know as our conceptual scheme corresponds to what it is in itself. Making that assumption, however, is tantamount to embracing the dogmatic faith of the correspondence theory of truth, which the idea of a conceptual scheme is supposed to overcome.

Furthermore, it can be questioned whether that assumption could possibly be true. In order for the conceptual scheme to determine itself, as the new orthodoxy must ultimately assume, it would have to be a self-determined framework. However, to be self-determined, the conceptual scheme could not have any given character by which it could stand as the antecedent ground to all intelligible content. If it did have such a nature, prior to the constitution of all intelligibility, it would have a content that it had not constituted for itself and thus fail to be self-determined. If, on the other hand, it was self-determined, generating its own intelligibility by means of its self-exposition, it would no longer comprise a ground of intelligibility, fundamentally prior to everything it grounded. Either way, the idea of a self-constituting conceptual scheme is incoherent.

Nevertheless, the idea of a self-determined conceptual development, making intelligible only itself, is precisely what allows Hegel's *Science of Logic* to escape the perplexities of the coherence theory of truth and its associate notion of a conceptual scheme. Admittedly, Hegel does acknowledge that the logical devlopment of categories concludes in an all-encompassing category, the Absolute Idea, providing the method or principle of intelligibility for all the preceding ones contained within itself. However, he emphasizes that the Absolute Idea can only be as a result (*SL* 70–72, 829, 838). This is because it does not have any given character, in the manner of a conceptual scheme serving as the foundation of intelligibility. Instead, what it is is mediated by the categorial development it consummates. It cannot be otherwise, for it is the established subject matter of a logic of self-determination, which, as such, can have no antecedent nature but must be what it determines itself to be. Accordingly, there can be no conceptual framework already operative at the outset of the *Science of Logic*, rendering intelligible the parade of categories that follows. If that were so, the work would be just one more version of foundationalism, determining its concepts through a given set of assumptions. If, on the contrary, logic is to establish the categories and their interrelations without taking them for granted—if, in other words, logic is to be the self-exposition of the categories—it must operate through a categorial immanence, where their order and intelligibility are produced as results rather than presupposed as dogmatic givens. Hence, the truth of the categories will reside not in their coherence with any given scheme but in their total freedom from determination by any prior principles, given standpoints, or other extraneous factors. Although they may achieve integration in the categorial whole that determines itself through their development, that integration does not underlie their exposition as an antecedent condition. For these reasons, the *Science of Logic,* to its own credit and viability, offers anything but support for the theoretical holism of the new orthodoxy.

CAN THE CONCRETE PRACTICES OF SPIRIT HISTORICIZE KNOWLEDGE AND ETHICS?

The *Phenomenology of Spirit* and the *Science of Logic* resist their enlistment by the new orthodoxy, but can the same be said of Hegel's Philosophy of Spirit? At every one of its levels, the Hegelian doctrine of spirit seems to offer an unshakeable basis for the new orthodoxy's turn to historical practices.

In the analysis of subjective spirit Hegel sets the stage by arguing three points: 1) Consciousness is irreducibly an embodied subject in the world; 2) self-consciousness has an intersubjective dimension; and 3) language is the necessary medium of thought. All have important significance for the new orthodoxy.

Hegel's argument that consciousness is an embodied awareness presupposing nature and individuated through a spaciotemporal being in the world[7] provides a first step away from the Cartesian picture of a disengaged ego, whose pure self-reflection is a source of knowledge independently of time and place and worldly practices. If, as Hegel argues, consciousness is a being in the world, wedded to a body caught in metabolism with nature and thereby endowed with a concretely embedded perspective framing all its internal and external sensations, is this not an almost Heideggerian encouragement to view cognition as something already conditioned by a pretheoretical practical engagement with the world?

This practical conditioning of knowing only seems to be confirmed when Hegel turns from consciousness to self-consciousness and analyzes it in terms of desire, the domination of nature, and a master-slave relation (*PM,* pars. 424–35). Here Hegel's argument seems to testify that self-consciousness is predicated upon what is not only a practical involvement with nature but one involving relations among selves. Many view Hegel's master-slave discussion as if it shows how self-consciousness is constituted through intersubjectivity. However, since the subjects who interact as master and slave can only do so by already bearing desire and recognizing their difference from one another, it would seem that they must already be self-conscious in some respect (*PM,* par. 430). Hence, what Hegel's argument would suggest is that the intersubjectivity of the master-slave relation establishes further forms of self-consciousness, if not self-consciousness per se. Nevertheless, even in this weakened form, the relation permits intersubjective practice to gain a foothold in the formation of awareness, a step that is fundamental for the new orthodoxy.

What seems to seal intersubjectivity's role as an indispensable condition of knowing is Hegel's analysis of language's contribution to thought. Treating thinking, like consciousness and self-consciousness, as a topic of *Realphilosophie,* he argues that thought is a real activity presupposing not only nature and the existence of embodied, practically engaged self-consciousness individuals, but language as well (*PM,* par. 465). Language is necessary for thinking, Hegel argues, because only words can provide the universal representations, freely generated by intelligence, that thought requires as the medium for its expression (*PM,* par. 459).

For the new orthodoxy, this involvement of language is doubly fundamental. On the one hand, it signifies that thinking is conditioned by linguistic usage, which is itself an intersubjective practice arising within history and subject to historical change. Hence, thinking is historically grounded. On the other hand, because language presupposes conscious intelligence to create signs, retain their meaning, and generate intelligible and understood speech, thinking remains bound to the foundational dilemmas of consciousness. Consequently, thought is not only historically framed but perennially dependent upon assumed standards of truth.

For the new orthodoxy, Hegel's appeal to history in his doctrines of objective and absolute spirit offers a final corroboration of this corrigibility of reason. Although Hegel discusses the historical development of art and religion just as prominently as the history of freedom and the history of philosophy, it is his treatments of right and philosophy that bear directly upon the character of theoretical and practical reason.

Although Hegel conceives objective spirit as the philosophy of right, detailing the institutions of freedom of which justice is composed, he views them as nonnatural conventions and accordingly concludes their analysis with an account of what must occur in history for them to arise. That account consists in a history of freedom that, by definition, concludes with the emergence of the institutions of right. Hence, the end of the history of freedom does not signify any halt to actual history.

Similarly, when Hegel addresses the reality of philosophy as the final cultural phenomenon of absolute spirit, he conceives a development of philosophical systems comprising the theoretical history by which his own system arises. Consequently, the history of philosophy he depicts comes to an end that signifies not the close of philosophical debate but rather the emergence of the form of philosophy the Hegelian system represents.

For the new orthodoxy, these dual histories express how systems of justice and philosophies are creatures of parallel institutional and intellectual developments where each new system arises through determinate negation of the tradition from which it springs. Since practical and theoretical systems thereby have their own problematics grounded in overcoming the antecedent dilemmas of their heritage, each is a product of its age. Hence, every system of justice and philosophy has its norms predicated upon a foundation given in history, a foundation consisting in the negation of preceding theory and practice. Hegel may wish to celebrate his own philosophy and the institutions of modernity as historical results that can never be bettered, but this is idle boasting if their principles are grounded in the equally conditioned practices of the past. A more honest appraisal would consist in recognizing that all practical and theoretical achievements are only final in respect to their own genesis. Because that historical genesis gives each ethic and philosophy its bearings, none can lay claim to an unconditioned validity. Therefore, the new orthodoxy concludes, Hegel's theory of objective and absolute spirit only reaffirms the lessons of subjective spirit: that reason and justice are corrigible conventions grounded in historical practices as transient as they.

Does this make any more sense than the coherence theory of truth and logical holism? Whether we turn to subjective spirit or the histories of objective and absolute spirit, the problem is the same.

Thinking may be an activity of a living individual, conscious of his or her own representations, self-conscious in virtue of certain relations to other individuals, and linguistically able to express his or her thoughts. Yet can any of these preconditions of thought be known to determine what counts as knowledge? To claim that either the structure of consciousness, intersubjectivity, or language predetermines the standards of objectivity requires some account of how we can have objective knowledge of what these conditions are and that they play their privileged role as foundations of knowledge. If, however, any of these putative foundations does determine what we know as true and right, how can we have any certainty that our knowledge of them is not a distorted vision that they themselves impose? So long as they underlie all our cognition, we can never remove their blinders and gain immediate access to what they or any other objects are in their own right. Conversely, if what they determine as true or false regarding their own role is true unconditionally, then what they contribute to the formation of this knowledge is of no consequence to its validity. But this means that in this instance, they do not function as foundations of knowledge, which is to say that they contradict the privileged character ascribed to them. Hence, either way, it is impossible to know that consciousness, intersubjectivity, or language are juridical conditions of knowledge. They may well be necessary preconditions of knowing, without which knowledge is impossible, but it makes no sense to argue that they play any role in the adjudication of knowledge claims.

Instead of treating any of these factors as foundations of knowledge, one must conceive them as conditions of knowing that leave utterly undetermined what can be known on their basis. Contrary to the interpretation of the new orthodoxy, this is precisely how Hegel addresses each one in his doctrine of subjective spirit. In conceiving consciousness as a being in the world, Hegel carefully refrains from ever asserting that the physical engagement of consciousness or the categories of its understanding enter in distinguishing which of the representations they make possible are true or false. Similarly, when he analyzes the master-slave relation, he acknowledges the type of self-knowledge it contains, but he never claims that its intersubjectivity decides what else counts as knowledge for the mode of self-consciousness it makes possible. Finally, when Hegel turns to language, his whole point is to show how it provides a medium for thought precisely by leaving thinking free of any dependence upon privileged givens. Language provides this service by furnishing signs, representations whose reference is freely determined by intelligence itself. Far from restricting thought to thinking representations tied to givens from whose bondage reason can never escape, language allows the conscious individual to have representations whose referent is a product of thought, or more accurately, a self-determination of thinking. Hence, language predetermines neither what can be thought nor which of the possible thoughts it can express are true or false. Language may have a given grammar and vocabulary, established in the practices of an historically situated linguistic community. Nevertheless, every language is and must be such as to allow any of its speakers to create whatever new meanings they choose without violating grammatical rules or current usage. By the same token, semantic analysis can never determine the truth of meanings that any language allows to be expressed. For, if grammatical language can express not just novel ideas but true and false theories, then linguistic structure leaves utterly undetermined which of its possible communications convey knowledge. Not only does the character of signs make this so, but it is impossible to argue the contrary with any coherence.

Hegel, unlike the new orthodoxy, grasps the true lesson of subjective spirit, that consciousness, intersubjectivity, and language all leave thought free of any limits other than those it imposes upon itself. And despite all appearances, Hegel does not lose sight of this lesson in his histories of freedom and philosophy.

By conceiving the genesis of the institutions of right after determining them in their concept, Hegel strictly demarcates the legitimation of these institutions from the historical process by which they emerge. What gives the institutions of right their exclusive justice is that they are structures of self-determination. As such, they have no antecedent foundations from which their character derives. Hence, the history from which they arise can contribute nothing to their validity, neither by providing prior standards for justice nor by imposing external limits upon what can count as right and wrong (see chapter 12).

If, on the contrary, one were to adopt the new orthodoxy's view that standards of justice are rooted in historically conditioned practices, as MacIntyre argues,[8] there is no way to escape the nihilist conclusion that all ethics are corrigible conventions relative to prevailing institutions. If one tries to circumvent nihilism by holding that history has an absolute character, leading to practices whose ethics are unconditionally valid, then one admits that at the end of history, an ethics emerges whose validity is no longer historically conditioned—a conclusion contradicting the claim that right and wrong are historically relative categories. Hence, it makes little sense for a new orthodoxy pundit like MacIntyre to denounce contemporary morals as the work of new barbarians, as if his appeal to historical practice still left room for objective ethical judgments.[9]

If this leaves the new orthodoxy in the clutches of nihilism, what undermines that embrace is the untenability of its claim that no practice can have its juridical character unconditioned by history. That claim is destroyed by Hegel's philosophy of right, which shows how the institutions of justice are structures of freedom, determined through their own practices and thus grounded upon themselves. Although nature and a plurality of choosing individuals are prerequisites for any institutions of right, they are conditions for just as well as unjust activity. Consequently, neither they nor any other enabling conditions comprise juridical foundations determining which of the practices they make possible are right or wrong.

The case of the history of philosophy is no different. Admittedly, Hegel seems to describe the genesis of his own system as if all prior philosophical history were guided by an internal necessity, logically linking each successive system to its predecessor in a continuous march towards true wisdom. If this be taken at face value, it leads to the new orthodoxy's view that every philosophical system is founded upon a conceptual result that is the product not of its own argument but of a prior incommensurable system. This condemns all philosophizing to foundationalism, save, perhaps, for the very first philosophy, which, if not grounded on assumptions generated by preceding philosophers, may still be founded on a conceptual framework rooted in some pre-philosophical practice. In any event, since the new orthodoxy must regard its own theory about philosophical development as something other than the first philosophy, it is at pains to account for the validity of its own philosophical position. Once again, if it admits that its metaphilosophical theory is itself conditioned by past philosophical history, then its view will be relativized unless that past history is an absolute development leading to an incorrigible wisdom unlike any prior theory. In that case, however, the truth of the new orthodoxy's position will not be conditioned by its genesis but be unconditionally valid, with the result that it will contradict the very view about philosophy that it advocates.

Despite first appearances, Hegel's doctrine of philosophy can escape this dilemma once it is no longer assumed to be a theory about how the actual history of philosophy is governed by a necessity mandating what can or cannot be conceived at any stage. To be consistent with Hegel's own claims concerning the presuppositionless, self-grounding character of his system, it must rather be understood as a rational reconstruction of theoretical history, showing how the greatest past thinkers have explored the possible options of thought, doing something that nothing compelled them to do: namely, recognizing the conceptual limits of their predecessors and then striking ahead on their own with what overcame those limits in the most direct fashion. Whether thinkers repeat the errors of the past or blunder into forgettable novelties is up to them. But if they are to make any abiding history in philosophy, they must go beyond all past developments while offering something that must be retained. If, further, the options of philosophical thought are logically limited and logically connected, then it should come as no surprise that one can order the history of philosophy in terms of the self-ordering of the different logical categories. That ordering is not an external necessity compelling philosophers how to think but testimony to how the autonomy of reason need not be without a logic of its own.

It is here, in philosophy's own development, that the new orthodoxy meets its Waterloo, freeing Hegelian theory from the truncated dogma to which it has been reduced. For us, this signifies both a liberation and an inexorable bondage. While we may escape enslavement to a corrigible, historical reason, the collapse of the new orthodoxy shows how no arguments can ever free us from the temptations of a systematic philosophy without foundations.

7
Can Philosophy Have a Rational History?

PHILOSOPHY'S EMBARRASSMENT WITH HISTORY

Although few philosophers have ever denied that they reason as historical individuals, born to a specific age and members of a particular culture, only recently have so many judged reason to be historical in character. This embrace of history cannot come easily for philosophy. From the moment thinkers assume the mantle of philosophy by enjoining reason to advance beyond opinion to truth, they set themselves a task whose fulfillment is impossible unless reason can legitimate the role of every factor that effects the course of its argument. If reason fails to validate each content and procedure it employs and instead allows philosophical argument to be guided by any influence whose authority has not been philosophically justified, reason's quest for truth stands condemned by the very reliance on unexamined opinion it seeks to surmount. If philosophy is not to abandon all claim to wisdom unbiased by arbitrary grounds, how can it fail to seek an unconditioned, universal, timeless validity completely indifferent to every particular, conditioned circumstance that historical convention might produce? Hence, when philosophers relegate reason to history, they seem to be eliminating the possibility of their own enterprise, as if fulfilling Socrates' warning that to do philosophy is to seek death, since eternal reason lies beyond human mortality.

Although philosophy's confession of its own historicity might seem to be the height of self-contradiction, it reflects just how great an embarrassment history can be for philosophical reflection. As much as philosophy's quest for truth may drive it to question the authority of all givens before the tribunal of autonomous reason, philosophy's own reality seems inescapably caught in the given frameworks of two parallel histories. As a cultural phenomenon, conceived in some time and place by living authors using some given language, philosophy is always situated within a world whose conventional practices and institutions have a history of their own providing the background and linguistic medium for every effort of reason. This history of institutions and activities external to philosophy is not the only history framing philosophical investigation. From the very start, every philosophical inquiry stands equally situated within a history internal to philosophical thought, the history of philosophy proper. Far from being an ex post facto construction, this latter history is reflected within the philosophies comprising it, as much by their own reference to their predecessor's argument as by the contrastive difference each must have simply to count as a philosophical development and not a mere restatement of past argument. Just as philosophy seems to incorporate the external history of nonphilosophical practices simply by employing the given language of its day, so it seems to direct its own course in reference to its internal history, finding its problems and approach by both rejecting and incorporating past theoretical achievements. On both counts, philosophy appears to be a child of its age, constitutively determined by the practical and theoretical heritage in and in reference to which it cannot help but emerge.

Granted this predicament, three basic possibilities lie at hand, each applying to philosophy's relation to the external and internal histories within which reasoning proceeds:

1. Philosophy is historically conditioned and therefore unable to achieve the unconditioned universality it traditionally claims. Because it is relative to the historical development of factors external and/or internal to philosophical debate, philosophy can never rise above opinion and exercise autonomous reason.
2. Philosophy is historically determined, but history has an absolute development leading to an unconditioned standpoint from which philosophical reason can attain wisdom.
3. Philosophy appears in history but presents what is eternally valid. Neither the history of institutions nor the history of philosophy

plays any role in determining philosophical problems or their proper resolution.

PHILOSOPHY'S TRADITIONAL FLIGHT FROM HISTORY

Traditionally, philosophy has affirmed the third of these possibilities by appealing to some ahistorical foundation as the wellspring of rational argument. Whether this foundation be characterized as a first principle of reality, the source of all being and knowledge, the ego, the transcendental conditions of experience, or the structure of communicative competence, it always provides a timeless privileged given on which objective truth is grounded.

Once the chosen foundation becomes characterized in cognitive rather than ontological terms, the denial of the historical character of reason readily carries with it a denial of the reality of history. For if all discourse is rooted in some eternal framework, such as intentionality or the structure of narrative, it may well be doubted whether history is any more than a meaning constituted by the timeless foundations of reference. Far from determining rational reflection, history would then be a product of the conditions of discourse, representing a construct no more privileged than any other object of knowledge.[1]

Needless to say, the growing acceptance of a historical reason has largely resulted from critical recognition of the insoluble dilemmas of any foundational appeal to privileged givens. The moment philosophers root objectivity in some foundation, they tie the justification of truth claims to a ground whose privileged role can never itself be justified. Any attempt to argue for the chosen foundation would undermine its supposed primacy simple by introducing other reasons in support of it. If, on the other hand, the proffered foundation be ascribed its privileged authority by virtue of its immediacy, there is no way to decide between it and any other competing candidate whose immediacy is similarly claimed. Hence, the only account that can be given of any putative foundation is one that explains how its given content has come to be granted its privileged role. This explanation would not comprise a justification of the chosen foundation but rather a deconstruction unraveling the genesis of the conceptual scheme it grounds. If it be accepted that philosophical theory must advance some given content as the standard and basis of argument in order to reason at all, there is little else to do but undertake a deconstruction that turns to the history of such a content's advance. In this way, the traditional appeal to ahistorical foundations has ended up inviting a turn to history, where the ground of argument is no longer sought in some self-evident principle or privileged standpoint but rather in the historically situated process wherein the fundamental terms of specific philosophies come to occupy their special place.

THE PROBLEM OF RELATIVIST HISTORICISM

In considering the historical genesis of philosophical theories, contemporary thinkers have generally cast their gaze beyond the history of philosophy to the history of cultural practices and institutions distinct from the phenomena of philosophical inquiry. Accordingly, it is worth first considering the possible ways in which philosophy can or cannot be determined by the history external to it.

To begin with, there is the widely embraced position of relativist historicism, which holds that philosophical thought is conditioned by the historical development of nonphilosophical factors, such that philosophical claims are always relative to the historical framework in which they are made. The proponents of this view have differed greatly in identifying which factors of convention have the privileged role of determining philosophical thought. However, whether they assign that role to current linguistic practice, economic organization, class interest, or cultural tradition, they all agree that since the determinant limits what problems and approaches philosophy entertains, it is folly to presume the unconditioned autonomy that philosophy has traditionally sought in its search for eternal truths. Instead, they argue, reason is governed by historical developments independent of philosophy, leaving philosophical argument endemically relative to its age and inherently corrigible.

As appealing as it may be, relativist historicism is plagued by the self-referential inconsistency that undermines every form of relativism. Despite their claims that rational argument is relative to historical conditions and hence incapable of justifying any unconditioned universal truths, relativist historicists advance universally binding truths of their own. These consist in none other than their description of the factors whose historical development conditions reason and their accompanying claim that these factors do determine philosophical thought, not just relative to our own historically conditioned views but throughout history. No matter what gets identified as having primacy as the historically conditioning factor, it figures as a suprahistorical foundation of which the relativist historicist somehow has privileged knowledge. If relativist historicists were to apply their characterization of philosophy to their own position, they would have to admit that their theory about history and philosophy has no universal validity but is merely a corrigible historical opinion, with no more weight than the opposing theories of this or any other age. If, conversely, they were to maintain the exclusive truth of their conception of the relation between history and philosophy, they would be contradicting their own claims concerning the historically relative character of philosophical discourse. Either way, the relativist historicist falls into self-contradiction.

The two most popular versions of relativist historicism, economic determinism and holism, exhibit most blatantly the dilemma involved. If, for instance, thought were conditioned by relations of production, how could one ever be sure that they permit access to valid knowledge of their own reality or of their conditioning role? Similarly, if, in line with holism, thought were conditioned by standards of justification rooted in given practices, how could this predicament be known with any certainty? If certainty is denied as the goal of a particular conceptual scheme, enshrined in its own specific practices, how can holists claim any validity for their description of that or any other practice, or, most importantly, for their ultimate claim that all thought is context-dependent? Relativist historicists may well ignore their own self-referential inconsistency, but they can never surmount its fatal consequences.

THE SUPERFLUITY OF ABSOLUTIST HISTORICISM

To escape this difficulty without denying the conditioning of reason by external historical factors, thinkers such as the young Marx and Lukács have advanced an absolutist historicism drawing its inspiration from certain remarks of Hegel.[2] They have recognized that no theory about history and philosophy can enjoy exclusive truth unless philosophy can somehow arise in an unqualified, unbiased form. Only when this has already occurred can a conception of philosophy's historical character pretend to be more than an opinion. Hence, the avatars of absolutist historicism have claimed that history has given rise to institutions and practices of an absolute character that permit philosophy to attain the wisdom it may have always sought but could never obtain due to external conditions prevailing in the past.

This view ascribes history an absolute development in two respects. On the one hand, it asserts that history comes to generate institutions that are rational—which is to say conceptually determinate or universal. This makes possible for the first time a philosophical understanding of historical reality, for only when convention takes a universal form, as some have said has occurred in modernity,[3] can convention be transparent to reason. Naturally, if convention were not to become conceptually determinate, there could be no philosophical knowledge of convention, nor for that matter of its role conditioning philosophical reason.

On the other hand, absolutist historicism presumes that historical development not only produces a reality that is rational, and thus philosophically conceivable, but produces practices that no longer prevent philosophy from exercising its long-sought autonomy. For only if current convention leaves philosophy free to legitimate its arguments without any given restraints, can reason provide truths whose justification is not jeopardized by a dependence upon unexamined factors. In this vein, the young Marx suggests, as Lukács later argues in *History and Class Consciousness,* that although all theory is predicated on class interest and thereby ideological, history generates a universal class, the proletariat, whose interests are free of all particular bias, such that those who adopt the proletarian point of view are adopting an unbiased view of modernity from which reality can be conceived without any distortion.

In this sense, the history leading to the present could be regarded as the prehistory of a timelessly universal order, just as the past succession of philosophical theories could be regarded as the prehistory of the one eternal philosophy, whose previous practitioners are mere pretenders, trying to pass off ideology—that is theory grounded on extraphilosophical interests—for wisdom.

Although this view has the virtue of not vitiating the authority of its own pronouncements, it suffers from too much success. By affirming an absolute development of history that makes possible a philosophy unimpaired by historical convention, absolutist historicism effectively eliminates the historical character of reason. Prephilosophical thinking may be dependent upon historical factors that its own thinking can never evaluate or justify. Knowledge of this very predicament, however, requires a cognition that does not share these limitations. Such is the cognition absolutist historicism is compelled to introduce. In laying claim to an absolute age, where the reality underlying discourse has developed so as to enable reason to grasp truth, absolutist historicism effectively sets philosophy in an eternal present, where the history conditioning discourse has come to a halt and thought jettisons its historical blinders. On these terms, all that is historically conditioned is the captive rhetoric of ideology, not the autonomous reasoning of philosophy that the absolutist historicists must themselves employ.

What their position reveals is that if philosophy can conceive its own relation to history without forsaking truth, it must view itself as a product of history whose argument is yet free from all dictates by the external historical conditions that may still have made it possible. This means that the reason purportedly set free by historical development would not refer to any historical conditions in determining philosophy's problems and approach, nor would the validity of any of its claims depend upon any contribution by history. In other words, absolutist historicism ends up leaving philosophy proper entirely free of historical determination.[4]

THE NATURE OF AN INTERNAL HISTORY OF PHILOSOPHY

Taken together, the examples of relativist and absolutist historicisms indicate how no coherent argument can be given to show that philosophy is determined by an external history. At most, nature and convention may provide the natural, psychological and linguistic prerequisites for philosophical discourse, but no factor external to reason can possibly be known to mandate what philosophy will accept or reject as true wisdom. Of course, this outcome does not automatically render philosophy an entirely ahistorical phenomena. It still leaves unresolved whether philosophy is determined by its own history and whether such determination could affect the validity of philosophical argument.

At first glance, the relation of philosophy to its internal history would seem to parallel that which holds between reason and external historical factors. Once again three options lie at hand, each involving the same problems encountered in the introduction of external history. First, philosophy might be just as juridically unconditioned by its own history as by the history of external institutions and practices. On the other hand, if philosophy is conditioned by its own history, there are these two alternatives: either wisdom is relative to the given conceptual schemes of the philosophical tradition, or this tradition reaches an absolute development, at which point the quest for wisdom sheds its self-biasing character and becomes actual wisdom.

Of crucial bearing on these options is what exactly the history of philosophy comprises. Does it consist in the history of elaborations of the selfsame philosophy or rather in the history of entirely different philosophical systems whose defining paradigms represent incommensurable frameworks?

The Genesis of the Selfsame Philosophy

That the history of philosophy be but the saga of one and, indeed, of the one and only philosophy sounds strange to anyone familiar with the mutually excluding arguments with which philosophers have waged their ceaseless wars. Nevertheless, there is something about this unrelenting combat that suggests an inescapable unity to philosophical thought. As Kant once asked, is it really possible for there to be more than a single philosophy?[5] If, objectively speaking, there be but one selfsame reason, how could more than one system of philosophy be founded on rational principles? The historical succession of different systems hardly rules out such a thought, for whenever a philosopher advances a new system, does he not, as Kant suggests, effectively declare that "there has been no other philosophy prior to his"?[6] After all, if any philosopher were to admit the existence of another philosophy—that is, another system of true wisdom—there would be "two different philosophies concerning the same thing, and that would be self-contradictory."[7]

Although the self-understanding of philosophers need not dictate the character of philosophical history, certainly the abiding unity of philosophy cannot be dismissed out of hand. If the history of philosophy were the genesis of one self-identical quest for truth, its history would have a prescriptive telos consisting in the complete development of the system of philosophy. Certainly, this normative goal would not entail that philosophical speculation would cease with its achievement, nor that thinkers could only conceive arguments in the order they would follow within that consummating system. It would mean that philosophical progress could be distinguished from either faulty elaborations or restatements of previously attained wisdom. Furthermore, if the nature of philosophical argument were such that no claims could count as wisdom unless the truth of their prerequisites were already established, genuine progress in the history of philosophy would duplicate the path of argument within the one system of philosophy.

One might ask to what extent the history of philosophy would be rational if this were the case. Granted that thinkers need not be familiar with past philosophy, nor understand it if they are, nor be aware that they are simply duplicating it when they restate it, nor realize that they advance arguments already refuted by past efforts, nor follow any predetermined route in their reflection, any *a priori* knowledge of the history of speculation would seem impossible. The historical progress of philosophy, however, would be another matter. Instead of concerning whatever may have been thought, this progress would involve solely those theoretical achievements that contribute to the advance of the one philosophy proper. Its course would be rationally determinable precisely because it would trace over time the same succession of arguments that logically follow within the system of philosophy. Valid philosophical argument would thus always stand determined by previous philosophical progress in the following manner: either it would limit itself to retracing that progress and make no history from a normative point of view, or it would make philosophical progress in its own right by appending its argument to that already achieved. In the latter case, its own addition could be made in ignorance or recognition of past accomplishments. Either way, the philosopher would have to work through and certify the arguments supporting his or her own novel contribution simply to present it in a justified form.

Of course, if the history of philosophy involves the elaboration of a unified system of wisdom, some thinkers will work out the initial arguments that rest on no others. For this reason, progress in the history of philosophy would proceed from an effort undetermined by any prior philosophical history. By contrast, subsequent contributions would rest on past achievements, either reproducing them or taking them as a given foundation on which to build. Nevertheless, this historical dependence would not condition philosophical argument, since it would involve nothing but the same order of conceptual precedence and succession by which the entire system of philosophy would unfold without reference to any antecedently given factor.

The History of Philosophy as a Succession of Discrete Systems

The situation is very different if the history of philosophy consists in the succession of disparate systems of philosophy. Conceivably, this succession could be arbitrary or necessary.

If it were arbitrary, there would be no need for one system to precede or follow another. In that case, philosophizing would have no determinate relation to the history of philosophy, and there could be no rational history of philosophy. This would be true from either a descriptive or normative point of view. Even if one were to admit that one system had exclusive truth, which, of course, would have to be the system within which one is arguing about philosophy, this system would not provide any normative ordering for philosophical progress. Since all other systems, being incommensurate theories, would not be stages in the completion of the true system, their succession would have no normative significance whatsoever.

If, however, the succession of philosophical systems involved necessity, the situation would be quite different. Such necessity might be thought to lie in an allegedly paradigmatic situation for making history in philosophy. Such a situation might be that wherein a thinker perceives the need for new arguments as a result of uncovering the shortcomings of past theory and then forwards a new theory to remedy these failings. On these terms, the history of philosophy might be thought to exhibit a necessary structure of determinate negation, where each new system negates or repudiates the errors of its predecessors, but carries their imprint within itself insofar as its novelty consists in an attempt to resolve the problems they have generated but failed to solve. Admittedly, such a situation might well reflect the experience of many a philosopher and be readily documented in many a case. Yet is it really necessary to the development of philosophy, and even when it does occur, are the direction and validity of philosophical argument really conditioned in any determinate way by this predicament?

Naturally, the first system of philosophy could not be determined in this manner, nor, indeed, would any other subsequent theory whose author reasoned either in ignorance of or without reflection upon prior philosophies. Of course, it might be argued that philosophies developed without reference to any other systems would either have a certain necessary form, from which a philosophical tradition could be born according to an internally determined sequence, or else have an arbitrary character that nevertheless would necessarily determine whatever tradition might arise on its basis.

Either way, if the history of philosophical systems is to determine their argument, reference to previous systems would have to direct either the method or content of subsequent systems, and not just be an item of psychological or scholarly interest. Insofar as discrete systems of philosophy comprise mutually exclusive totalities of philosophical thought, rather than sections of one philosophical theory, the dependence of one system upon its predecessors signifies that philosophical argument would be founded upon something falling outside its reach. It would mean that philosophy operates from some given standpoint, conceptual scheme, or set of problems that it has not generated itself but received from an antecedent body of thought incommensurate with its own. If this were not true, the internal history of philosophy would have no bearing on reason, and any philosopher could work out a new system bearing no imprint of prior philosophies.

Consequently, whether the history of philosophy determines the development of philosophical systems rests on whether philosophical argument can be determined by any given standpoint or conceptual framework. This problem concerns not just subsequent systems but the first philosophical system as well. Even though it has no prior philosophical history to mold its thought, it could still issue from the establishment of a philosophical viewpoint determined by a prephilosophical discourse. Hence, the problem at stake is whether philosophical discourse in general can be known to be bound by conceptual foundations. This problem is not answered by noting how it is certainly possible for a discourse on truth to be predicated on a given framework. What lies at stake is rather whether any argument can succeed if all philosophical discourse has that foundational structure.

DECONSTRUCTION VERSUS RATIONAL RECONSTRUCTION OF THE HISTORY OF PHILOSOPHY

If philosophy were conditioned by an internal history consisting in the succession of mutually exclusive philosophical systems, speculative reason would be inherently foundational, provided it did not arrive at an absolute threshold from which philosophy could argue without being biased by the theoretical heritage shaping all previous thought. Of course, if the internal history of philosophy did take an absolute turn, analogous to the one absolutist historicists ascribe to external history, valid philosophical knowledge would once again be ahistorical, in contrast to those earlier efforts of thought whose dependence on past theories rendered them prephilosophical impersonators of wisdom. If, however, such an absolute outcome were denied, philosophy would be deprived of all autonomous reason. Instead, it would stand reduced to a foundation-ridden endeavor whose quest for truth would always be frustrated by its attachment to given conceptual frameworks whose determining role could never be questioned without being presupposed.

On these terms, the only plausible approach to philosophy and its history would appear to be deconstruction. This would consist in an exercise in doxology, unmasking the antecedently given conceptual schemes underlying different systems of philosophy. Such deconstruction could provide no wisdom but at best offer an edifying service promoting an opined self-awareness of our own assumptions. Deconstruction, however, cannot be coherently advanced as a replacement for philosophical investigation. Presenting it as the sole option for the study of philosophy is tantamount to claiming exclusive knowledge that philosophy is inherently foundational and hence a self-contradictory delusion requiring a sobering cure. As popular as that claim has become, particularly in the wake of Wittgenstein, it resurrects all the self-referential dilemmas afflicting relativist historicism. If all philosophy is burdened by assumptions determined by past philosophical tradition, how can the advocates of deconstruction consistently maintain that their approach has any more validity than that of any opposing view? If the deconstructionists were to admit that their conception of philosophy is itself relative to some given foundation, they would have to offer their description of the history of philosophy as a mere opinion with no privileged authority. If, however, they still affirmed the exclusive truth of their characterization of philosophy, they would be contradicting the relative character that they ascribe to all discourse.

The conclusion is unambiguous: if the history of philosophy is a history of discrete philosophical systems, these cannot be known to follow one another in any necessary order. Although most philosophers have indeed developed foundation-ridden theories, it makes no sense to argue that all philosophy must rest upon given conceptual schemes. That would be just as absurd as seeking to cure us of philosophical speculation by engaging in rational argument.

Hence, there can be no rational history of philosophy in any traditional meaning of the term. Whether philosophical history consists in contributions to the one abiding philosophy or in successions of different philosophical systems, the development of philosophical argument must be just as undetermined by the work of past thinkers as it must be free from external control. Any claim to the contrary is nothing less than nonsense.

Does this mean that philosophy must maintain silence regarding its own history? Not at all. The impossibility of arguing against a foundation-free, historically unconditioned philosophy does not leave the history of philosophy a matter solely for intellectual historians.

The conceptual dilemmas of historicism and universal deconstruction themselves indicate essential features of philosophical history. Since philosophy cannot and should not be bound by antecedent frameworks, philosophical argument does not depend upon any antecedent theorizing. Therefore, there can be no necessity to any temporal sequence of philosophical systems. If there is to be any rational ordering of successive philosophies, it can only be a conceptual one, completely independent of temporal considerations. Thus, to argue that it is impossible to be a Platonist today can only mean that, conceptually speaking, current positions successfully repudiate Plato's views, not that it is impossible to philosophize in line with Plato's argument, either with knowledge or in ignorance of his theories.

This leaves open the philosophical task of a rational reconstruction of the history of philosophy. Unlike deconstruction, which unmasks the presuppositions underlying philosophical systems as testimony to the impotence of reason, rational reconstruction seeks what conceptual connection can be found in past philosophy in order to retrieve what is rational and incorporate it as a building block in conceiving truth. This, after all, is what all philosophers engage in when employing other theories as critical foils and supports for their own arguments. What this involves is tracing back the presuppositions on which past theories rest and then ordering them with regard to one another in view of how some account for the presuppositions of others while relying on the achievements of further theories for their own starting points. If any past theories can thereby be integrated into a unitary argument that somehow accounts for all its claims, they will be grasped in a rational ordering revealing their conceptual dependence upon one another and certifying their own theoretical achievement. On these terms, the argument to which they contribute will neither depend upon nor necessarily follow their actual temporal succession. Although their history just might follow their rational order, this would be but a contingent development that no reasoning could foresee.

The same situation applies to the use philosophical argument makes of current usages, references to other theories, and introductions of other given contents. All do provide material contributing to the expression of philosophical theory. However, this does not mean that they have any role in determining the validity of those arguments that employ them. If they were to be ascribed any juridical status, it would have no legitimacy, until the philosophy in question established their authority through its own argument. In this sense, we, as contemporary philosophers, stand on the shoulders of our predecessors only insofar as we are able to establish that their feet do not rest on arbitrary foundations. To do this, there is no need to deny that our speculation could not take place unless we inhabited a historical world providing us with language and particular intellectual traditions as well as the natural prerequisites for rational life. Nevertheless, all these factors are conditions of consistent as well as inconsistent, valid as well as invalid theory. The moment any is assigned the status of a principle of knowledge, determining what can and cannot be considered true, all the absurdities of foundationalism get reintroduced. There is little choice but to recognize that the existence of these factors leaves entirely undecided the course that philosophical inquiry will take.

Like Socrates, we must ultimately admit that philosophy's quest for wisdom can be guided by but two things: recognition of our own ignorance and an opined understanding that there is a difference in meaning between opinion and truth. There can be no other rational grounds for taking up philosophy, since any appeal to guiding reasons would presuppose prior knowledge, signifying that philosophizing had already begun. All that can coherently urge us forward are divine voices, feelings of wonder, or some such name for an ignorant arbitrariness that leaves utterly undetermined what will follow.

No matter where we stand in history, the self-conscious ignorance from which philosophizing begins deprives us of all right to claim any given knowledge including any knowledge of which questions to ask. Nevertheless, we can immediately engage in dialogue with past theory, just as Socrates listened and questioned the claims advanced by his interlocutors. Here we need not be burdened with deciding which questions to ask, for it is the assertions of past thinkers that provide us with direction. From the point of radical ignorance at which the quest for truth begins, all we can ask of these philosophers is to legitimate their claims. If we have yet to develop our own philosophy and thus lack wisdom with which to judge their truth, we can do little more than observe whether past thinkers provide consistent or inconsistent arguments for the theses we have called into question. Either way, all our dialogue with the tradition can establish is its coherence or incoherence, not the truth or falsity of its claims. Thus, *before* we philosophize in our own right, determining what is true, previous thought can only offer us opinions whose philosophical worth remains to be established. Consequently, the philosophical tradition cannot impose itself upon our thought unless we arrive at the same ideas through our own independent argument. If such rational reconstruction fails to reappropriate prior theories, the history of philosophy remains an antiquarian study, of no bearing on philosophical argument. Today and tomorrow, only by reasoning in freedom from history can we determine whether the routes of the past are paths we must follow.

II
THE FOUNDATION-FREE ETHICS OF FREEDOM

8
The Limits of Morality

The new fashion in ethics warns us that morality has come of age. Far from being an irremovable keystone of the human condition, morality, it is said, is a modern creation. Born of reflection on the inability of given convention to impose obligations upon us without the confirmation of our personal deliberations, morality allegedly introduced a new demand: that we disengage ourselves from the psychological mechanisms of desire and disposition and the cultural patterns of custom and law so as to make our unencumbered selves the ultimate arbiters of conduct.[1] Under its tutelage, ethics became transformed into an individual striving to fulfill self-imposed obligations limited to no particular field or condition and from whose reach no asylum could be found. Yet, in achieving this very disengagement from all prior interests and attachments, morality arouses the suspicion that its purity deprives the individual of the means to specify any norms of conduct that do not express subjective arbitrariness. Hence, we stand before an ethical either/or: either we cling on to morality in the vain hope of transcending mere personal preference, or we abandon its disengaged standpoint for an ethic of community, in which the shared practices of a given institutional framework provide common ends and common roles in which ethical norms can be sustained.

According to current wisdom, to opt for one is to repudiate the other. If we adopt morality, we deny the presence of a unity of ought and is in nature or convention, rescinding prescriptive authority from the given order of the world we inhabit, choosing instead to be self-defining subjects, creating our own obligations by applying the universality and consistency of reason to our will, striving to realize what should but will not be unless we take our personal initiative.[2] Although we thereby risk failing to uphold any distinction between subjective caprice and our moral norms, we at least transcend the hold of the contingent practices of a given community and operate at the only level where truly universal obligations seem attainable. If, alternately, we adopt the ethic of community, we reject the normative primacy of the disengaged moral subject and acknowledge instead obligations rooted in the established norms and practices of an ethical framework to which we belong, obligations that enjoin us to pursue a common life in which we already participate, where what ought to be is no longer separated by any gap from what is, where our membership in the ethical community involves fulfilling roles tied to shared values and character that bring about what already prevails.[3]

Moreover, current wisdom instructs, this choice is a sobering one. If we embrace the project of morality, we end up unable to determine any obligations that are certifiably objective. If, on the other hand, we embrace the ethic of community, we must abandon the universal claims of the moral standpoint and accept the particularity of the community in which we find ourselves, recognizing both that the norms we observe hold true only within its bounds and that any attempt to uncover norms of unlimited scope only lands us in the emptiness of morality.[4]

Despite the widespread conviction that ethics has no other prospect than this either/or, there is another alternative, originally advanced by Hegel, that recognizes the limits of the moral project, yet conceives it as reconcilable with the ethic of community. This view grants morality a limited but affirmative value of its own, according to which, morality, far from being antithetical to the ethic of community, provides a prerequisite for the latter while warranting a place, albeit circumscribed, within its domain. Further, whereas this gives morality a positive, if subordinate significance, the encompassing ethical community is conceived not as merely particular but as a universally valid order in which what is and what ought to be are unconditionally united.

To explore the validity of this alternative, no better resource is available than Hegel's own thematic analysis of morality in the second part of his *Philosophy of Right*. Although Hegel's critique of Kantian morality has not lacked for commentators, Hegel's positive exposition of the moral project has hardly been discussed by subsequent philosophers. If it is to illuminate our current quandary in ethics, we must determine to what extent Hegel's analysis uncovers the logic of the moral project, where the limits and affirmative value of this project may lie, and to what extent morality can figure as both a prerequisite for the forms of ethical community and an incorporated element within their life.

THE MINIMAL STRUCTURE OF MORALITY

Given the systematic construction of Hegel's *Philosophy of Right*, where concepts are introduced only after their prerequisites have been established, it is important to take into account both the place of morality within the whole of ethics and the internal division of the concept of the moral project.

Hegel's theory of right treats morality following upon abstract right and preceding ethical life. This places morality between the property relations that comprise abstract right and the institutions of family, civil society, and state that build ethical life's three divisions. Conceptually speaking, this ordering signifies that morality presupposes property relations, which are conceivable independently of either the moral project or ethical community, whereas ethical life presupposes both property relations and morality. In other words, whereas participation in ethical community requires moral agency and personhood, moral agency is not defined by membership in a family, civil society, and the state, but does involve personhood, the recognized status of property owner. Of course, whether these implications hold true depends upon what morality itself turns out to be.

In this regard, the internal ordering of Hegel's account of morality deserves notice. In the *Philosophy of Right*, he conceives the moral project in terms of three sets of relations that successively determine moral agency with respect to purpose and responsibility, intention and welfare, and the good and conscience. Although morality as a whole contains all three aspects, their order implies that the minimal structure of moral agency is defined in light of purpose and responsibility, that the role of intention and welfare depends upon the former, and that moral agency's determination of the good as conscience presupposes the two prior relationships. Hence, we can assess Hegel's account on its own terms by examining to what extent these relationships hold.

To begin with, the minimally defining feature of morality must be ascertained, the feature that presupposes no other moral factor yet is ingredient in all other aspects of moral agency. Given the elementarity of abstract right and morality's independence from ethical community, our sole resources are the plurality of persons, individuated through their property by which they recognize each other as self-determined owners, embodying their will in some external entity. In their capacity as property owners, who have inalienable ownership of their own bodily existence, persons cannot be slaves, whose entire being is subsumed under the will of another as the factor of its objectification. As owners, persons enjoy the minimal respected freedom that permits their activities to recognizably express their own, rather than another's, will. Although this makes possible all further engagement in relations of freedom, including moral agency, persons exercise their rights and duties as proprietors irrespective of any specific aims that might motivate their choice of what objects to own and what contracts to enter. What counts in their interaction as free owners is simply that they exercise the right to embody their will in some recognized external factor and observe the coordinate duty of respecting the like embodiment on the part of others. What their intentions and interests may be in acquiring and disposing over property is a matter of indifference as far as their self-determination as property owners is concerned, just as what and how much they own are irrelevant. So long as they dispose over some external domain in which their will has a respected existence, their freedom as persons is realized.

In terms of moral agency, by contrast, individuals interact not with respect to external factors giving an immediate embodiment to their wills, but with regard to their actions as they are internally determined by the agent. To move from property relations to moral interaction, persons need do no more than shift their concern from the objectification of their freedom in property to their actions as the vehicle for their recognized and respected self-determination. The need to make this shift is implicit in property relations, to the degree that malicious and nonmalicious property disputes underline how the realization of right, as initially defined in terms of the rights and duties of property owners, depends upon the initiative of individuals, who must undertake the action that they have determined will reaffirm the property rights that have been violated by the particular acts of others. Moreover, no other resources must be introduced to account for this move, since the choosing will with which persons are endowed gives them all they need to make their actions the focal point for the realization of their respective freedom and to recognize the freedom of each other in the actions they undertake.

However, if the actions of persons are to be those in which their self-determination as moral subjects is recognized, their actions must contain a dimension that recognizably owes its character to the determining of the agent. Since an action, as voluntary, is preceded by an antecedent representation of an end that serves as the ground of its achievement, morality immediately involves two parallel distinctions: that between the internal and external aspects of agency, comprising the inner decision and outer act following upon it, and that between that aspect of the outer act that is recognizably prefigured in the decision and that aspect which is not.[5]

Hegel identifies as purpose the common content that is prefigured in the represented aim of the agent and equally objectified through an outer act resulting in some alteration of the given state of affairs with respect to which the agent acts.[6] Because the agent in question is finite, he or she faces an independently given world with a character and connectedness of its own, whose every detail and relationship can only be imperfectly and incompletely known. Hence, the purpose is determined only in relation to the given situation as it is perceived and understood by the agent, whereas the alteration produced by the action will involve results manifesting the purposeful determining of the agent as well as unforeseen and unintended effects. Although the act of the agent is a contributing factor to all aspects of the altered situation that would not have arisen without it, a distinction can still be drawn between those results of the act that are prefigured in the chosen purpose and those that are not. Thereby, the agent can be held accountable not simply for the act and its consequences but for those features of it that express the knowing and willing of the agent as that agent sought to determine him- or herself through the chosen purpose (PR, par. 117). Hegel calls this prefigured dimension of the act the action, in distinction from the deed, which designates the act in its entirety. (PR, par. 115). This contrast of action and deed carries with it the distinction between imputability for the deed and "responsibility," the latter designating the special accountability that is limited to the action (PR, addition to par. 115). Hegel's initial claim is that moral agency has its minimal determination in the doing of such action, where the agent is held accountable only for that part of the deed that is expressly determined by the antecedent knowing and willing of the individual. This should first provide an identifiably moral action and moral responsibility.

However, far from being special to moral agency, these features appear rather to be generic to voluntary action, pertaining just as well to property relations as to actions that have no normative significance at all. Instead of providing the differentia for distinguishing moral from non-moral action, the categories of purpose and responsibility seem thematic to Hegel's discussion of practical intelligence in his theory of subjective spirit, where agency in general is conceived without regard for whatever additional factors render action a mode of normative conduct.[7]

Admittedly, every self-determination of persons involves purpose and responsibility to the extent that proprietors acquire and dispose of property only insofar as they recognize each other's actions to be purposeful objectifications of their wills, establishing entitled domains by proceeding with knowledge of what kind of act is required to win the recognition of others. This is particularly evident in the entering of contracts and the distinction between nonmalicious wrong and malicious acts of fraud and crime, none of which could occur if the participants' actions were merely unintended deeds, where knowledge of the situation was a matter of indifference. Similarly, actions of no ethical significance at all, such as technical manipulations of objects, can be done with purpose and manifest responsibility.

If purpose and responsibility are to be specifically moral, something more must be involved. Although Hegel may not sufficiently emphasize what else renders purpose and responsibility elementary categories of moral agency, he does add two features that could allow a line to be drawn between nonmoral and moral action and imputability. First, moral action is always addressed to other individuals in their capacity as like agents (*PR*, par. 112). What counts, morally speaking, is not altering the material corporeal world but having an impact upon the agency of others, as expressed in their aims and activities.[8] Secondly, moral purpose and responsibility involve right and duty, such that moral agents are entitled to be held responsible for their actions and not their deeds, while being bound by the correlative duty of acting with such responsibility while holding other moral agents accountable in the same way. On both counts, purpose and responsibility figure as elements of a special structure of interaction, rather than as generic features of purposive activity that could just as easily apply to functions of a single individual and things. To act with putatively moral purpose here involves realizing a preconceived end relating in some manner to the affairs of similarly engaged individuals and doing so both with the right of being held responsible for the action and not the deed that results and with due regard for the corresponding responsibility of others. Within this interaction, purpose and responsibility provide the factors by which individuals enjoy a nonnatural, mutually respected autonomy, which, thanks to the relations of right and duty ingredient in it, cannot operate independently of this interrelationship. Through it, individuals exercise an artificial agency that individuates itself in acting with a preconceived end relating to others such that each agent is held responsible for his or her act as it is determined by that agent's prior knowing and willing. Here individuals figure as subjects who are what they do (PR, par. 124), interrelating and recognizing each other in regard to the aspect of their actions whose content derives from the individuals as agents.[9] In this way, purpose and responsibility can be seen to be basic categories of a particular form of self-determined agency that is not given as a function of the self but arises in and through a specific mode of interaction.

Yet despite its intersubjective character, this interaction does not comprise the framework of an ethic of community. Its participants interrelate in terms of their individual accountability as determiners of the character of their own actions, not as members of institutions who occupy roles and pursue ends reproducing an order in which right is already embodied. In this respect, the right and duty of purpose and responsibility go beyond the parameters of agency in general, without introducing anything specific to ethical community.

Distinguishing action from deed in terms of right and duty may import a normative dimension into the proceedings compatible with morality, but it neither establishes why the right and duty of purpose and responsibility have validity, nor what content the purposes in question should or should not have. The former question of validity need not be raised at this point, since the validity of morality itself remains an open matter. However, it must be asked whether the absence of any specifications for the content of purpose beyond its reference to other purposive agents prevents action, purpose, and responsibility from providing the minimal categories of moral agency. If purpose has no other restrictions upon it, how can its pursuit be emblematic of morality, when morality must distinguish among different purposes in order to differentiate immoral and moral conduct? This "problem" of the indeterminacy of purpose dissipates once we grant that morality involves agents determining and realizing what is right in a situation where the good in question is an ought whose specification and coming into being depend on individual initiative. In that case, what characterizes specifically moral purpose cannot lie in any prior prescription of its content. Instead, what makes purpose special to moral agency must rather lie in the form it has within the complex of moral action. Only on this basis can that further aspect of moral agency that involves determining the proper content of purpose be conceived. Hence, it makes sense for Hegel to remark that the moral is first determined in reference to the subjectivity of the will without being opposed to the immoral (PR, remark to par. 108).

It still is tempting to add the general proviso that purpose not only addresses the affairs of other moral agents in a context of right and duty but aims at realizing right. Hegel suggests this addition in remarking that moral action not only is known to be the agent's own and a relation to the will of others but has an essential relation to the concept of right, taken as an ought (PR, par. 113). Nevertheless, reference to realizing an ideal of right would here be empty talk in two regards. First, right has no independently given determination for moral agency, other than property entitlements, whose own adjudication and enforcement calls for personal intervention[10] and whose moral significance remains to be established. Secondly, purpose and responsibility involve their own realization of right, namely that right of being held accountable for one's action that is internal to the interaction in which purpose and responsibility figure. Hence, if purpose and responsibility are to be vindicated as minimal categories of moral agency, it will suffice to show that they figure as prerequisite components of all further features of moral agency, such that morality is unthinkable without their elementary presence. In regard to Hegel's discussion, this can be substantiated by turning to his next categories of morality, intention and welfare, and examining their relation to purpose and responsibility.

INTENTION AND WELFARE

If, following Hegel's suggestion, we accept purpose and responsibility as minimal features of morality, we confront a coordinate set of moral rights and duties: on the one hand, the right of moral subjects to be held accountable for their actions, as determined by their knowledge of the situation and their conscious aim, and on the other hand, the duty of moral subjects to take responsibility for their so-determined actions and to extend to other moral subjects the same right and duty. As already noted, these prescriptions have a formal character in that they leave out of account the content of purpose and merely focus on the agent's recognized determining of the action's morally relevant character. The only limitation upon purpose is the purely negative proscription that its realization cannot transgress the right and duty of responsibility of others.

Purpose, however, has a particular content, which the right to responsibility for action leaves otherwise undetermined just as the right to property leaves undetermined which objects should or should not be owned by persons, with the proviso that property acquisitions not violate the person and property of others. This content of purpose is at hand in the aim that precipitates action as well as in the act that realizes it. In both cases, this content stands in relation to other contents. In the preconceived aim, the content stands related to further aims, to which it may be subordinated as a means to an end. In the realized action, it connects to consequences that can correspond to the further aims to which purpose may be subordinate. If a justification were to be sought for the content of a purpose, a standard would be required, and if this standard were to be decided by the agent, in conformity with the determining role of subjectivity in moral agency, then this justifying standard could consist in a further aim that the purpose would be intended to serve as a means to its achievement. If the purpose served such an aim, the action would be moral, whereas if the purpose conflicted with it, immoral action would result. Hence, purpose and responsibility provide the resources for a further dimension of moral agency, where the content of purpose is determined in light of a second-order aim. By knowing and willing such a second-order aim, the agent can pursue justified purposes—justified in terms of a chosen intention that the purpose serves.

Taken in the abstract, pursuing a purpose with intention can, like purpose itself, figure as a generic feature of voluntary action. An amoral purely technical act can be undertaken with intention, as in the case of a shoemaker who purposely cuts a sole in order to repair a shoe, just as an amoral but normative action can be done with intention, as in entering a contract in order to obtain monetary gain. Nonetheless, like purpose, intention can have moral specificity by being understood to be ingredient in a structure of right and duty, where first, intentions relate to consequences affecting the affairs of other moral agents and where second, moral agents are, on the one hand, entitled to be held accountable only for those consequences of their action that are prefigured in their intention and, on the other hand, duty-bound to hold themselves and others accountable solely for the intended consequences of their respective actions. Intention thereby provides moral agency with a further dimension of autonomy. Whereas moral purpose rendered the action attributable to the agent in terms of how the agent has determined it through knowing the situation and willing an aim, moral intention makes the consequences of the action count as matters of responsibility only insofar as they conform to the goal for which the agent pursued the purpose. Although this right and duty of intention no more specifies what counts as a valid intention than the right and duty of purpose determines which purposes are moral and which immoral, the problem of moral justification now shifts to the content of the intention, setting the stage for a further determination of the moral project.

Hegel's analysis of intention and welfare draws out the implications of these basic moves that follow from the categories of purpose and responsibility. To begin with, however, his account raises the same suspicion that accompanies his introduction of purpose and responsibility, the suspicion that the categories at stake are not specific to moral agency. The first distinction drawn applies to the action as an empirical, concrete whole, having a manifold of particular sides and connections. Within this complex lies an essential nature, manifest in the causal relations by which specific consequences follow from it. To the extent that the agent knows this essential nature and wills it, the agent's aim is no longer a mere purpose concerning the immediate existence of the deed but rather an intention concerning the action's substance and ultimate aim.[11]

Insofar as this aim of the action is something represented by the agent prior to its execution, it is not something external but rather a particular aim residing in the agent. Comprising the particular goal chosen by the agent, it comprises the interest of the agent in its impending act, an interest whose fulfillment in the executed action and its consequences constitutes the welfare of the agent to the extent that this is determined in reference to the intention motivating the action (*PM,* par. 506).

So conceived, intention, interest, and welfare would seem to represent features of any voluntary action whose motive lies in the attainment of some consequence of the action. As we have seen above, if intention simply signifies the aim motivating the attainment of a purpose, intention can figure in all types of voluntary action, save for those with no regard for the consequences of the deed. As for interest, Hegel himself points out that virtually every voluntary action is done with interest, since unless a deed is performed aimlessly, some particular end serves as its motivation and provides an interest in its undertaking (*PR*, par. 124). Of course, if intention and interest are generic to voluntary action, so must welfare be if all it comprises is the fulfillment of interest.

As with purpose and responsibility, further qualifications must be made to render these categories constitutive of moral agency, and Hegel introduces additional features to make intention, interest, and welfare morally significant. The key additions are what he calls the "right of intention" and the "right of welfare" (*PM*, par. 505). On their basis, what distinguishes moral intention and moral welfare from intention and welfare in general is that the former are matters of right. This signifies that they figure within a structure of interaction comprising a mode of recognized and respected self-determination on the part of the participating subjects whose intention and welfare are at stake. Like any rights, these have as their counterpart the corresponding duties to respect their exercise by others. Hence, exercising the rights of intention and welfare necessarily involves reference to the intentions and welfare of others, such that morally specific intention and welfare constitutively concern undertaking actions whose consequences bear upon the motivating aims and fulfillment of interest of others.

What, then, is the content of the right of intention? As we have seen, intention aims at consequences expressing the essential nature of the action—consequences that are willed on the basis of knowledge of what that essential nature is and what it entails. Although every act may have a universal character connecting it to certain results, each act is equally embedded in external circumstances, leaving it prey to outside forces, including the wills of others, that lead to consequences foreign to its nature (*PR*, par. 118). The right of intention extends imputability only to those consequences that were aimed at by the agent with due understanding of the nature and circumstances of the action and its likely results. Just as the right of purpose limited responsibility to those aspects of the deed that were prefigured in the aim of an agent cognizant of the situation of the deed, so the right of intention makes moral agents accountable solely for the intended consequences of their acts. In this respect, the right of intention insures that the universal character of the particular content realized by the moral will shall not be something self-subsistent, but rather should count as only what the agent has recognized it to be in the antecedent intention motivating the act (*VR, 3:350*). Hence, although each act is of a certain type, such as arson or murder, to use Hegel's examples (*PR*, note to par. 120), what the agent acting with moral intention is accountable for is not this universal quality, which serves merely as a means to achieving the intended aim, but rather the import of the act that the agent understood and willed. In this way, what counts morally is the nature of the act as determined by the intention of the subject.

As should be evident, purpose enters in as a constitutive, albeit subordinate, element in the right of intention. One cannot act with intention unless one already acts with purpose, providing a deed with a universal character that can serve as the instrument for satisfying a further motivating aim. Hence, intention has a double structure, encompassing the universal content contained in the purpose and the particular aim of the intention that provides the subjectively determined motive making the consequences entailed in the purpose of value to the agent (*PR*, addition to par. 121). Needless to say, unless one already holds an agent accountable for those aspects of the deed prefigured in a chosen purpose, it makes no sense to hold that agent accountable for any intended consequences of the action.

If the right of intention means that moral agency should have its autonomy honored in the consequences as well as in the act itself, this also broadens the responsibility of the moral agent, making morality a matter not just of performing right actions with the right purpose but of producing right consequences with the right intentions. As Hegel maintains, this implies that one should know not merely one's action in its immediate singularity but the ramifications entailed by its universal nature (*PR*, addition to par. 118). Moral accountability thereby demands greater powers of insight than the right of purpose alone would require, leaving children, imbeciles, and lunatics, who might be competent to act with some degree of moral purpose, incompetent to act with moral intentions (*PR*, remark to par. 120).

Yet, this second type of responsibility, which extends accountability to the universal import of the action as known and willed by the agent

(*VR* 3:369), is still formal in that the right of intention does not prescribe which consequences and which intentions are to be sought. The moral subject is still left to determine both and to seek their justification through some other resource. The only restriction contained in the right of intention is that the moral agent act on motives congruent with holding others accountable for the consequences of their actions so far as these were intended with knowledge of the nature of the acts and their circumstances.

The right of intention may thus leave unresolved the problem of adjudicating among intentions, but the very fact that each intention is a self-chosen particular content carries with it a further right, which Hegel calls the "right of welfare." Because the content of the intention remains a matter of discretion for the moral agent, it derives from the individual and represents the agent's personal interest in the universal quality of the action (*VR* 3:373). Given the self-selected, particular character of this interest, which is simply the subjectively determined value that the action's consequences have for the moral agent (*PR*, par. 122), its satisfaction comprises an equally individual welfare, defined not simply by any given physical or psychological needs but in terms of moral self-determination, which involves the particular moral agent's deciding what is of worth. Since the welfare at issue is nothing more than the achieved aim of the intention, its realization is automatically at stake whenever a moral agent acts with intention. Hence, if moral agents have a right of intention, they equally enjoy a right of welfare, a right to pursue the satisfaction of their interests as these lie determined in their intentions.

As Hegel points out, this right to welfare is not a right to egoism (*VR* 3:334). Since the content of a moral intention is directed at the affairs of others with respect to their equal right, the accompanying pursuit of welfare is personal in the purely formal sense of attending to the intentions of the moral agent, whatever those intentions may be. Satisfying the chosen interest of the moral agent will realize that individual's own welfare even if the intention at issue concerns the welfare of another. This is because an altruistic intention, as something self-chosen, remains the personal aim motivating the agent's action and thereby counts as a personal interest whose realization represents that agent's particular welfare. For this reason, moral conduct can no more be disinterested than egoistic in character (*PR*, par. 124).

If this allows personal welfare to encompass the welfare of others, freeing the right of welfare from any bondage to self-seeking indulgence or self-abnegating disinterest, the mutual respect such entitlement entails introduces a more positive connection between personal and general welfare. Since the right of welfare, as the recognized prerogative of all moral agents, obliges each subject to honor the like entitlement of others, the aim of intention should be such as to conform to the promotion of the welfare of others. As a whole, the aim of moral intention can thereby be said to be the welfare of the moral subject and the welfare of others (VR 4:324). Although this might make it appear that intention obtains a universal content by aiming at the welfare of all, every one of the welfares in question consists in the satisfaction of interests with a particular self-chosen content still left undetermined by the structure of moral right and duty (VR 4:324; PR, par. 125). Insofar as the interests at stake are all particular contents of merely personally assigned value, each may just as well be the means for a further interest rather than an end in itself (PR, par. 122). None possesses any mark that would distinguish it as more objectively valid than another. Besides being subject to the proviso of harmonizing with one another, the contents of these welfares remain unrestricted by the rights of intention and welfare, leaving undecided whether they are otherwise valid.[12]

Accordingly, the right of welfare is just as formal in character as the right of intention. All it prescribes is that moral agents find self-selected value in their actions, without hindrance to the like quests of others (PR, par. 123). If moral agents are to give content to their pursuit of welfare and actually determine their intentions without relying upon any extraneous authority, the only resource at hand from which they can draw is their natural subjective existence—that is, the given complex of the needs, desires, passions, opinions, and preferences that they possess in their capacity as selves, irrespective of any institutional norms (PR, par. 123). Taken up as an aim, this content figures as the happiness of the individual, a happiness that comprises the moral agent's welfare, not as this content lies naturally given in the self but as transposed within the framework of moral right and duty, where it acquires a universal significance for the agent as a matter of entitlement linked to the like right of others.[13] In this respect, the moral agent stands as arbiter over these desires and inclinations in a situation where welfare obtains its content from them, but still lacks a necessary relation to any particular one (VR 3:387, 4:332). Because the universal aspect of welfare has no specific bearing upon which inclinations are made the aim of intention, the formality of welfare remains, leaving still open the question as to whether it is right to satisfy one's inclinations (*VR* 3:384). Since welfare, be it of the individual or of all other agents, concerns the particular aims chosen personally by each and every moral subject, it can collide with right, especially when the only other universal content of right to which reference can here be made are the property entitlements of persons (*VR* 4:339).

This possibility of conflict raises the question of whether acting with intention to promote my welfare as well as the welfare of others can justify an action that otherwise violates right (*PR*, par. 126). Granted that moral agency presupposes the right of personhood but abstracts from all norms of an ethic of community, right and welfare here figure as the rights of persons and the particular welfare of moral subjects, respectively (*PR*, remark to par. 126). As Hegel suggests, two contrasting rankings seem to be inherent in the competing entitlements of property rights and moral welfare. On the one hand, the claims of welfare cannot supersede those of personhood insofar as property relations provide individual freedom with the elementary respected existence that first allows agents an opportunity to be held accountable for their actions. Moral subjects would thus only be undermining their own right of welfare if they were to assert the expendability of the rights of persons (*PR*, par. 126; *VR* 3:399). On the other hand, the right of welfare should supersede particular property entitlements when upholding them threatens the very life of an agent whose survival depends on acquiring what another owns. In that case, a right of distress takes precedence since death extinguishes the totality of the agent's autonomy, eliminating all personhood and moral agency (*PR*, par. 127), whereas the violation of the property of another only infringes on a particular side of that owner's freedom as a person and, depending upon that owner's moral aims, of his or her moral welfare (*VR* 3:35).

In either case, the discrepancy between right and welfare persists, leaving each only contingently related to the other. This discrepancy should be overcome, for welfare without right is no more acceptable than right without welfare, when moral agents are equally persons. Although Hegel maintains that only in the institutions of ethical community and, in particular, in the state, can right and welfare actually be joined together (*VR* 4:334), he claims that moral agency constitutively addresses the issue and that, indeed, once the rights of intention and welfare are at hand, moral agency has nothing other on its agenda than confronting this task. This is what lies at stake in Hegel's analysis of the moral categories of the good and conscience, where moral agency is determined with respect to its own attempt to act with intentions whose particular content it has certified to be right.

The outcome of the moral self-determination involved in acting with intention in pursuit of welfare confirms this move. Due to the formality of the rights of intention and welfare, whereby all that is upheld is an entitlement to be held accountable for the intended consequences of one's actions in conformity with the like right of others, moral agency immediately faces the problem of determining which intentions are valid and then acting upon them to promote a welfare in accord with right. The very rights to intention and welfare make this obligatory, since if one is held accountable for what one knows of the universal ramifications of one's action, then one is equally obliged to intend those consequences that one establishes to be valid. Does moral agency have the resources to fulfill this imperative? Hegel's analysis of the good and conscience serves to answer this question by exploring the remaining options of the moral project. The first task is charting the logic of this development.

THE GOOD AND CONSCIENCE

Moral agency addresses the good when the particular intention making the purpose of action of interest to the subject is determined to be universally valid so as to realize a welfare that is right and thereby integrate the particularizing activity of the subjective will into the ideal of right. The moral good poses this unification of welfare and right, of particular aim and universal norm as the task of moral agency. In undertaking to determine and realize the good on the basis of its own subjective resources, moral agency is conscience. As such, conscience incorporates purpose and responsibility and intention and welfare with the coordinate rights and duties that make these factors constituents of moral self-determination. Yet conscience adds a new dimension that brings to a head the limits of the moral project.

Once more, conceiving the new relation requires first identifying what is specifically moral about it. The good, comprising the unification of welfare and right, might well appear to be just as applicable to the ethics of community as to moral agency, especially when Hegel himself suggests that the family, civil society, and the state each unites welfare and right within existing institutional bonds. In the family, each member plays a role upholding a common welfare whose right is already enshrined in the household to which all owe allegiance. In the market place of civil society, each commodity owner pursues a private welfare that there can only be advanced by satisfying the welfare of some other market participant. And in the state, which ultimately insures that all get their due, the legitimate aims of citizens are brought to realization while illegitimate pursuits are frustrated. What then, makes the good a moral good, and what makes the subjective stance aiming at its realization a moral agency?

It cannot simply be that the moral good is, to paraphrase Hegel, the intention that has right as its content and the right that exists through being willed with intention (*VR* 3:407). The good embodied in ethical community equally involves actions with right intentions insofar as its roles are performed with interest and consciously reproduce the framework of right they constitute. Nor is it enough to characterize the good as the universality of the will in its capacity as self-determining (*VR* 4:345), since members of ethical community can equally exhibit universality in the institutional freedoms they exercise. The moral good must have further features of its own that make it and conscience emblematic of morality. If unsystematic assumptions are to be avoided, these features must be composed of no further resources than what moral agency already provides.

To his credit, Hegel does point to key aspects that serve to distinguish the moral good from the good of the family, the social good, and the good of the state, without violating the strictures of systematic immanence. First, the moral good is an ought, comprising a unity of right and welfare that has yet to be brought into existence and can only be brought into being through the initiative of subjects who are obliged to realize it. This contrasts with the good of each form of ethical community, which is already realized in the institutions whose particular unification of right and welfare figures as the defining aim of their members' conduct. Whereas the good of ethical community thereby contains within itself the willing that realizes its own unity of right and welfare, the moral good is something to which the moral agent stands in an external relation, facing it as something not yet at hand in the world the moral agent inhabits (*PR*, par. 131). Indeed, it is precisely this absence that obliges the subject to make this good's realization a personal aim.

This relational character of the moral good, whereby its unity of right and welfare does not yet contain the activity realizing it, further entails that the source for its content must lie in the will of the moral subject who engages in bringing it into being. A good that is an ought, requiring realization by an agent unencumbered by any existing relations that embody that good, cannot already have a content determined independently of that agent's will. If it did, it would lack the component of welfare, which must be united with right. Because welfare is the satisfaction of the chosen aims of agents, an antecedently determined good that does not contain the realizing activity of moral agents would leave their choice of intention out of account, rendering their welfare equally excluded and thus incapable of being in any unity with right. Consequently, the subjective will to which the moral good is externally related is not just that on which its realization depends. The subjective will bringing it into being is equally responsible for deciding what content the good should have.

Moreover, because the good that conscience faces is unrealized and thus does not contain the moral agent or any institution to which he or she belongs, conscience's obligation is not based on membership in any community. Rather, it is as an individual will, unencumbered by any attachments that mandate what the good should be, that conscience stands obliged to strive for what it alone can specify and bring into being.[14]

These morally specific features of the good already contain the salient points that distinguish conscience from the agencies animating family, civil society, and state. Insofar as the moral good is an ought in an external relation to the agency obliged to both determine and realize it, conscience consists in an agency that aims at such a good, deciding what content its intention must have to unite right with the welfare of itself and others, and then undertakes to fulfill that aim. In this capacity, conscience assumes the burden of determining the content of the moral good independently of any given interests, attachments, or practices that the order of things imposes from without. Conscience cannot rely upon any such factors precisely because the good it should realize is an ought not yet at hand in the given. Conscience has no choice but to turn inward, for no external resources can mandate prescriptive norms for a good of such a character. Yet, because the good stands outside it, as something in which the subjective will is not yet contained and integrated, the given purposes and aims of the moral subject need not conform to what the good should be. In this respect, the good stands as an ought not only because it is not yet at hand but because moral agents may or may not determine themselves in conformity with what they know the good to be (*PR*, par. 131). Accordingly, conscience places moral agents in a situation entirely different from the defining predicament of family members, civilians, or citizens. The latter are obliged to maintain an order already embodied in the institutions that provide them their constitutive roles. By contrast, moral agents exercise conscience by facing one another as subjects obliged to act on right intentions aiming at something not yet at hand, whose goodness it is the responsibility of the subject to determine, know, and bring into being. Whereas a just family, civil society, and state provide institutions within which their members' rights and welfare are guaranteed, moral agents appeal to conscience in a situation where it is just as contingent whether the external world will permit them to realize their moral intentions as whether each and every conscience will aim at what it knows to be good rather than evil (*PM*, par. 510).

Despite the determining role of the subject, moral agency as conscience once again involves a structure of right and duty, which remains a structure of interaction. Since the unity of right and welfare comprising the moral good pertains to the affairs of other moral agents as well, acting on conscience constitutively relates to the right and welfare of other moral agents. Further, as a prerogative pertaining to every moral subject, it entails its own right and duty, adding a third dimension of accountability to the rights of purpose and intention. Acting with conscience, moral agents are not just entitled to be held accountable for their actions rather than their deeds and for those consequences of their actions which they intended. Now they are fully responsible only insofar as they knew and willed the good or evil contained in their aims (*PM*, par. 132; *VR* 3:410). Once more, the requirements of moral competency are increased, for now agents must not only be able to act with purpose and understand the ramifications of their actions but be able to determine and know the difference between good and evil (*VR* 4:351). Enjoying the right to be held accountable as subjects of conscience, moral agents are equally obliged to hold others accountable on the same grounds and to act on conscience, knowing and willing intentions that bring right and welfare into harmony for all. Although this third dimension of accountability finally brings in reference to the objective validity of intention, it still retains a formal character. For, as Hegel notes, the right to be held accountable only for what I see as universally valid in no way determines what particular content I ascribe to this good, nor whether my consciousness of the good is erroneous or true (VR 3:413; PR, remark to par. 132).

This formality underlies the abiding problem of how these rights and duties of conscience can actually be carried out. The basic difficulty concerns how conscience can fulfill its task of determining the good. Whereas moral agency can readily give itself a purpose permitting its action to be distinguished from its deed and further decide upon an intention by which certain consequences of its action acquire subjective value and imputability, it is far from clear how conscience is to set about determining the very principle on which moral validity rests. As such, the good that conscience is obliged to determine and realize should hold valid for all moral agents. In principle, what the individual moral agent decides the good to be should count as an aim that every moral agent has a duty to know and will. However, because acting on conscience is their common right, each moral agent is entitled to determine the content of the good and be held accountable with respect to what he or she knows and wills it to be. This presents a dilemma, for if moral agents are to honor each other's right to conscience, each must leave it to the discretion of others whether they arrive at the same determination of the good. If there is a conflict, each moral agent falls into the predicament of either having to deny the objectivity of the conflicting determinations of others, which is tantamount to violating the duty of recognizing their right of conscience, or denying the objectivity of his or her own specification of the good and accepting the authority of others, which is tantamount to abandoning the responsibility of conscience. The only means of escape from this quandary would seem to be the contingent occurrence of concordant determinations of the good by each agent's independent conscience. Such fortuitous harmony would, however, offer but paradoxical relief, for each appeal to conscience would still depend for its viability upon the extraneous decisions of others, something undercutting the generic autonomy of each conscience.[15]

Can moral agency overcome this difficulty, or can it only be resolved by leaving conscience behind and embracing the standpoint of the ethic of community, where the congruence of determinations of the good is achieved through an institutional framework wherein agents realize the universal welfare they share by pursuing common aims generic to their roles as participating members?[16] And if the moral project is doomed to fail in its attempt to determine and realize the good, does this deprive morality of all affirmative value?

Hegel's analysis of conscience helps us answer the first question by exploring the possible options open to moral agency in face of the good.

The starting point is the external relation between the moral good, the universal unity of right and welfare yet lacking the subjective activity both determining and realizing it, and the plurality of moral subjects obliged to act on conscience. Given the character that it has, this relationship involves three stages: first, the apprehension by conscience of the abstract idea of the good and conscience's determination of its content in regard to what particular action the individual should undertake to realize it; second, the moral agent's willing in respect to this privileged aim; and third, the realization in the world of the willed good. Each stage relies upon the determining role of the individual moral subject, yet each stage no less involves reference to the affairs of others. Of course, to the extent that moral agency can proceed through the first stage in different ways that affect how it wills the good and how that good is realized, the two subsequent stages will take correspondingly multiple forms. What Hegel's account shows is that not only are the second and third stages always plagued with contingency, making the realization of the moral good something problematic, but the first stage is beset by difficulties that persistently blur the line between morality and immorality.

THE DIALECTIC OF CONSCIENCE

Moral agency first relates to the good as to sheer duty. Because the good opposes the moral agent as the unity of right and welfare that does not yet contain the subjective willing by which it is realized, the good is, on the one hand, the moral essentiality that exists neither in the external world nor in the given aims of the agent and, on the other hand, a universal end without any further particular content. Consequently, the good immediately stands as a universally valid aim, with no further qualification than that it ought unconditionally to be known and willed by the moral agent. As such, the good is simply duty, to be realized not owing to any particular content but because it has the form of being whose realization is the universally valid obligation of the agent (*PR*, par. 133). Of itself, the good prescribes no other rule than that duty be done for duty's sake.

Yet, to carry out duty in deed, the moral agent must will a particular intention to be effected by achieving a specific purpose in a particular action. Hence, the very demand of duty requires for its translation into practice that the abstract universality of duty, which the good represents for the moral agent, be further determined. The moral agent must therefore answer the question: What is duty? Hegel consistently points out that the only content at hand for duty is the intentional doing of right and caring for the welfare of both oneself and other moral agents (*PR*, par. 134). Insofar as the good consists in the unity of both right and welfare, it must be understood that right and welfare here figure no longer as independent considerations, that may conflict with each other, but as factors that are conditioned and limited by one another (*VR* 3:421). A good will, which warrants the title by realizing the good, is accordingly defined by doing right with care for welfare and attending to welfare that conforms to right.

These precisions are, however, of little help in giving a practical specification for duty. Given morality's presupposition of personhood and abstraction from the authority of ethical community, doing right in conformity with welfare simply signifies upholding property relations that allow moral subjects to pursue self-selected aims in recognition of the accountability they are due. Since property relations are fraught with conflicting claims and wrongs that cannot be resolved by means of their own resources and since welfare can involve aims that conflict with one another and with the aims of other moral subjects, adding the proviso that right be done in accord with welfare adds little precision of content to the edict that duty be done for duty's sake. The problem confronting the moral agent remains one of determining how the general aim of the good can be achieved in a particular action.

Hegel's basic claim is that the moral standpoint cannot develop any immanent doctrine of specific duties from the resources at hand (*PR*, remark to par. 135). The good, facing the moral agent as duty, prescribes that duty be particularized, but, lacking the determining activity of its own realization, the good remains an abstraction, offering no guide to what is demanded (*VR* 4:356). Since there is no unequivocal way of locating a particular duty inherent in the universal duty of the moral good, each specific duty, as particular and limited, is different from good and can only find its sanction by sharing the general form of being a duty, a form that is indifferent to its content. Hence, there are no absolute particular duties, antecedently mandated by the good. Rather, every particular duty enjoys its normative character merely by being posited in that form (*VR* 4:356).

This positing can be the work of no other than the moral agent, which signifies that if the moral good is to be particularized and translated into action, the moral agent must independently determine which contents will be subsumed under the form of duty. In other words, the very reality of the moral good can lie nowhere else but in conscience, the moral standpoint that invests in its own subjective knowing and willing the authority and obligation to independently decide the particular aims giving good conduct its direction. Hegel aptly describes conscience as absolute self-certainty, which is reflected into itself in its universality (*PR*, par. 136). Conscience is absolutely self-certain insofar as it ascribes absolute authority to its own independent determination of which aims are good. Moreover, conscience is self-reflected in its universality insofar as the universal validity it enjoys in determining good aims is entirely self-imposed with full awareness that its own knowing and willing are the source of the universal validity conferred upon its chosen aims. In each respect, conscience treats its own subjectivity as determining the good, recognizing its own individual will as the moral universal for which no external particulars have any binding value (*VR* 3:426).

Yet, in determining what is good exclusively from out of itself (*PR*, par. 138), conscience faces a discrepancy between its own resources and their intended product. With respect to content, conscience confronts the fact that the duties it must determine are not properties peculiar to the moral agent as an individual but obligations binding upon all. With respect to form, conscience must grapple with the fact that insofar as the good is essentially universal, its content should not take the shape of feeling or anything else that is individual but should rather be determined through laws and principles. By appealing to its individual self as the ultimate arbiter of the good, conscience thus opposes what it aims to be: the principle of universally valid conduct (*PR*, remark to par. 137).

Hence, conscience, in the very act of determining itself as the realization of the good, is indistinguishable from what comprises its own antithesis—evil, which signifies the immoral subjective willing that determines its aims in independence and difference from the universal duty of the good.

That conscience renders itself evil is most evident in its relation to other moral agents. Since acting with conscience is the duty of all moral agents in face of the good, each conscience treats as determinative of the good not only its own subjectivity but subjectivity in general. Hence, as each conscience relies exclusively upon its own individual resources to determine what duty is, its determination precludes the legitimacy of any different determination by other moral agents. From their competing points of view, however, its chosen aims appear to be evil, standing opposed as they do to what these other consciences have determined the good to be. If conscience replies by denying the authority of their aims, they must hold it to be evil once more for failing to honor their right to conscience. Indeed, conscience must regard itself as evil as well, for the moment it condemns other agents for committing the evil of willing aims contrary to what conscience has determined to be good, it knows itself to be rescinding its recognition of their right to conscience, which is a violation of its own duty. Thus, so long as there is any diversity of chosen aims, conscience finds itself confronting evil in itself and in others, condemned in reference to determinations of goodness of equally self-annulling character.

Even when the private determinations of each conscience miraculously correspond, evil still haunts each agent. This is because no conscience can provide more than a subjective assurance to distinguish whatever determination it gives the good from a determination of evil. In either case, a particular aim is willed that cannot be deduced from the abstract ideal of the good. Its particular content must derive from determinations of the subjective will, whose desires and inclinations may just as well be sanctioned as condemned (*PR,* remark to par. 139). Insofar as conscience is the privileged determiner of the good, for whom no given particulars have independent validity, no content in the self can be said to be intrinsically good or evil. Hence unison in intentions still leaves the line between good and evil a mere stipulation, subject to repudiation at any moment.

This predicament leaves conscience with a variety of options, none of which can remedy the abiding difficulty.[17] All these options are premised upon conscience having determined itself, selecting some particular aim as the realization of the good. This selection draws a distinction between good and evil, since determining a valid intention stamps any contrary intention as immoral. Given that the moral agent is at liberty to implement or not implement the particular content it has determined for the good, the moral agent may act, relative to conscience, in a manifestly good or evil fashion or act in a fashion that is evil but appears to be good. When the show of goodness is directed to others, the agent acts with moral hypocrisy, whereas when the show of goodness takes in the agent him- or herself, it is moral self-deception (*PR*, par. 140).

Needless to say, the difficulty in sustaining the universal validity of conscience's distinction between good and evil injects a dialectical element into what it means to act manifestly morally or immorally as well as hypocritically or self-deceivingly. How this difficulty renders manifestly good action susceptibly evil and vice versa has already been documented. The cases of hypocrisy and moral self-deception, which both depend upon a prior determination by conscience of good and evil, follow an analogous course.

Moral hypocrisy involves, first, that conscience has decided what aim counts as a particularization of the good; second, that the moral agent wills a particular aim conflicting with this aim; third, that the moral agent knows of their conflict; and fourth, that the agent yet asserts to others that the resulting action is good (*PR*, remark to par. 140). The dissemblance in moral hypocrisy might appear immune to dissolution from challenges to conscience's determination of the good, since what hypocrisy rests upon is not so much the truth or falsity of conscience's selection of the good aim but the duplicity in its attempt to pass off as good to others what it knows to be evil. However, if the very distinction between good and evil drawn by conscience is recognized to be merely subjective—which, as we shall see, occurs when moral agency succumbs to moral irony—the moral significance of hypocrisy collapses as well.

Moral self-deception leads to a similar result. To begin with, moral self-deception could appear to be impossible, since it requires seemingly contradictory features: first, that the moral agent as conscience determine the good; second, that that same agent intentionally perform an action that he or she knows to transgress what he or she has determined the good to be; and third, that that same agent still consider the action to be good. Clearly, if moral self-deception is to make any sense, the self-deceiving conscience must appeal to some further factor permitting the action, already acknowledged to be evil, to be subsumed under the good. Moreover, since moral self-deception is predicated upon conscience, this additional factor must not be an external given but something that plays its role due to the determining reflection of conscience itself.

This signifies that moral self-deception will, in the first instance, involve an agent appealing to self-selected "good grounds" to sanction an action that his or her conscience already has determined to be otherwise evil. Elevated to a principle, this moral self-deception comprises what Hegel calls "probabilism" (*PR*, remark to par. 140), the ethic that insists that an action violating what is right can count as morally good provided the moral agent can find some probable good ground for its performance. The good ground need only be probable insofar as it, like any ramification of an action, does not occur with ironclad necessity but is subject to the contingencies affecting the execution of any aim. Although probabilism's appeal to good grounds to sanction evil is an attempt by conscience to get at the objectivity of the matter, what makes a ground count as good is still the subjective decision of conscience. Hence, insofar as moral conduct is performed in regard to others, conscience is here not only deceiving itself as to the validity of the evil act but equally engaging in the hypocrisy of presenting evil to others as if it were objectively good (*PR*, remark to par. 140).

In effect, probabilism's appeal to good grounds is equivalent to making the moral agent's selection of "good grounds," rather than the objective content of the grounds, the factor that turns evil into good. In other words, what makes an otherwise evil action good is that is was done with good intentions—intentions that have no intrinsic link to the action and its ramifications but are attached by conscience as the legitimating factor. This provides for a further form of moral self-deception, the ethic of good intentions (*PR*, remark to par. 140). Here the moral agent recognizes an act that conscience has determined to be wrong to be nonetheless good, provided it is performed with good motivating aims. Self-deception enters in because the appeal to good intention is no better at rendering evil good than the appeal to good grounds. Once again, the content of the sanctioning factor is not what gives it its power to subsume evil under good. Just as no internal inspection can distinguish a good from a bad ground, so none can distinguish a good from a bad intention, especially when each intention can count as the means to some further motivating aim, which may be either good or evil. In each case, the deciding element lies in the stipulation by conscience that the factor involved, be it ground or intention, is good, whatever its content may be. The ethic of good intention may thereby leave little evil or hypocrisy remaining when every agent can find good intentions for performing each and every act (*PR*, remark to par. 140). Yet the inability to rank particular duties and intentions that this entails equally reflects the emptiness of good intention as a redeeming principle (*VR* 4:383). Because good intentions have no identifiable filling that makes them irrevocably good, they cannot fulfill the pardoning role that they are assigned. As a result, conscience only deceives itself in appealing to them. To act merely on good intentions is thus no different than evil, for what it amounts to is the same willing of subjective aims at the expense of the good (*PR*, remark to par. 140).

Hence, conscience must look elsewhere to be able to subsume evil under good, and the only resource left is precisely what rendered intentions good or evil: namely, conscience's mere conviction that they were so. Making this count provides an ethic of conviction where conscience elevates the mere arbitrariness of the moral agent in choosing intentions to the privileged role of making evil the good. Any pretention of appealing to some other content is now left behind as conscience regards its own singular subjective conviction as the moral universal, empowered to invert whatever particular determinations have been assigned to evil. It no longer matters what grounds an action may have or with what intentions it be done. What renders an otherwise evil action good is simply that it be performed with conviction.

This outcome brings to a head the self-contradictory character of conscience. In treating conviction as what is universally valid, conscience invests legitimacy in a private subjective attitude that, as singular, excludes all others, depriving the convictions of other agents of the same deciding privilege ascribed to its own (*VR* 3:465). Acting on conviction therefore cannot be affirmed as a moral right, for its very exercise requires either suspending recognition of the same right on the part of others or else reneging on the authority invested in one's own conviction and submitting to their arbitrariness. With the last remnant of moral objectivity denied, there is simply nothing left to decide between competing convictions than force (*VR* 4:387).

Once conscience takes cognizance of this outcome, it has no other option, without abandoning the moral project, than to embrace a moral irony, retaining the certainty that the good can only be determined by subjectivity, but recognizing that this means that its content is at the mercy of personal arbitrariness, whose every decision is no more certifiably good than evil (*VR* 4:389; *PR*, remark to par. 140). From this vantage, the moral agent can no longer take seriously his or her own conscience, for now the agent recognizes that conscience, as purely arbitrary and subjective, is master over the good, whose every determination by the moral agent can be countered and set aside like a plaything for personal entertainment. Moral irony may thereby undermine the bases for hypocrisy and self-deception by subverting all acknowledgement of any action being good or evil in itself (*PR*, remark to par. 140). Yet, moral irony does not stand entirely detached from conscience. It still accepts the absolute standing of moral subjectivity, upholding the moral agent's quandary in face of a yet to be determined good as definitive for ethics—a commitment that may well represent the final moral self-deception. Hence, moral irony marks not a departure from the moral project but its most extreme expression.

THE NORMATIVITY OF MORALITY

As determined by purpose and responsibility, intention and welfare, and the good and conscience, moral agency displays a perennial inability to specify and realize what is unequivocally right through its personal initiative. In each of its possible forms, the moral project founders by seeking to determine the principle of objective validity as a subjective positing.[18] Emancipating agency from the authority of any externally given laws, conscience has left the moral subject with no rule actually capable of determining valid personal action. Yet, since action must be determined by something, does this not mean that in reality moral action is determined by the purely particular elements of desire and passion that duty is supposed to counter? In the end, is moral freedom anything other than the natural freedom of obeying desire? If, as Michael Foster suggests, this were the conclusion of Hegel's analysis of morality, it is hard to see how the moral project could retain any affirmative value of its own.[19]

In face of this difficulty, it seems that one must look beyond morality to secure any redeeming value for the moral project. Hegel himself seems to suggest such a path by the systematic ordering of his *Philoso-*

phy of Right. In principle, those structures of right that come first have their place both by providing prerequisites of the structures that follow and by being incorporated within them. In regard to morality, this implies that the institutions of ethical life doubly extend normative value to the moral project, first by rendering it a necessary precondition for ethical community in all its forms and second by extending to it the legitimacy of ethical institutions by inserting moral agency within them as a component element of their functioning. In the first case, morality would receive an instrumental value by making possible normative relations in distinction to which its own essence is antecedently determined. In the second case, the moral project would obtain an intrinsic validity by becoming an element contained within normatively valid institutions. In each respect, the moral project would be reconciled with the ethic of community and receive its abiding value through this reconciliation.

How, then, might moral agency first be a prerequisite for the institutions of ethical community? One common suggestion is that morality provides a formative training for the will, bringing it to renounce all particular desires and will the universal, which finally obtains properly objective determination and reality in the common life of ethical institutions.[20] Although the universal willed by the moral agent is acknowledged to be a deficiently formal principle, unable to specify a content that is not arbitrary, it is still maintained that the will must first attain the moral standpoint before it can will the universal bonds of ethical community, whose realization is qualitatively different from the satisfaction of particular desires.[21] If, however, what moral agency wills as the universal is really nothing more than its own particular caprice, how does morality provide any training at all, let alone one that family members, civilians, and citizens would have to have undergone in order to engage in valid household affairs, economic relations, or political activities?

Granted that the foundering of the moral project leaves it with no independent normative value, morality's role as a prerequisite of ethical community would have to find support in the second aspect of its proposed reconciliation with ethical life, that it be a component of ethical institutions themselves. Hegel lends support to this view by making parallel claims concerning the conceptual and real relation between morality and ethical life. On the one hand, he asserts that the deduction of the concept of ethical life lies in how abstract right and moral self-consciousness conceptually result in ethical life as something into which they are absorbed (*PR,* remark to par. 141). On the other hand, he maintains that abstract right and morality cannot exist independently, since abstract right lacks the element of subjectivity by which right is realized, whereas morality has only that element. Each has no self-sustaining reality but can only exist as part of a whole, as part of the institutional system of ethical life (*PR,* addition to par. 141). Taken literally, these remarks imply that the moral project, like property relations, is not only contained within ethical institutions but can only be sustained by being integrated within their compass.

This integration seems plausible in the case of abstract right, for property relations only obtain a secured reality under the protective implementation of civil law as enacted and enforced through the state. Yet how can moral agency, defined as it is in reference to a good that is an ought, find a place in an ethic of community where agents will a good already embodied in the existing institutions to which they belong? The common refrain is that morality enters in because ethical institutions, in the form in which they are conceived by Hegel, integrate subjective freedom within their forms of community (*PR,* remark to par. 124). This integration can be thought of as fundamental to the ethic of community, for what sustains ethical life as a self-realizing good is the subjective willing of an objective law.[22] Hence, if ethical life is to be possible, the laws of the ethical community must be capable both of governing the wills of its members and of being fulfilled through their voluntary acts. To satisfy the first requirement, ethical community must actually enact such laws and enforce them. To satisfy the latter, the laws of the ethical community must be compatible with the subjective freedom of those who are to obey and realize them.[23] The key question is what is the identity of the subjective freedom at issue.

In the family, the subjective element of feeling and personal attraction is given sway as a contributing element in the free entering and dissolution of the marriage bond. In civil society, civilians pursue the satisfaction of their personally chosen economic interests in the market and have their actions judged in reference to their intentions in legal proceedings. And in the state, citizens have their freedom of opinion regarding what is right honored in institutions of political freedom. Yet, in each case, are the subjective freedoms at issue instances of moral autonomy?

An exact identity should not be awaited. Regardless of any right of conscience, moral agency cannot have free sway within ethical community, for, as Hegel argues, the dictates of conscience must be constrained when they do not conform to the objective laws by which right and welfare are upheld in the state (*PR*, remarks to pars. 137 and 337). Still, granted these limitations, is the subjective freedom ingredient in ethical community identifiable as moral freedom? Spouses may exercise the right of marrying and divorcing on the basis of their personal feelings, but is this prerogative what is involved in the rights of conscience? The family good, which unites right and welfare just as do the social and political goods, is not simply an unrealized abstraction awaiting determination by the moral subject. It represents a common good, albeit particular to that household, which is a shared aim for family members only insofar as it has objective existence in the home to which they belong.

The contrast of moral freedom with the "subjective freedom" ingredient in civil society is no different. Commodity owners may exercise a right of interest and welfare by engaging in market activity, but the interest they there realize is not simply a subjectively determined aim that *should* conform with the welfare of others. Rather, it is an economic need for commodities that can only be pursued in an existing institutional structure, the exchange system of the market, where its satisfaction is necessarily tied to the satisfaction of another commodity owner and is subject to a public regulation ensuring the economic welfare of all. Here, what might be called the freedom of desire or appetite is indeed realized by the laws governing the civil economy, but this occurs not in the manner of a moral intending of those laws but only by harnessing this freedom in such a way that it sustains an order that the needy agent does not intend as the conscious aim of his or her market activity.[24]

As for civil law proceedings, individuals are held accountable not for their deeds but for their actions, and only for those of their consequences that are prefigured in intention with knowledge of the likely ramifications of their conduct. Moreover, individuals are only judged fully responsible in due consideration of their knowledge of right and wrong (*VR* 3:359). However, this does not mean that the administration of civil law incorporates the moral rights of responsibility, intention, and conscience without alteration, for the right and wrong that legal subjects should know is not the moral good and evil but the legal and illegal, as mandated by positive law (*PR*, remark to par. 132). Accordingly, determining whether an action is a crime is a different matter from determining its moral worth (*PR*, remark to par. 113; *VR* 3:414).

Finally, the state may permit its citizens freedom of conscience in the sense of not attempting to intrude upon their beliefs or preventing them from expressing their convictions. This might be thought of as respect for moral freedom if it were not that, as Hegel himself points out, the self-determination of the moral subject in purposes, intentions, and conscience is completely untouchable by outside force, having a purely internal existence that makes public legislation and enforcement of morality an impossibly ridiculous venture (*PR*, additions to pars. 94 and 106). However, it still might be thought that moral freedom enters directly into the subjective initiative that citizens exercise in participating in self-government. Here, one could argue, following Michael Foster, that the citizen only realizes the ethical community of the state by recognizing in its law a rational authority binding upon his or her conscience.[25] Admittedly, citizens can always adopt a moral attitude towards the law of the state and judge and obey it according to the dictates of conscience. However, what characterizes the entitled political freedom of citizens is that it is always directed at realizing the constitutional aims enshrined in the political order they inhabit. The subjective discretion this involves by no means conforms to the private deliberations of conscience in face of an unrealized, undetermined good.

In each case, the subjective freedom of ethical community either fails to correspond to moral autonomy or else contains elements of moral self-determination that have been subjected to a thoroughgoing transformation. This should not be surprising, for the very structure of ethical life tends to preclude any inclusion of the moral standpoint within the activities constitutive of ethical community. In contrast to the moral good, the governing aim of every form of ethical association is a good containing the activity of its realization. That is why the types of agency that are defined in pursuit of such an aim are always already situated within the form of community at which their actions are directed. For this reason, the external relation between agent and good that characterizes morality has an incommensurability with the unification of ought and is that ethical community continually realizes by prescribing to its members a common end already at hand in their institutional framework. To claim, nevertheless, that ethical life realizes morality in public life, bringing the perennial "ought" of the moral good into mundane existence with moral freedom, is to forget that the ethical good is of an entirely different sort.[26]

The only relation moral agency could seem to have to ethical community is either peripheral or revolutionary. In the former case, morality would enter in at the interstices of institutions where personal actions are required for which no objective guidelines are already at hand. Hegel refers to just such an example in his discussion of civil society, when he maintains that there morality has a place insofar as neither the workings of the market nor the interventions of the public welfare administration can remove all instances where private charity is needed (PR, pars. 207, 242). To the extent that the family and the state have similar "imperfections," where ethical concerns are left unrealized and undetermined by existing institutions, the moral predicament would inescapably reassert itself.

In a revolutionary situation, by contrast, morality would have a role to play because individuals would then confront an existing order bereft of legitimacy, provoking them to realize a good whose institutional embodiment would be yet to be established. Although the principles of ethical community might supply guidelines for what should be erected, the actual tasks of tearing down the old and replacing it with the ideal new would require determining what founding measures should be taken. Since such measures aim at founding an ethical order as the product of their activity, they are not themselves the ethical functions by which ethical community reproduces itself. They are rather moral undertakings, where the appeal to conscience, with all its attendant perplexities, cannot fail to enter.

If the moral project achieves reconciliation with ethical community only at these margins, it is less than clear whether morality wins a borrowed legitimacy or simply represents an inescapable role to which present and future members of ethical institutions are condemned. For even if morality carries over to the founding of ethical institutions and the sustaining of their relations at the borders of discretion, the normativity of the moral project would at best be incidental.

There is another alternative, however, that gives morality its own integral validity and, in so doing, provides ethical community with a legitimacy independent of historical conventions. This alternative involves simply recognizing the normativity of self-determination and observing how both moral agency and ethical community comprise different structures of freedom while sharing the validity that comes with the reality of self-determination. What gives self-determination normativity is the self-grounding, unconditionally universal character that the reality of freedom alone can possess. Normatively valid conduct and institutions cannot owe their legitimacy to anything that lacks the same validity without forfeiting their justice. The only way that they can avoid this self-defeating dependence upon external foundations is by owing their character to themselves, by being self-determined and providing a self-ordered system of the institutions of freedom, a system that grounds itself and is conditioned by no independently given normative factor. Leaving aside the details of the argument that underlies these basic moves (an argument I have developed at length elsewhere),[27] it will suffice here to review how the moral project, despite all its inherent limitations and dilemmas, still comprises a mode of self-determination, which, as such, enjoys legitimacy as it stands integrated within the system of freedom that ethical institutions crown.

Morality comprises a mode of self-determination by being a structure of interaction wherein the interrelating individuals determine both the content of their aims and actions as well as the form of their agency, doing so such that both these contents and forms individuate each agent as self-determined. If morality were merely an endeavor of the self in relation to objects, it could not achieve actual self-determination, for all its actions would issue from an agency, the natural will comprising the capacity of choice, whose form is given prior to each action as its enabling precondition. Yet, because the moral project is something involving a plurality of agents acting in relation to one another, as Hegel's account uniquely emphasizes, morality can comprise a system of rights and duties where individuals employ their given capacity of choice to exercise an artificial agency defined in terms of the complementary activities they engage in. This artificial agency is that of being a moral subject, something one attains only by acting in regard to others so that one's actions count solely as they are determined by one's knowing and willing, recognized as such by other agents to whom the same recognition is extended. By participating in this structure of moral right and duty, individuals determine both what they will as well as who they are in their capacity as agents, something they cannot do without interacting with others. In exercising and observing their right and duty of purpose and responsibility, individuals render themselves responsible agents whose imputable actions are determined by their own insight and purposes. In exercising and observing their right and duty of intention and welfare, they further render themselves agents responsible for the consequences of their actions, to the extent that these are determined by their own knowledge and intentions. And finally, in exercising their right of conscience, individuals render themselves responsible for knowing and realizing good through their actions while determining their actions in view of this aspect of their agency. In each case, individuals succeed in determining the very form of their moral subjectivity while determining the content of their recognized actions as something for which they are responsible. By entering the moral project, individuals therefore secure for themselves a recognized self-determination, acquiring a type of agency they impose upon themselves in function of their coordinate activities.

Admittedly, the freedom of moral subjects is limited by an inability to determine and realize the good that morality concerns. Yet this inability does not eliminate the fact that in this endeavor, individuals still exercise a mode of entitled self-determination, making their actions the focal point in which their freedom is recognized by others and thereby attaining a form of autonomous agency that is the product, rather than the independently imposed condition, of their activity. It is achieving this self-determination, defined in and through an interactive structure of right and duty, that sets the subjective willing of the moral agent apart from the freedom of desire with which the natural self is endowed.

Moreover, the inability of morality to attain its good does not radically distinguish moral freedom from the other modes of self-determination. The self-determinations that persons achieve in property relations are endemically prey to conflicting interpretations and transgressions. Yet, the fact that persons are subject to nonmalicious wrong, fraud, and crime does not eliminate the rights and duties of property relations or the self-determination individuals achieve as owners. Similarly, family members cannot have their household rights and duties guaranteed by the resources of the family alone, yet this does not destroy the entitlements and obligations in terms of which they enjoy the freedom of family membership. And even in civil society and the state, where public resources are organized to give all their due, citizens are still subject to usurpations and abuses of power that endanger their social and political freedoms. Yet, once more, this predicament does not undermine their social and political rights but rather represents an endemic possibility against which vigilance must be directed.

Finally, although moral striving is not equivalent to the subjective freedom at hand in ethical institutions, the moral project is not antithetical to the institutions of household, social, and political justice. Actions dictated by conscience that violate just affairs of family, society, and state can be publicly curtailed like any other infraction without eliminating moral freedom. Indeed, owing to the internal dimension of purpose, intention, and conscience, morality has an untouchability that makes it unsusceptible to public legislation and enforcement. Wherever other modes of free agency are operative, be they in the family, society, or the state, the moral standpoint can always surface, whether or not the freedom of conscience is upheld by the state. Furthermore, this possibility is not just a superfluity for ethical community. At those margins where ethical institutions leave room for unguided individual initiative in behalf of right, the normativity of freedom makes it imperative for morality to enter the gap of ought and is and cast its net. For all its limits, the moral project thus remains a right and duty for us all, complementing rather than precluding the other claims of ethical community, wherein good may be objectively determined after all.

9
Capital, Civil Society, and the Deformation of Politics

THE COMMON DEFORMATIONS OF MODERN POLITICS

Ever since the American Revolution made freedom the legitimating principle of public life, politics has grappled with the problem of establishing the just society and state upon its basis rather than that of given authority or interests, set virtues or means of conduct, or a transcendent form of goodness. If subsequent history has not resolved how self-determination can be the substance of public life, it has focused attention upon two central aspects of the problem: first, the place of capital within the just society, and second, the valid relation between society and state.

This has come about not so much through the disagreement of competing political movements or the antagonisms of differing regimes as through the convergence of approach underlying all modern political conflict. No matter how irreconcilable opposing positions have been, their controversy has always rested upon a shared conception of social and political life, characterized by a dual reductionism. On the one hand, the state has been conceived as a function of social relations of one form or another, while on the other hand, society has been reduced to a sphere determined through natural relations. On this basis, the relation between capital and society and between society and state has been called into question by nothing less than a challenge to the actual distinction between these spheres and to their capacity to realize freedom.

The Reductions of Liberalism in Theory and Practice

Liberalism provides both the most familiar and the earliest example of this reductionism. Although the liberal tradition first introduces freedom as the determining principle of public affairs, it does so by construing freedom as liberty, a given capacity of choice granted to all men by birth. Since what freedom is is here determined by nature, rather than by an exercise of willing itself, liberty is not actually self-determined. To really be autonomous, liberty would have to determine itself rather than stand determined by something else. For this to be, liberty would have to give itself its own character through its own action and do so such that the particular end it wills would be one specific to it, owing its content to no other source. Liberty, however, is a mere faculty of choice, whose form is given to it by nature and whose particular chosen ends derive from the given array of alternatives from which it is at liberty to choose. Consequently, liberty is always bound to a content that it has not brought into being, leaving it a formal potency of willing whose particular ends do not follow from its own structure. Liberty is therefore relative to the given array of alternatives before it and so can never have the nonrelative, unconditioned character required for normativity.

Because liberty finds its particular content in the given alternatives outside it, what differentiates one will from another cannot be the structure of liberty common to all by birth. That structure is itself something universal, without being individual. Since liberty is incapable of being an individuating factor, what here must supply each will with a distinguishable content are ends independently determined by reason, particular interests, desires, outer circumstance, or some other source. However, insofar as they have their origin outside the will, they leave individual bearers of liberty pursuing particular ends that may conflict with and cancel the free choice of others.

For this reason, the liberal tradition recognizes that the inviolable liberty of all has no secured reality in a state of nature and requires the institution of some common public authority to protect and guarantee its existence. Since liberty remains the principle of justice, such public authority can only legitimately arise, if it does so, through the free consent of the individuals falling under its jurisdiction.

Furthermore, because the instituted authority has no other legitimate mandate than securing the liberty given to all by birth, public life is not a sovereign, self-determined body politic, existing for the sake of a freedom specific to its own activity. It is rather a conditioned external authority that can take any form so long as it is instituted through the consent of all and preserves and protects the exercise of liberty defined by nature, prior to all social or political relations. As the classic figure of liberal theory, John Locke, himself admits in chapter 10 of his *Second Treatise On Government,* public authority can be democratic, oligarchic, or monarchical without affront to the justice of liberty, since here the structure of government is only a chosen means to secure the prepolitical exercise of a natural will and no more an end in itself than political participation.

On this basis, all legitimate public life gets reduced to a single sphere of civil government where individuals are left to pursue their particular interests and desires so long as they accord with the same liberty of others. Consequently, public freedom is here not a matter of a political or social engagement consisting in actual participation in self-government or specific social institutions. It is rather reduced to an exercise of civil rights simply involving a natural liberty of individuals to will their particular interests and desires without restraint by any authority to which they have not given their consent.

Through this line of argument, the liberal tradition has come to conceive the state as a *civil* government, subordinate to the free play of particular personal interests whose harmonious existence it is mandated to secure and preserve. Any political life independent of this relative function of civil administration is excluded.

Conversely, for liberal theory, the activity of civil authority is the one and only form of public life that stands in accord with the human rights of liberty. All other instituted, nonnatural associations impose distinctions contradicting its principle and are therefore subject to regulation by civil government. In other words, there is no just society that can be distinguished from the activity of civil government, nor can the state be distinguished from the public realm in which individuals have the right to pursue their particular ends. Accordingly, in the liberal tradition, civil society and civil government are interchangeable terms, signifying the absence of any difference between social and political freedom and any recognition of separate spheres of civil society and state with distinct ends of their own. Insofar as civil freedom derives its content from the natural will of liberty, however, the reduction of state to civil government involves not only a conflation of state and society but a reduction of the civil sphere to an embodiment of a naturally determined relation.

Political economy extends this double reductionism to the conception of the economy and the relation of capital to society and state. To begin with, it adopts the liberal conflation of civil society and civil government by conceiving a political economy where economic relations fall within a society whose pursuit of particular interests provides the end to which government is subordinated.[1] On this basis, the economy can be labelled "political" because politics here consists in nothing but the protection and maintenance of the same self-seeking liberty at work in market relations. Secondly, because the specific freedom exercised by the participant in the "political economy" is the natural liberty to pursue particular ends of one's own choosing, the society entailed in economic activity is ultimately determined by presocial relations of humans and nature. Thus, although political economy attempts to conceive the economy as an emphatically social sphere distinguishing civilized society from the life of savages, as Adam Smith affirms,[2] it ends up deriving the specific structures of economic activity from natural relations.

The classic formulations of *The Wealth of Nations* exhibit most plainly this one side of political economy's conflation of the social with the natural. From the start, economic need and the goods satisfying it get characterized with respect to humans' physical requirements, just as labor gets reduced to the technical process of an individual working directly upon objects of nature (p. 5). Accordingly, the division of labor here develops not from any social process but from the propensity in human nature to truck and barter (p. 13). Consequently, it arises as a division between private producers who each first work technically upon nature and only subsequently exchange what they do not directly consume of their own product (p. 11). The resulting exchange relations are then left governed by a labor theory of value, which determines the prices at which commodities are bought and sold by the labor embodied in their production. The latter here consists in a technically defined labor process mandated by the anthropological necessity of humans' metabolism with nature (p. 30). Finally, even capital gets introduced via the presocial scheme of private producers. Despite its attested social power and indifference to any natural limits upon the magnitude of wealth, it gets originally characterized as the stock of subsistence goods required to tide over the private producers while they await the sale of their respective products (p. 259).

Of course, in offering these natural specifications, political economy is attempting to conceive how a social system of market relations works itself out through them, building a sphere of civil association in which the satisfaction of needs has its place. What economic structures thereby arise do so as exercises of that same natural right to pursue the particular interests of one's own choice that here gives the freedom of civil society/civil government its defining content. Consequently, so long as the system of economic relations can be seen to operate through each individual's liberty to satisfy needs of his or her own choosing by freely entering into relations of commodity exchange, it has a legitimacy in perfect accord with the workings of civil government. To the degree, then, that capital be conceived as an economic structure composed entirely out of such freely convened market relations, it itself becomes a realization of liberty, a work of free enterprise that requires no special civil regulation beyond the public legal protection of private interest accorded all action in civil society. Indeed, since government here has no other function than securing the exercise of liberty, the protection of capital would become an affair of state, with no less than the existence of human rights hanging in the balance. The economy here becomes a political concern, just as politics becomes no more than a civil matter, bound to realize a natural freedom that alone lends them both their legitimacy.

Leaving aside the theoretical problems entailed in the double reductionism of liberal theory,[3] it is important to note how its practical consequences for society and state have been realized within those regimes espousing the liberal credo.

With regard to the internal sovereignty of the liberal state, contemporary history well exhibits the reduction of political freedom to civil rights that follows from the civil conception of government. While the citizens at large exercise their right to pursue their particular interests and livelihoods under the protection of public law, actual governing has become the prerogative of political parties. With the consent of the electorate, the party politicians have acquired a monopoly over political action, which they exercise as members of a particular profession, entered into through the same vocational, rather than political, self-election that applies to any career choice in civil society.

Under this regime, the citizens have been left little option, politically speaking. On the one hand, they can go to the polls or some can become professional politicians themselves. Either way, their involvement only serves to reestablish the same gulf between ruler and subject. On the other hand, they can forgo these limited opportunities of electoral participation and take to the streets in the fashion of the extraparliamentary opposition of recent decades. In doing so, however, they stand once again outside the organs of government, attempting to influence those who govern rather than wielding any political power themselves.

In these circumstances, the politicians consistently appeal to their constituencies not as groups of political agents, actively participating in self-rule, but as members of society, as taxpayers, members of a particular class, and bearers of certain ethnic interests. As such, the governed answer back through the voice of public opinion, where they step into the political arena not as participants in an organized exercise of political power but as an atomized mass of passively expressed personal opinion.

While this has left individual citizens with little more than a civil freedom to pursue their private interests in security, the politics monopolized by parties has itself largely lost the character of self-government for the sake of political ends. Instead, it has become reduced ever more to an activity of administration with no other internal matter to attend to than addressing particular social interests and realizing civil rights. Consequently, just as government has tended towards bureaucracy, its policies have tended to be determined not so much by political principles as by the particular ends of different social pressure groups, whose lobbying activity is but one more side of the civil reduction of politics. Whether this takes the form of corporate domination or union influence, the subordinate character of political action remains the same. What compounds this subordination is that the very means of political action that require social resources, such as the publicity afforded by the media, and the ability to sustain political organizations and mount electoral campaigns, still remain more accessible to those with power and influence in society.[4]

All these internal ramifications of the liberal reductionism cannot help but be reflected in the external relations of the state. Insofar as internal sovereignty is not preeminently a matter of self-rule for its own sake but government for the sake of realizing social interests and civil liberties, the liberal state pursues and has pursued a foreign policy issuing from the latter consideration. On these terms, international relations cease to be a sphere in which respect for political autonomy is at stake, a sphere where national "interest" can correspond with political justice to the degree that any legitimate state has for its one and only raison d'être the wholly common end of self-government. Because the liberal state has no such universal principle of *political* justice for its end, its national interest is irreducibly particular in character, deriving its content from the given array of social interests within it according to how they make themselves felt in their struggle to influence government. Consequently, its foreign policy seeks to promote what has corresponding social benefit to the nation, be it in response to the needs of particular corporations or industries, capital accumulation in general, the demands of unions, or the threat of foreign injury to or conquest of its civil society. In other words, contrary to Marxist and Weberian conceptions, it is the *political* factor of the liberal reduction of the state to civil government that here allows for an imperialist foreign policy—imperialist in that it advances a socially defined national interest without regard for the political autonomy of other nations.

The Socialist Reduction

If these familiar aspects of the historical fulfilment of liberal theory indicate the significance of the double reduction of politics to society and society to nature, the example of socialist theory and practice serves to suggest only more the prevalence and severity of the problem.

By its very name, "socialism" proclaims its advocacy of the primacy of society over all other dimensions of public life, immediately indicating its challenge to any abiding distinction between civil society and state. In its least extreme form, social democracy, this entails a social subordination of politics analogous to the double reduction of liberal theory.

On the one hand, social democracy views the state as a public authority whose function is to assure the satisfaction of the needs and interests generated within civil society. Unlike strict liberal government, the social democratic state does not simply protect and guarantee the given property of its citizens and their pursuit of private interest. Rather, it further recognizes their right to have their economic needs be actually satisfied through their own efforts. To the degree that society offers only this opportunity, but not its guaranteed fulfillment, the state steps in to enforce it through whatever measures can be taken that do not suppress the social rights of individuals to decide what they need and will consume, to enter into exchange relations as they see fit, and to earn their living in occupations of their own choosing. Resolving this social question is the content of politics, and government accordingly has the public welfare for its end. As such, the state is here a welfare state.

On the other hand, social democracy prescribes a democratic form to this public administration of welfare. Since the terrain of this democracy remains civil society, it proceeds in recognition of the same civil right to pursue private interest under the protection of public authority that liberal civil government granted. Beyond this right, however, the democracy of the welfare state can grant its citizens nothing more than the right to be subject only to that administration of welfare to which they have given their consent. Any more substantial political freedom is precluded for precisely the same reasons that left the citizen of the liberal state voluntarily handing over the monopoly of political action to the governing "politicians."

Although the social concerns of social democracy indeed have a different focus than those of liberalism, the welfare state does not have any specific political activity for its end, any more than does the liberal state. Its business is the management of social policy, and the governing aim of its administration is the purely social matter of securing the public welfare with the agreement of the members of society. Consequently, the welfare state, like liberal civil government, can take any form so long as it accords with its determining social proviso and has the consent of the governed.

On this basis, social democracy bears the same formal character as that democracy that might be claimed by liberalism and accordingly stands limited in a dual way. On the one hand, its citizens do not themselves manage the public welfare but only give their consent to those who actually minister over it. On the other hand, the government legitimized through their support is not preeminently an organ of political self-rule existing for its own sake but a conditioned authority committed to ends determined independently within society. The democracy of the welfare state can only determine the means to these ends and not these ends themselves. As a result, its political freedom is limited to setting social policy for a civil society given to it. Its governing activity is accordingly administrative in character and bureaucratic in organization.

As for capital, its status is already mandated in the subordinate relation of the welfare state to the predetermined structure of society. To the degree that capital is a relation comprised entirely out of the interrelated, yet freely chosen pursuits of particular interest constitutive of civil society, it cannot rightfully be abolished without violating the social freedom giving social democracy its highest aim. Alternately, to the degree that the relations of capital do not themselves effect an automatic satisfaction of the needs generated within them, capital and the economy as a whole must come under public regulation to secure the realization of social welfare. On both counts, capital stands as an affair of state for a government with no more than social concerns.

With these internal foundations, the welfare state is left to pursue its foreign relations on the same footing as the liberal state. Once again national interest has a purely civil content, providing foreign policy with no other necessary principle than the defense and furtherance of domestic social welfare. Of course, here the welfare in question is not that of whatever particular class or interest group can most influence government, but rather the general welfare addressed by the social democratic principle of guaranteeing the satisfaction of the needs of all members of the nation's own society. Since, however, this general interest is still one of a particular given society, there is nothing about its character that allows its advancement to coincide with a foreign policy based upon the political principle of universal respect and furtherance of self-government. In other words, the imperial prerogative remains, albeit in a very faceless, general form.

Marxist Socialism and the Withering Away of Politics

If the social democratic solution thus leaves a world of civil rights, satisfied needs, and political emptiness, the socialism of Marxist theory and communist practice offers a much more radical version of the modern reductionism universally challenging the justice of separate social and political spheres of freedom.

Although it can be argued that Marx's concept of capital actually requires the valid separation of civil society and state,[5] his theory of communist society directly reduces one to the other before eliminating all vestige of nonnatural and nontechnical relations.

To begin with, Marxist theory accepts the liberal and social democratic convention that politics per se is constitutively determined by social factors of some kind. It diverges from their conceptions, however, first by identifying the determining social factor as class interest rather than civil rights or public welfare. Second, it considers this social foundation of politics to be not the source of its legitimation, but precisely the restrictive particularity that robs it of all legitimacy.

Consequently, when Marx criticizes the modern republic for actually being a bourgeois state, whose sham democratic universality cannot mask its actual class rule, he does not call for a new body politic that will truly realize a universal self-rule above all particular interest. Instead, he champions the seizure of the state by the proletariat so that it can impose its own particular class rule in order to do away with the state and politics altogether. In other words, the dictatorship of the proletariat is instituted precisely to carry through to its logical conclusion the reduction of politics to society already expressed in the doctrine that the state is but an instrument of class interest. The proletarian dictatorship supposedly accomplishes this by eliminating class differences in society, thereby annulling its own class rule and allowing the state to wither away and leave in its wake nothing but a communist society of free, associated producers.

This total collapse of all political life into society is but one side of Marxism's double reduction. At the same time that the state is rendered a mere function of class interest, society itself is left determined by an economic base ultimately comprising a sphere of natural necessity endemic to the human condition and thus underlying, rather than emerging within, human history.

Indeed, in his mature economic theory, Marx does attempt to conceive capital as a social relation. However, he never succeeds in completely freeing his conception of the natural reductions of political economy, as is evident in his presocial conception of need and use value, his derivation of both commodity fetishism and the labor theory of value from a sphere of private producers, and his reduction of labor power and labor's use value production to anthropological and technically determined givens, respectively.[6] What is of more decisive significance for Marxist political thought and the regimes it has inspired is that in Marx's theory of communist society, it is this vestigial natural aspect that comes to the fore.

Marx himself makes this most clear in his famous sketch of the communist ideal in the third volume of *Capital*.[7] There he explicitly delivers the natural reduction underlying the whole conception of communism. He declares that economic relations comprise a sphere of natural necessity beyond which first begins the realm of freedom. In other words, the economy is not itself a historically emergent social structure composed of the interdependent yet autonomous self-seeking of members of society but a suprahistorical base, an inescapable natural feature of the human condition that can only limit, rather than realize human freedom. Consequently, if humanity is to build for itself a realm of freedom, mankind must restrict the hold of economic relations upon human activity. Because these economic relations are but matters of natural necessity, they can be managed through a purely technical domination.

This mandates the exclusive task of communist society: it is to free humanity from natural necessity by realizing an administration of the economy that will replace the social system of the market and reduce the working day to a minimum through an unrestricted automation of production and an automatic distribution of its products. The "society" of communism thus entails a transformation of the economy into an econometrician's dream: a purely technical sphere in which all social relations of commodity exchange, wage labor, and capital have given way to a collective "administration of things," as Engels forthrightly puts it.[8]

Not surprisingly, since such communism achieves itself through the annulment of civil society and the withering away of the state, the realm of freedom it establishes is one of purely private activity, of hunting in the morning, fishing in the afternoon, writing poetry in the evening, and so on.[9] Communist humanity has here indeed reappropriated human species being, for without any society or state to engage in, humanity has nothing left but the natural liberty of its anthropological existence. Such is the promise that is to motivate and legitimate the class dictatorship of proletarian revolution.

Needless to say, the Marxist regimes of our day have not succeeded in establishing the world of hobbies for which civil society and state are to be sacrificed. They have, however, gone a considerable way towards collapsing state and society and reducing both to spheres of administered necessity.

From the start, wherever Communist movements have succeeded in taking over the state for themselves, they have directly deprived it of any independent universality. In the name of a Communist future, they have made the body politic a "workers'" state, where government purportedly serves the working class by being in the hands of those canonically representing its interests. Here not only is government constitutionally subordinated to the social interest of the proletariat, but the right to political action is itself restricted on the social basis of class background and allegiance.

If such regimes have in no way allowed their state power to wither away, the dictatorship of their Communist party rule has everywhere supplanted the interaction of wills constitutive of political life with an unrestricted administration of the "masses' interests." By prohibiting all opposing political groups while imposing "democratic centralism" within its own ranks, their ruling party has banished political plurality and thereby set government above the bonds of mutual agreement that alone save political authority from collapsing into the arbitrary domination of a single power. In this way, the political hegemony of the Communist movement has largely succeeded in making politics wither away into an instrument of "class" domination, which would be bureaucratic in character if the substantive factor of party allegiance did not overrule matters of technical efficiency.

What, however, has made these workers' states such questionable representatives of proletarian interest is not just the inherent arbitrariness of their rule, which by itself might conceivably allow for a benevolent despotism from the proletariat's point of view. This possibility is overshadowed by the fact that Communist regimes have concomitantly undermined the structures of civil society through which the classes both have and advance their particular interests.

Most immediately, this has involved curtailing the civil rights of individuals to choose what commodities they need and how they will earn a corresponding livelihood. Communist regimes have generally effected this by supplanting the market relations in which these rights are exercised with the technical domination of a central economic management under the party's state control. It manages to set levels of production and distribution of goods independently of the social interaction of commodity relations not only by eliminating autonomous units of capital but by assailing the free sale of labor power. That has been achieved by imposing rationing, restricting the movement of individuals, mandating their employment, and prohibiting their being without officially prescribed work.

Whatever security such measures may provide, they prevent individuals from entering employment through free contractual agreement, thus leaving them more like wage slaves than free laborers who can choose their own vocation and bargain over the conditions of their employment.

If all this undercuts the freedom of action of individual workers, the party's concomitant hegemony over society excludes their common pursuit of interest as well. To be consistent with its political dictatorship and direct state management of the economy, the party cannot help but prohibit independent trade unions and all other autonomous social organizations. To the degree that this occurs, the ruling party representing the interests of the working class actually eliminates any public space in which social groups can act to advance their particular interests. Thus, subordinating politics to class interest, Communist regimes have undercut their own legitimacy by reducing civil society to a technically administered sphere.

The Final Natural Reduction of Fascism

Although communism in theory and practice thus carries the liberal conflation of politics and society and society and nature to a further extreme, fascism has brought it to its ultimate conclusion. Making no amends to social and political freedom, fascist rule has openly sought to determine public life through natural principles whose content is given independently of what issues from mutually respected willing.

In its initial, comparatively tentative development by Italian Fascists and their Phalange successors, fascism presented its defining challenge in a twofold way.

Under the guise of saving politics as much from submergence in the class struggle as from the formal rule of liberal civil government, fascism struck its own first blow at the independence of society and state by injecting corporatism into the structure of government. In so doing, it treated social classes as if they were estates, making their social divisions directly political in character, while branding the state with the marks of social interest.

At the same time, fascism proceeded to undercut the remaining autonomy of its conflated social and political spheres by subjecting them to the absolute rule of the Fascist movement. It claimed to represent not some social interest, in the manner of the Communist movement, but rather an aristocratic ethos, utterly extraneous to civil society and politics and instead rooted in the given character of a particular people.

The full consequence of these moves were then drawn by the Nazis, who took to its logical conclusion the natural notion that the people is the basis of political and social order. Rejecting all claims of freedom, the Nazis subordinated state and society to the self-assertion of the German people, openly admitting that its defining character was not the result of any social or political enactment but a natural unity determined by race. Within Germany, the Nazis accordingly eliminated all social and political standing for those not part of the "Aryan race," while placing all social and political power into the hands of the designated representative of the people's will. Since that will was natural in character, its only appropriate embodiment could be the equally given particular will of a leader, whose authority would be unrestricted by any relations of mutual respect and agreement.

On this basis, Nazi rule could be consistent with itself in its foreign policy only by embarking on a campaign of world conquest. Since it legitimated itself by championing the natural particularity of the German people as the sole foundation of public life, the Nazi state was bound to challenge the right of other nations to govern themselves and run their societies unbeholden to the Aryan principle. Accordingly, the Nazi affirmation of the particularity of the German people turned itself outward as the self-assertion of a master race whose will requires hegemony over all other peoples to be true to itself.

In so seeking to stamp out social and political freedom by imposing the absolute rule of natural difference, Nazi facism brings to a head the double reductions of state and society already forwarded by its fiercest opponents.

THE ALTERNATIVE CONCEPTION OF INTERACTION THEORY

If the contingencies of history have so far prevented the Nazi extreme from taking hold, they have not stopped liberal, social democratic, and communist regimes from making the conflation of society and state a universal feature of the present world order. Although no alternative regimes have arisen that exclude natural determination from public life by erecting society and state as irreducible spheres of freedom, an alternative has nevertheless been developed in theory. It is provided by the interaction conception of civil society and state introduced by Hegel and left largely undeveloped since his death. Although Hegel did not consistently work out this alternative conception of justice, he did lay down its basic argument for thinking society and state as separate domains necessary for the realization of freedom.

This argument challenges the common reduction of politics to society and society to nature in a threefold way.

To begin with, interaction theory argues that freedom is the sole substance of justice. This is true because normative validity requires unconditioned universality, and only what is self-determined can have that character.

For relations between individuals to be just and not merely operative practice, they must be relations that ought to be maintained no matter what particular circumstances are at hand, so long as the latter are not themselves just relations commanding the same validity. If a relation or institution were relative to any particular conditions that were not just themselves, it would be determined by what lies outside justice and thereby forfeit its own normative status. Since just relations are thus justified in any situation that is not already a specific relation of justice, they are universally valid. Furthermore, because a relation of justice can only be legitimately limited by another just relation, the universality of justice is unconditioned.

Consequently, justice cannot be caused or grounded by any independently given factors. Justice must instead be its own ground and accordingly exist for its own sake alone. This can be the case, however, only if justice has its specific character through its own relations and not from any separate ends or procedures of construction. Therefore, the relations of justice must be self-determined, giving themselves their entire content through their own freedom. This means that justice does not have foundations. It rather consists in freedom, for self-determination is precisely what has unconditioned universality by being determined by nothing but itself.

Any attempt to base justice on prescribed virtues, given means of conduct, a fixed essence of goodness, or some other factor separate from freedom thus founders insofar as it leaves action not for its own sake, as right conduct would require, but for the sake of those predetermined ends here supplying it with its character. Accordingly, as long as justice be so conceived as a given form that action must embody to be valid, its specific content cannot be legitimated without invoking some absolute authority to determine it. Plato and Aristotle recognized this problem and sought to save such justice from relativism by introducing an unconditioned agent to frame and implement its given standards. However, whether their redeeming figure be a philosopher-king[10] or an absolutely good man,[11] his own autonomous rule contradicts the whole framework of prescribed justice it is meant to realize.

If, instead, justice be grounded in natural law or the nature of the self, as in traditional liberal theory, or constructed with a privileged procedure, as in Rawls, or reduced to a matter of convention, it is left determined by something other than itself yet again. Consequently, the resulting relations of justice stand relative to what is outside justice and therefore cannot have the legitimacy justice must command.

If this indicates that freedom is the sole content of action for its own sake, interaction theory further argues that freedom cannot itself be conceived as a principle of justice, out of which structures of right are derived. This basic strategy of liberal theory is intrinsically aporetic because treating freedom as a principle contradicts the very structure of self-determination.

When one makes the free will that from which justice is derived, the free will is reduced to something that determines what is other than itself. Therefore, the free will does not exercise any *self*-determination in the relations of justice derived from it. Instead of giving itself any further determination in them, it rather determines what is secondary to and distinct from its principle. On the other hand, since these derivative relations are determined by a principle of freedom prior to and separate from them, they are not self-determined either. Consequently, making freedom the principle of justice ends up depriving freedom of any objective realization, while leaving the structures of justice incapable of embodying the very principle that is supposed to legitimate them.

This dilemma persists as long as the free will is conceived either as a natural liberty all people are born with or as a structure of the single self.

If, following classical liberal theorists such as Hobbes, Locke, and Rousseau, freedom be construed as liberty, that natural capacity to choose among given alternatives, then the will is left beholden to whatever array of choices it faces. Consequently, what it wills is always conditioned by given circumstance and can never claim the unconditioned universality just action requires. Furthermore, since liberty leaves the will in the natural predicament of choosing from among independently determined alternatives, it precludes the real autonomy consisting in willing a content deriving from the will itself instead of from something other.

If, on the one hand, the Kantian strategy by followed, of eliminating the heteronomy of liberty by determining the content of free willing through a principle specific to the will's own structure, the same impasse is reached. Insofar as freedom here remains defined in terms of the self per se, it gets reduced to a universal capacity common to all, with no individuating character of its own. With self-determination characterized monologically—that is, as a feature of the single self—what differentiates free wills from one another, providing them both with their individuality and contrastive relation to others, are particulars whose source has to lie elsewhere than in freedom. Because autonomy is here merely universal in form, the particular content of every will is once again left undetermined by freedom. Consequently, self-determination has no reality, for like liberty, monological freedom cannot give itself a content of its own.

In the face of these problems of any natural or monological conception of freedom, interaction theory first holds that the unconditioned freedom granting normative validity to action can only be realized if the will actually wills a particular content that is not only independent of inner desire and outer circumstance but also serves to individuate the will through its own act. Then, in decisive departure from the liberal and Kantian conceptions, interaction theory argues that the free will can so particularize itself only by relating to other wills, and doing so voluntarily.

To begin with, the self-determination of the free will must have a form common to the will in general and a content exclusively its own if its action is to have a particular end specific to freedom. The will can only do so through a contrastive relation to other willings, wherein it stands individuated as a particular instance of a commonly existing structure of willing. So long as the will acts in a solitary fashion and deals only with nature, it cannot achieve this individuality of freedom, for its act refers only to what is not a will.

The relation to other wills is therefore required, interaction theory argues, but not as a given condition from which free action proceeds. If it were something independently at hand and thereby imposed upon willing, the particularity afforded the will would not be self-determined, but determined through a contrastive relation given without its consent. Thus, the free will must not just stand in relation to others but will that relation as part of its own self-determination.

Further, these other wills can provide the requisite contrast terms for the first will's individuation only if they are self-determined themselves. For that to be the case, their relation to it and other wills must also be voluntarily established by their own particular self-determination.

Therefore, interaction theory concludes, freedom is not a natural or monological relation, but an irreducibly intersubjective one whereby individuals each will their own particular end and relation to others by simultaneously honoring the correlative self-determination these others will as part of the same process. In other words, self-determination is an interaction of a plurality of individuals whereby each freely engages in an objectively respected act of willing by recognizing and being recognized by similarly self-determining individuals.

Admittedly, individuals can only enter into this relation if they already possess a natural body and a thinking and choosing self with which to recognize what others will, choose a particular content to will with respect to that of others, and lastly determine themselves in a way recognizable in the world. Nevertheless, their willing first acquires the further status of free action through the reciprocal recognition of an enacted interaction.

Since, furthermore, the intersubjective structure of freedom is such that it involves mutual respect for the contrasted self-determination figuring within it, free action has normative validity as well. Therefore, interaction theory argues, freedom is not a principle of justice, from which laws and institutions are to be derived, but an existing structure of right, whose exercise of freedom is directly accompanied by the respect securing its objective reality.

If one ignores this inherent actuality of interaction and instead treats freedom's reciprocal recognition as a noninstitutional ideal legitimating derivative structures, as Hannah Arendt and Jurgen Habermas have done, one only reinstates the dilemmas of liberal theory. To avoid this course, it must be recognized that the basic concept of interaction is itself a particular structure of right, building the most elementary type of justice. This right is not that of either society or state, nor does it directly shed light on how a separate civil society and state could be necessary institutions of freedom. Nevertheless, it provides the indispensable starting point for conceiving the total reality of freedom and so opens the line of argument that legitimates the justice of civil society and state in opposition to the prevailing regimes of our day.

Property as the Minimal Structure of Interaction

This minimal structure of right comprising freedom without further qualification is the relationship of individuals wherein each objectifies his or her will in a particular embodiment that accords with those that others give their own wills in recognition and respect of one another's self-determination. Within this reciprocal relationship, each will freely objectifies itself in a recognized and recognizing manner such that its sole individuating feature as a free will is the specific external embodiment it has chosen and that others respect as its own. This external entity here functions only as the recognizable medium of the will's self-determination. The independently given features of this recognized object of the will are a matter of indifference, for the will does not will them but rather its own objectification. They only figure as subordinate accidents of the will's respected embodiment.

Although individuals do here achieve an objectively recognized self-determination, their realized freedom is abstract insofar as the particularity they have given their wills lies outside in the form of an external thing. In other words, the basic structure of interaction comprises an existing right limited to acquiring and disposing over property of one's own in recognition of that of others.

The significance of this elementary abstract right for the consideration of civil society and state is twofold.

On the one hand, the rightful relationship of persons through property is not determined by social or political relations but is a nonnatural structure of interaction irreducible to any other. If this be ignored, civil society and state cannot be properly conceived in their own right. The familiar Marxist doctrine of economic determinism and base and superstructure founders on just this point by claiming that property relations derive from relations of production. It fails to recognize that the commodity, contained in all economic relations as their most basic element, itself presupposes abstract right insofar as there could be no exchange relations in which objects could bear value and figure as commodities without goods already being held as property by different persons.

However, precisely because the relation of persons through property rests on no more than their reciprocal recognition of each other's embodied will, abstract right is, on the other hand, subject to conflicts requiring further relations of right not only to ensure the stability of property relations themselves, but to give freedom an unconditioned realization. Because abstract right leaves it to the arbitrariness of individuals to choose which object shall embody their will and what they shall thereby acknowledge as the domain of others, persons can always fall into collisions of nonmalicious wrong when they disagree over what objects are the entitled property they have recognized, befraud one another by employing the reciprocal relation of contract to obtain property through misrepresentation, and commit open crime by choosing to violate the property rights of others. Since abstract right simply involves persons on an equal footing, it contains no higher authority empowered to settle entitlement disputes, nor can it provide any objectively sanctioned use of force to punish fraud and crime. Any time a person attempts to right wrong through her own use of force, her action is subject to being an illegitimate act of revenge so long as others refuse to recognize it as rightful retribution.[12]

As a result, the interaction of abstract right calls for further structures of justice to resolve the problems endemic to property relations. Although this does not immediately justify the existence of a civil society and state, it does indicate that freedom cannot be restricted to the self-determination of persons through property.

Needless to say, the required move beyond abstract right cannot consist in making the interaction of personhood a first principle of justice from which additional institutions are derived. To avoid reinstating the dilemmas of liberty, one must rather take abstract right as the most elementary component of the reality of freedom, incorporated in all further relations without, however, being their determining ground. Certainly, if individuals do not have recognized possession of their own bodies, that most basic property presupposed by all other property relations, they are unable to engage in any further independent activity and exercise the rights at stake in moral, family, social, or political relations. Nevertheless, disposing over property does not determine what are the other freedoms one ought to enjoy.

Morality and the Unresolved Problem of Right

What follows from the internal problems of abstract right is not civil society or the state, but morality, understood as the interaction in which individuals seek to bring right into existence through their autonomous action towards others, recognizing that only in so doing will their own conduct be just. This mode of freedom refers to personhood without depending upon any additional relation of right. On the other hand, morality is not reducible to abstract right since moral subjects do not interact just as persons, embodying their wills in property, but as individuals who act with the intention of doing right in general. Accordingly, moral subjects recognize one another not merely as owning property, but as rightfully responsible for their own actions. On this basis, morality is an integral structure of interaction in which individuals exercise the mutually respected right and duty of relating to one another through self-determined actions recognizably prefigured in a conscious purpose aimed at each other's right and welfare.

However, although the unresolved wrong within abstract right calls for persons to interact in this moral way, the situation of moral action is problematic in itself, as Hegel has pointed out.[13] Whereas the subject exercises moral autonomy only by acting to realize the good encompassing right and welfare, this moral good has no particular content in itself precisely because it is an ought that requires the action of the moral subject to bring it into being. Therefore, the putatively objective good that the moral subject ought to intend and realize can obtain its actual content only through the subjective determination of individual conscience. However, since conscience has nothing but its own subjective arbitrariness to decide what is good, it cannot come to any unquestionably valid moral determinations. Consequently, every moral action remains a moral problem for both its author and the others who interact with her in view of her responsibility for her deed.

Although morality still has as much legitimacy as abstract right, by being a mode of mutually respected self-determination, the correlative abstractness of the good and the inability of conscience to determine it objectively leave moral interaction anything but the crowning form of freedom. Besides failing to resolve the wrongs endemic to abstract right, morality introduces the additional problem of establishing a structure of freedom in which the recognized reality of right and welfare is objectively at hand in the self-determination of interacting individuals.

Taken together, the deficiencies of abstract right and morality clearly indicate that freedom cannot be restricted to personhood and moral autonomy, as traditional liberal theory and Kantian practical philosophy have done in their own naturally determined versions of these relationships. What is required to supplement these freedoms is a domain where individuals can interact within an existing institutional framework already embodying the reality of their respected rights. In such a domain, the good their actions realize is the very order making those actions possible. The legitimate reality of civil society and the state will consist in just such a context of ethical institutions.

However, their introduction and determination cannot be made as yet, because the ethical life called for by the limits of property relations and morality involves an institution that is neither social nor political yet is presupposed and incorporated by both society and state. This ethical institution is the family, and without understanding the outlines of its valid organization as a structure of freedom, the justification and proper form of civil society cannot be understood.

The Family as an Ethical Institution of Freedom

The new mode of freedom the family adds to personhood and morality without introducing social or political relations is that of establishing an association with another through mutual consent, wherein these individuals freely unite into a joint person with a common property and welfare, sustained by the reciprocally recognized feeling to make that bond the end of their action towards one another. Since the joint person and property of this association requires the recognition of other persons to have rightful existence, the enactment of its bond must be made in a publicly recognizable and recognized form. Thus, the family is situated from the start within a context of other persons, such that being a family member means acting both with regard to other members in terms of family right and acting with regard to individuals outside the family not merely as a person and moral subject but as a representative of the family itself.

On this basis, one has a household of freedom, erected through the recognized agreement of its founders and having no other restriction than that they share the ethical love consisting not in a psychological feeling but in the felt commitment to trust one another as members of a common person and property with the right and duty to act for that end. This household unity comprises the minimal ethical institution in that its association immediately arises out of mutual choice and provides a context determined by willing within which its members can exercise a form of autonomy whose existing reality and end is that association itself.

Whether or not these family members indulge in the natural function of procreation is a matter of circumstance and choice on which the free family unity does not depend. Similarly, the ethical relation of parent and child within the family is an optional one, which has no direct connection to the natural relation between biological parents and offspring. The young figure as children in the family not by blood but by the publicly accepted commitment of the parents to treat them as individuals who need the shelter and care of the parents to allow them to develop into autonomous persons, moral subjects, and family members.

Although historically both marriage and childrearing have been limited to couples of the opposite sex, while the generic family relations to those within and without the household have been separately allotted to man and woman as distinct masculine and feminine roles, the free family cannot be bound by these customs. Only when all aspects of its organization are determined by the autonomous agreement of its founding members does the family become an ethical institution of freedom, existing for its own sake with rights and duties proper to itself. Unlike moral action, which always seeks to realize a right not yet at hand, the self-determination specific to the family member realizes the same freely established association that already comprises the existing framework in which such action occurs. Consequently, the free family embodies the actual unity of subjective autonomy and realized right that morality could not achieve.

Nevertheless, the freedom of the family is still deficient on two grounds.

First of all, family relations by themselves have no means to ensure that members of the household abide by the rights and duties that apply both between spouses and between parents and children. If conflicts arise between spouses concerning management of the common household property or the upbringing of children, there is no third party available within the family to adjudicate the dispute. Alternately, the mere plurality of persons and families provides no binding authority outside the individual family that can either objectively establish when a marriage has been duly convened or annulled or rightfully compel spouses both to respect each other's equal stake in the household property and to act responsibly for the welfare of their children and the family as a whole.

Since the family thereby leaves the respect for its right at the mercy of the arbitrariness of its members, the family requires some further institution of justice to secure its own exercise of freedom. The content of that freedom, however, is itself limited insofar as the autonomy realized in the existing bonds of the family has its sole legitimate end in the commonweal of the household. This commonweal is merely particular, since it is the right and welfare of a single family, and contingent at that, since it rests on a shared feeling of ethical love that may dissipate at any time. Furthermore, the common personhood and welfare of the household provides no room for its members to interact on the basis of different particular ends of their own separate choosing. All they have a right to will in their roles as members of the same family are actions that maintain and forward its common bond. The moment spouses begin to interact as individuals with divergent welfares and private domains, the household has lost its constitutive unity of ethical love.

What is therefore lacking in the family is the mutually respected freedom to act towards others in pursuit of one's own independent interests within an existing association that is universal in scope yet consists in nothing but the reality of such self-determination. Given the abiding problems of securing both abstract right and the limited freedoms of the family, this community of interest would also have to insure the property relations and welfare of its members.

This then is the dual mandate that abstract right, morality, and the free family together provide for a further structure of interaction. It must incorporate them all, publicly securing property and family rights while adding its own normative community of interest.

What is called for here is not a body politic concerned with matters of government and political right. The mandate is rather for a civil society consisting in the institutions wherein individuals enjoy the recognized freedom to pursue particular ends of their own choosing in public, so far as their action forwards the similar pursuit of interest by others.

Without this sphere, individuals may dispose over property, act and be treated as moral subjects, and participate in the commonweal of the family, but they cannot interact with others in terms of their own freely chosen interest. This may not be the most sovereign freedom, but if it is lacking, the structures of right are left at odds with the interest of individuals.

The Normative Structure of Civil Society

The great challenge of civil society is to provide the institutional framework in which the pursuit of independent interest builds a normative mode of freedom instead of an exercise of natural liberty, where all do as they please irrespective of any mutual recognition of right.

The key lies in determining the individual pursuit of interest such that it can only take place through the realization of the interests of others. If that can be achieved, action towards others for particular ends of one's own choosing becomes a legitimate mode of self-determination since it is bound up with similar action by others in a context where all interact exclusively by virtue of exercising and respecting one another's right to determine themselves in this manner. The elementary resolution of this challenge is provided by commodity relations, which thereby comprise the basic structure of civil society's community of interest. This becomes evident simply by examining what is minimally entailed in civil freedom.

The irreducible starting point is a willing of particular ends of one's own choosing where those ends are of such a character that they can only be realized through a correlative realization of the similarly chosen ends of others. As such, these ends must comprise independent interests that cannot be satisfied by either what is directly available from nature or what one already has within the private domain of one's person and household. If that were not the case, willing them would involve no interaction at all. These interests must rather require acquisition of something that only others can supply and that these others can so supply only by voluntarily receiving in return what satisfies their own chosen ends.

In other words, the particular ends at issue comprise a need whose content is entirely a matter of personal preference yet can only be satisfied by what someone else has to offer under the condition that the bearer of the first need have and be willing to offer in return what satisfies some analogously chosen need of the latter. Such need is not a natural want for what the body requires, nor a psychological desire for what the soul may long for, but an *economic* need for means of satisfaction that can only be obtained from correlatively needy individuals. Although the particular content of this economic need is a matter of personal preference and may coincide with some physical or psychological want, it is constitutively predicated upon the relations between the individuals bearing them. If it so happens that they can satisfy certain biological or psychological needs, such as for the air they breathe or the affections they desire, without engaging in a reciprocal interaction with one another as independent owners of the objects sought, then these needs have no economic reality nor any civil character.

Accordingly, what comprise the exclusive objects satisfying economic need are *commodities,* goods expressly owned by other individuals who are willing to exchange them to satisfy their own correlatively determined wants. Only within this social context of a plurality of commodity owners can need have an economic character, and only in the interrelation of individuals who need what others have and have what others need can property function as a commodity, related not only to the respected will of its owner, but to the social need of others with commodities of their own.

In this way, the minimal determination of civil society resolves itself into a market where individuals face one another at one and the same time as bearers of needs for the commodities of others and as bearers of some commodity that others need. Only by both choosing to need a commodity and possessing a needed good can an individual participate in this society of interest. Its reciprocal satisfaction of need offers individuals the opportunity of realizing a particular end of their own choice with the normativity consisting in the mutual recognition of each other's right to make their need the factor of their self-determination.

Contrary to the views of political economists and Marxists alike, commodities bear utility that is social and not natural in character, for they satisfy not the wants of human nature but the specifically social needs of others who can offer something wanted in return. Consequently, the multitude and diversity of utilities are as free of natural limit as that of the economic needs individuals choose to have. A commodity can be anything so long as it is an object of property needed by some one other than its owner, just as an economic need can have any content so long as what satisfies it is possessed by someone else.

Accordingly, the production of goods bearing utility is equally predicated upon the social relation of interdependent needs, rather than being a feature of the human predicament. Because a product can have economic utility only by being fashioned as a commodity for the needs of other individuals, use-value production is specific to the enacted context of civil relations, be they only partially or universally realized. All natural, subsistence production, on the other hand, has no economic normativity, for the wants, work, and products it involves relate humans and nature under either physical or psychological necessity or the demands of the household. Only the production of commodities, whatever form it may take, relates individuals to one another through the pursuit and respect for each other's freely chosen ends.

What all this indicates is that the basic relation between the members of civil society's community of interest consists in commodity exchange, where individuals acquire what they need from some one else by voluntarily giving in return some good of their own that that other individual seeks to have. Within this freely entered relation of exchange, commodities acquire the further social quality of exchange value, which consists in the equivalence of one commodity for another as realized in their exchange. Since their exchangeability depends simply upon the choice of the two parties involved, which need not reflect any particular outside considerations nor obey any preconceived idea of "economic rationality," exchange value is neither something intrinsic in the objects exchanged nor something determined by any process preceding the act of exchange itself. All labor theories of value that determine the proportions at which commodities are exchanged by the conditions of their production ignore the fact that commodity exchange is determined by the free mutual agreement of the parties to the exchange. It is the constitutive reality of exchange that allows nonproduced items, such as labor power and land, to have exchange value just as well as products, so long as someone can be found to trade another commodity for them.

Although commodity relations thus proceed wholly in terms of a reciprocal exercise of willing, their legitimacy has been challenged by Marx on the ground that commodity exchange entails a commodity fetishism where the social relations between individuals figure as relations between things ruling over people's lives.

The constitutive structure of commodity relations, however, entails the very opposite of what Marx fears. To begin with, the goods individuals exchange are not things but socially determined objects bearing both utility and exchange value by virtue of the interdependent relations of their owners. In order for these goods to be exchanged rather than unilaterally appropriated, the parties to the transaction must recognize one another both as free persons, objectively owning their respective goods, and as free members of a community of interest, exercising the common right of satisfying needs of their own choosing. In the act of exchange, individuals thus relate to one another not as subjects of things but as masters of commodities, using them as subordinate means to interact as independent bearers of need and enjoy the respected freedom to pursue particular ends of their own choosing in public. Consequently, commodity exchange is not an injustice, but a civil right, in as much as it realizes the particular self-determination of individuals in unity with one another through mutual respect.

The Status of Capital Within the Civil Economy

Granted this basic legitimacy of the elementary structure of commodity relations, the question arises as to what is the status of capital in relation to them? Does capital have normative validity as a necessary component of civil society, consonant with the freedom of particularity realized in commodity exchange? Or does capital entail injustice by restricting self-determination by something other than the content freedom gives itself? And if capital does entail any such illegitimate "natural determination," is it a distortion of commodity relations that can be purged from them, or is it an inseparable outgrowth that undermines their legitimacy as well as that of civil society as a whole?

The key to resolving these questions lies in understanding the minimal structure of capital underlying all its forms. This consists in the sequence of two commodity exchanges, schematically represented by the formula M-C-M', where one individual first purchases a commodity from another (M-C) and then sells that commodity for a greater amount of money than was paid for it (C-M').

Marxists have argued against the legitimacy of capital by claiming that the added exchange value received at the end of the second transaction contradicts the form of equivalence constitutive of commodity exchange. In their view, this surplus value can only be accounted for by a creation of new exchange value, which occurs not in the realm of exchange but in that of commodity production. There, so the argument goes, the individual who advances money to receive more in return obtains his or her increment by paying the laborer less for labor power than the exchange value his or her labor produces. This so-called "exploitation" of labor is achieved insofar as the exchange value of commodities is determined by the labor expended in their production. In *Capital*, Marx, unlike many of his followers, does admit that such "exploitation" involves no juridical wrong, for what the laborer is paid is the equivalent exchange value of his or her labor power, whereas the putatively value-producing labor is not something ever belonging to the laborer, nor even a commodity with exchange value, but rather the form in which the purchased labor power already belonging to the capitalist is consumed.[14] Nevertheless, even if the capital-labor relation does not directly violate the freedom of exchange, the determination of exchange value by expended labor would do so by comprising a "natural" principle that rules over exchange independently of the wills of individuals. The basic structure of capital, however, precludes this very possibility.

In the first place, not only is the M-C-M' exchange sequence providing the minimal reality of capital completely accountable in terms of commodity exchange, but the commodity relations it consists in proscribe any other factors from determining it. All that is required for an individual to purchase a commodity and then sell it for a profit is that she find in the market individuals willing to sell her that commodity and then purchase it at prices enabling her to realize a surplus. As in any commodity exchange, both sequences of M-C-M' proceed in terms of equivalencies that are established on no other basis than that the parties to these exchanges agree to trade their respective commodities for one another. This can occur regardless of whether the commodities are products, which is why the capital relation need not involve a production process at all but can merely consist in a speculative purchase and resale of goods.

In any event, there is nothing automatic about the sequence of exchanges comprising the capital circuit. Each depends upon the concurring choices of the parties to the transaction to determine what exchange value equivalents will actually be realized. The prospective bearer of capital may find it utterly impossible to sell the commodity resulting from the first advance of money in the M-C exchange, or the bearer may only be able to sell it at a loss or a break-even price. No factor independent of the arbitrariness of the other individuals in the market can mandate that a profit be realized or that it have a certain magnitude without violating the principle of mutual voluntary agreement constitutive of every commodity exchange. It is precisely this inherent contingency and variability in the sale of commodities that makes competition possible by confronting bearers of capital with the necessity of dealing with the independent wills of the commodity owners who form their market. This can entail altering the price, the publicity, or the character of the marketed commodity, but whatever is involved, the mutual decision to exchange still remains the ultimate arbiter of realized exchange value. Contrary to the labor theory of value, capital always faces a realization problem.

With regard to the identity of the bearer of capital, the M-C-M' relation presents no restriction other than that this bearer stand recognized in the market as a commodity owner needing commodities of others to make a profit and therefore obligated to respect the property and social need of the individuals to whom it relates. On this basis, the bearer of capital can be a single individual, a family, a corporation, a public enterprise, or, for that matter, a workers' cooperative, so long as that agent enters into the sequence of exchanges comprising the M-C-M' circuit.

Whatever the case, the minimal structure of capital remains in total conformity with commodity exchange, for it consists in nothing else. Commodity exchange, however, is not reducible to a relation of capital, for there is nothing about the former that precludes transactions in which profit is neither sought nor realized. Consequently, the M-C-M' circuit represents but one possible form that commodity exchange may take.

As for commodity production, it is not only irreducible to capital, but optional for the latter as well. On the one hand, commodity production need not proceed as a relation of capital, for a commodity can be produced and sold without profit, either when an employee or the owner of the means of production manufactures it. On the other hand, capital need not produce commodities, for although capital cannot be capital without involving an M-C-M' exchange sequence, it can achieve that entirely within the sphere of exchange through a speculative buying and selling of commodities.

If, however, capital is to involve commodity production, it must do so on terms compatible with the M-C-M' relation. As it turns out, these terms preclude any labor theory of value and therefore preclude the exploitation and natural determination of exchange relations for which Marx and his followers have challenged the legitimacy of capital.

These terms do so simply because the M-C-M' exchange sequence leaves the realization of capital's profit through the sale of its product something that is not independently determined by what occurs within its production process. Insofar as capital attains its profit only by concluding the two transactions of its M-C-M' circuit, what profit it realizes is instead dependent upon what exchange agreement is actually reached between capital and its prospective consumers. Although the bearer of capital may wish to sell a product at a price equalling the sum of the prices paid for the factors consumed in its production plus a certain increment, which, as a good Marxist, she may measure against the expended labor, she will succeed in doing so only if buyers be willing to pay that price. If not, the product will only be saleable at a different price, and it will then be that price that represents the realizable exchange value of the product. Capital cannot escape this realization problem because its relation as a producer to its consumers is one of exchange that issues from mutual agreement rather than from any unilateral determination. Consequently, neither the expended labor nor any other factor in the production of the commodity can determine the exchange value realized in its sale and the profit that may result. All the factors of production do determine is the exchange value that must be exceeded in the sale of the product if a surplus is to be gained, and this they provide not by virtue of their role in production but by virtue of the price at which they were purchased.

For these reasons, the M-C-M' exchange sequence that incorporates commodity production does not thereby subordinate the determination of exchange value to factors independent of the wills of the parties to its two exchanges, the purchase of the factors of production, and the subsequent sale of the product. Commodity production by capital thus does not impose a natural determination upon exchange relations in violation of civil freedom.

Accordingly, the relation between capital and labor involves no exploitation. Since the purchase of the worker's labor power by the owner of capital is itself a commodity exchange, what determines the actual exchange value of the traded labor power is the free agreement of that transaction. Since no independent standard can set that value, there can be nothing unequal about the exchange. Furthermore, since the labor capital consumes cannot determine the realized exchange value of the product, it only contributes to producing the new utility that helps make the product a marketable good. Therefore, there is no labor-posited exchange value of any determinate measure, let along one that would exceed the price of the purchased labor power and so seal the exploitation of labor to which Marx refers.

The inability of capital's own production process to determine either the price at which its product is sold or the magnitude of the resulting profit here reflects how the civil economy cannot be conceived as merely a system of capitals. Because commodity exchange and commodity production are irreducible to relations of capital, just as exchange value is not determined by the latter's production process, the theory of normative economic relations cannot make the accumulation of capital the all-determining principle of the economy. Capital accumulation must instead be conceived as a subordinate process within commodity relations that is affected by market factors exogenous to capital but endogenous to the total commodity interaction of the market within which capitals exist.

So situated, capital realizes in its own specific manner the same freedom of particularity that commodity relations provide. Neither capital's minimal form as M-C-M' exchange nor its particular shape as profit-making commodity production violate the normativity of commodity interaction in any way.

The Inability of Commodity Relations to Secure Civil Justice

However, the whole system of commodity relations, including those of capital, is tainted by a problem that necessitates that civil society not be restricted to an economy, but contain further institutions. Although these institutions presuppose the economy, their mandate is to intervene upon it such that the economy is rendered the subordinate rather than the determining base of civil society.

The problem at issue consists in the endemic inability of the civil economy to guarantee the satisfaction of the very needs generated in its interaction as matters of right. This inability has three bases.

First, insofar as the civil economy consists in commodity relations resting on mutual agreements of exchange, it is always contingent whether its members encounter other willing parties whose respective needs and commodities correlate with their own. This is true of every commodity relation, whether the commodities involved are products or nonproduced goods such as money, labor power, or land. On the basis of economic relations alone, every individual's ability to satisfy his or her need for commodities depends upon the free and therefore arbitrary decisions of others both to provide and market the required goods, and to accept in exchange what the individual has to offer, be it money, labor power, or some other commodity. This predicament is no different when the exchange is part of an M-C-M' sequence or when the capital involved is advanced by an individual, a private corporation, a public enterprise, or a worker cooperative. So long as the economic agents must enter into commodity relations, they can have no assurance of finding consumers or producers willing to conclude any desired exchange.

Second, there is nothing in commodity relations to prevent economic agents from amassing commodities through exchanges that then make it easier for them to engage in further exchanges while making it more difficult for others to do so and thereby satisfy their own needs. Once again, the constitutive willfulness of commodity relations makes this an irrepressible eventuality no matter which of the possible forms of commodity ownership happen to predominate. Whether there be nonprofit or profit-making corporations, privately or publicly owned enterprises, corporate or worker self-managed firms, nothing in their internal organization can preclude the relative enrichment of some and the impoverishment of others so long as they interact through commodities. Insofar as any economic agent in a civil society faces the general predicament of operating on the basis of mutual agreements with other independent agents, no economic form can prevent the ongoing process of commodity exchange from continually producing the disparities in commodity ownership that can subvert the equal opportunity of individuals to satisfy their chosen needs. For these reasons, there is no invisible hand to guarantee the economic welfare for all members of civil society, no matter if the market be dominated by private corporations, public enterprises, or worker self-managed cooperatives.

What compounds this problem is that although all commodity relations proceed in terms of mutual respect for the ownership of the exchanged items, these transactions themselves provide nothing to prevent violations of the property relations they proceed upon. Just as persons are subject to non-malicious wrong, fraud, and outright crime they cannot remedy just by acting as persons to others and just as the family has no means of its own to enforce the rights its members enjoy, so the civil economy cannot secure the commodity ownership of its members through the commodity exchanges in which its interaction consists. Thus, even if an individual does manage to acquire the commodity she needs, no economic relation can prevent another individual from taking it away nor punish the malfactor and retribute the victim.

All this means that the opportunity to participate in the civil economy and realize particular ends of one's own choosing by spending money, finding work, or trading goods is left unsecured by the very relations comprising the exercise of that right. Although commodity relations always involve reciprocal satisfaction of need, they are endemically incapable of guaranteeing the satisfaction of the needs of all members of civil society. For this reason no principle of organization endogenous to the civil economy, be it "free enterprise" or workers self-management, can resolve the problem of satisfying need as a normative relation of freedom.

This failure has special significance due to the civil character of the need for commodities.

First of all, the need in question does not have a natural limit given by the physical requirements of individuals and the natural scarcity of those things that can satisfy bodily wants. The need for commodities can have anything as its object, so long as the individual chooses it as an end and others rightfully possess it. Furthermore, to acquire the object satisfying such need, one does not confront the obstacle of nature's stubbornness, which technical activity can overcome. One rather faces the barrier of entitled commodity ownership, which can only be removed through the free consent of the owner to enter into exchange. Because of these socially specific features, the unsatisfied need for commodities comprises the endless poverty of a limitless want facing an unnatural plethora of goods utterly unattainable without a commodity of one's own that others want in exchange.

Nevertheless, what makes the poverty endemic to commodity relations a social *wrong* is not its unrestricted magnitude but rather the rightful status that commodity relations accord to the satisfaction of an individual's need for commodities through action of his or her own choice. Independently of commodity relations, the satisfaction of physical or emotional need has no normativity except in view of maintaining the bodily and psychological preconditions for a person acting in relation to others. By contrast, the satisfaction of the need for commodities has normativity for its own sake, since it is itself an exercise of freedom involving mutually respected and respecting realizations of freely chosen particular ends. Consequently, it is an unconditioned civil right that members of society be guaranteed the opportunity to satisfy their need for commodities by entering into an exchange of their choice, involving the acquisition of what they need in return for their money, their labor power, or any other commodity they are willing to part with.

Because, however, commodity relations cannot ensure this civil right that requires them for its realization, let alone protect the given property and family rights of economic agents, civil society must contain further institutions.

The Limited Justice of Civil Law and Social Interest Groups

On the one hand, there must be a public administration of justice to enforce the property and household rights of the participants in the market by standing over it as the recognized arbiter in conflicts in these matters. The rights over which this authority has jurisdiction do indeed derive their basic content from the prior interactions of persons and of family members. However, this office's mandate is to implement these rights within the further context of the civil economy and to do so by virtue of its own activity, with all the specific formalities that entails. Consequently, the public administration of justice engenders an irreducible civil right of its own consisting in the right of members of civil society to enjoy their property and family freedoms under the protection and arbitration of a recognized public authority. The exercise of this right can be seen to involve aspects of civil law and the activities of civil courts, penal institutions, and police that apply and uphold it.

No matter how this function works itself out, however, the public administration of justice cannot itself remedy the social wrong of unsatisfied need for commodities. Although this civil authority realizes a valid civil right by publicly protecting persons and households, it does so by preserving the given state of commodity ownership. Therefore, its activity cannot breach the problem of altering that ownership such that every member of civil society has the actual opportunity to satisfy her need through action of her own choosing.

For this reason, civil justice requires that the public enforcement of property and household rights be supplemented by social institutions that specifically attend to the unrealized needs continually generated by commodity relations themselves. Since what lies at stake is guaranteeing all members of society the freedom to satisfy their chosen needs through freely entered exchange, these institutions cannot annul commodity relations, which, after all, comprise the very exercise of the freedom to be realized. Instead, these social institutions must somehow intervene upon commodity relations so that their reciprocal satisfaction of need is not suspended but made available and actual for all.

The framework of the civil community of interest allows for two types of institutions to address this task.

On the one hand, individuals have the civil right to join together into social interest groups to forward a common need through joint action in conformity with the market and the institutions enforcing property and household rights. These organizations have civil legitimacy insofar as they are voluntary and seek to advance particular interests that can only be realized by reciprocally satisfying the different needs of others. Given the limitless variegation of need within the market, the interests motivating such groups can be any social need that its members have chosen to pursue in common. Since this jointly held interest forms the basis for the group, membership in it cannot be legitimately restricted with regard to other factors but must be open to any one sharing the particular interest championed by the group and the free resolve to join in its common action.

What here provide the just bounds for the actual activity of social interest groups are nothing other than the commodity relations and civil law procedures to which all civilians are party. Since social interest groups rightfully aim at realizing the freedom of their members to satisfy their particular needs in reciprocity with others, they can only do so by participating in rather than supplanting civil institutions. This means that social interest groups have two fields of direct action: the market and the public administration of civil law.

Before the law, social interest groups face the same limits that individual civilians do. Although a social interest group may make common suit in the courts, it cannot overcome the fact that the public enforcement of property and household rights in no way alters the given distribution of property resulting from commodity relations. Joint action by an interest group may expedite the protection of its members' property but not resolve the problem of their unsatisfied need. To attend to the latter, action in the market is required.

Within its limits, the members of a social interest group have the opportunity to try to arrange commodity exchanges to their satisfaction by collectively deciding under what terms to enter into exchange.

The options available for achieving this goal naturally reflect the different types of exchange and economic agents that commodity relations can involve. In this respect, the market itself allows for labor unions and professional groups to withhold the services of their members until their employers or clients agree to an acceptable payment, for consumer groups to withhold their purchasing power until their demands be met, or for associations of worker self-managed concerns, private corporations, or even public enterprises to control their production in common to advance their own ends in the market. All such activities remain in accord with the reciprocity of civil right, for they do not involve any unilateral appropriation of what others have but rather comprise acts of persuasion whereby one group in society aims at reaching a desired *agreement* with some other parties to exchange.

Although this aspect of respect for the social autonomy of others grants legitimacy to the market activities of social interest groups, it also leaves them burdened with the same problem of the contingency of satisfaction that gives rise to them in the first place. No matter what a social interest group jointly does with the commodities of its members (be it their money, their labor power, or their products), it cannot eliminate the arbitrariness of others upon whose exchange decisions depends the satisfaction of its members' shared needs. Consequently, although a social interest group may succeed in arranging the exchange its members seek, its own activity can never guarantee the satisfaction of their needs. Consumer groups, business associations, labor unions, and federations of worker self-managed enterprises all bear this limit simply because they are but particular groups having to deal with other independent agents in the market. For this same reason, the success of one social interest group in promoting the welfare of its members need not benefit those in other groups nor those individuals standing unorganized outside them all. Although a group can advance its interest only by reciprocally satisfying the needs of others, the terms of their exchange may leave the latter at a disadvantage for their next entry into the market while leaving the uninvolved individuals no better off. Just as commodity relations among individuals can preclude neither growing disparities in their commodity ownership nor the inability of some to enter into the exchanges they desire, so the market engagements of social interest groups cannot prevent the development of poverty and social inequalities that prejudice the opportunity of all to satisfy their needs.

For this reason, civil freedom requires more for its realization than commodity relations, public enforcement of property and family rights, and social interest-group activity. If social justice is to be achieved, these institutions must be supplemented by an enforcement of welfare that is not restricted to the members of a particular interest group nor exercised by particular agents in society, limited by the choices of others. The needed enforcement must instead extend to all individuals in society and emanate from a universally recognized authority empowered to secure for all the opportunity to satisfy their freely selected needs through economic action of their own choosing.

The Needed Tasks of the Public Administration of Welfare

In order for society to be civil, it must therefore incorporate a public administration of welfare whose mandate is given by the social freedom of particularity already at hand. The universal realization of that freedom is precisely what lies at stake, and, accordingly, the enforcement of welfare cannot consist in eliminating commodity relations and social interest-group activity nor the property and household rights upon which they rest. Because the freedom to satisfy one's chosen needs in reciprocity with others requires these structures for its exercise, the public administration of welfare cannot supplant but only intervene upon them.

Nevertheless, the required public intervention has a very radical scope yet unrealized in any existing regime. Since its aim is to guarantee the reciprocal satisfaction of freely chosen needs through freely entered exchange relations, the public administration of welfare must act on two fronts simultaneously.

On the one hand, it must ensure that all members of society have at their disposal sufficient commodities with which to enter into exchange with others to obtain what they need. On the other hand, public authority must guarantee that the commodities needed by the members of society be made available in the market in adequate quantities.

What lies at stake here is something more than ensuring the physical subsistence of individuals. That is indeed a civil right that members of society enjoy in their capacity as persons whose physical preconditions of personhood must be publicly protected together with their property. The public enforcement of welfare, however, extends beyond the physical requirements of the members of society to their social needs.

To achieve their guaranteed satisfaction, public institutions cannot unilaterally give individuals goods to consume. That would deprive them of their civil freedom to choose both what they need and how they will satisfy that need in reciprocity with others. By the same token, the public administration of welfare cannot mandate that the commodity ownership of individuals be equivalent, with respect to either the specific utilities involved, or their aggregate exchange value. Since individuals may freely desire both different commodities and different levels of wealth, imposing uniformity on either score actually undermines the freedoms to be realized.

Civil authority must rather strive to insure that all individuals can acquire the commodities they need by having at hand what others will accept in return. Instead of doling out goods to be consumed directly, public institutions must provide that every member of society has sufficient goods to exchange. These include a marketable labor power, adequately trained to the individual's choice, as well as whatever money or commodities are necessary to secure his or her livelihood through exchange with others. At the same time, public authority must insure that there be jobs available as well as an adequate supply of affordable commodities.

Two factors that necessarily complicate this task are the unrestricted character of social need and the inequalities of wealth endemic to commodity relations.

Since individuals can choose to need any variety and amount of commodities, the public administration can never completely eliminate the possibility of discrepancies between the needs of individuals and the available supply of commodities, including desired terms of exchange for labor power. Consequently, the public authority will have to limit the needs whose satisfaction it guarantees in accord with the actual resources of the economy. This restriction involves no violation of right, for it applies to all individuals without discrimination and enables them to realize their social freedom of satisfying needs of their own choosing in reciprocity with others. Although the choice of needs whose satisfaction is publicly guaranteed is here restricted, the limit is determined solely by the conditions allowing for reciprocal satisfaction, where the needs involved remain matters of personal preference. Thus, as in all cases of right, it is free willing that here limits itself.

Similarly, the public administration of welfare must take further positive measures in face of the disparities of wealth that can continually emerge from commodity exchange, no matter who participates in the market. In themselves, inequalities in commodity ownership need not involve any social wrong. Since members of a civil society have the respected right to choose their own needs, what and how much they will seek to acquire for their satisfaction, and the type and degree of activity they will undertake in that pursuit, different individuals can fully satisfy all their needs through completely unequal livelihoods. Indeed, given the different preferences of individuals, it can even be said that they can *only* satisfy their chosen needs through unequal acquisitions of wealth.

Nevertheless, disparities in commodity ownership can reach a point where the great wealth of certain market participants gives them such an advantage in making further transactions that others with lesser means find themselves unable to conclude the commodity exchanges they require through economic activity of their choice. Their disadvantage comprises the social wrong that public action must rectify.

The required corrective does not consist in imposing equal incomes across society but rather in ensuring that all do have sufficient means to earn the livelihood they wish through whatever economic engagement they choose. What determines the social measures necessary to accomplish this is once again the given resources of the economy, which sets the de facto upper limit of the needs that all can satisfy in reciprocity. Only if the economic situation leaves no other alternative, such as adequate self-renewing public works, need the satisfaction of the disadvantaged involve an administered redistribution of wealth from the privileged, be they private individuals, corporations, workers' cooperatives, or even public enterprises. In order to maintain the social freedom of need of all concerned, the redistribution cannot comprise the dispossession of specific utilities. It must instead proceed through monetary taxation—that is, the public appropriation and redistribution of exchange value, which leaves it to the individuals to decide what goods to dispose of or acquire. Although the equalization of incomes is not an end in itself, the redistribution of wealth through taxation has no *a priori* limit. Whatever may be required to eliminate social disadvantage is justified so long as it preserves the constitutive freedoms of commodity relations.

The inherent contingencies of these relations make public intervention a continually recurring endeavour, whose measures must constantly be revised in accord with the situation in the market. No matter how extensive is public involvement, so long as the members of society maintain their autonomy, any unilateral, planned social policy will require constant adjustment. Because the order of the economy is not determined by any single will but is the result of the independent willings of the different participants in the market, no public plan can ever be assured of achieving its ends.

Consequently, the public administration of welfare entails a constant and continually revised intervention in the economy in reaction to the positive circumstances of the market. Although the required measure thus have a specific content that cannot be derived in any *a priori* way, they nevertheless must fall within those general guidelines mandated by the concept of civil freedom. On these terms, public authority does not eliminate and supplant commodity relations but rather regulates them so that the ethical right of economic activity is externally secured for all. Since both the public protection of property and family rights and the administration of welfare here relate to the economy as that upon which they act, the economy remains the basic structure of civil society presupposed by all the rest. However, under their combined regulation, the economy is rendered the subordinate and not the determining base of society. The justice of commodity relations requires that this be so, and only when society's own public institutions free it from subservience to capital or any other economic factor can society be civil and realize social freedom. A free enterprise system that leaves the market unregulated is therefore an unfree society, failing to institutionally secure the civil right to satisfy one's need for commodities through activity of one's own choosing.

The Requirement of an Independent State Ruling Over Civil Society

Although the public administrations of civil law and welfare rightly lord over the economy, they remain social institutions confined to the community of interest of civil society. All their activity affords the members of society are the respected civil rights to enjoy their person, property, and family freedoms under the protection of public law and authority and to have the publicly guaranteed opportunity to satisfy their needs through actions of their choice. These institutions do not provide any political rights to participate in self-government, nor does their public regulation comprise a self-determining government whose ruling activity is for its own sake and thereby politically sovereign. Instead of determining its aims, the public enforcement of civil law and welfare is strictly limited to advancing the independently determined particular interests of the members of society. Even if these interests be taken together as the public welfare, they still constitute an end to which the administration of society is the separate means. Consequently, the activities of civil institutions are irreducibly relative to the distinct pursuits of individuals and never ends in themselves.

As such, the public institutions of civil society have power neither to make the laws they enforce nor to legitimate and determine their own authority. If they did, they would be able to set their own ends and act for their own sake, which would contradict their relative, civil character. Without these self-grounding capacities, however, these institutions cannot independently command recognition as the public administrator of civil right and welfare. Although the social freedoms of civilians cannot be universally realized without the intervention of these civil institutions, the public administration of right and welfare cannot provide itself with the conditions for its own existence. It may rule over the economy and completely realize civil freedom, but it is still not the source of the law it applies nor of the authority it needs to fullfil its mandate. As a consequence, the public administration of civil society, on which all other civil relations depend, has no independence of its own.

This means that the public administration of civil society and civil society as a whole cannot be the crowning order of freedom. By themselves, civil institutions leave the whole domain of right subject either to collapse or to a law and authority of an extraneous origin, whose independent givenness upsets the whole framework of unconditionally universal freedom upon which normative validity rests.

Accordingly, civil society's own lack of independence makes necessary a further sphere which can give civil institutions their law and authority. Because the reality of freedom would be undercut if its order were imposed upon it by something else, the distinct activity of this higher sphere must itself be a domain of freedom consisting in a respected exercise of self-determination. Nonetheless, its right must be irreducible to no other, for its task is to determine and realize all relations of right including its own.

Therefore, what civil society requires is an additional structure of public freedom with a dual mandate. On the one hand, this new structure must provide civil authority with all the means necessary to secure social freedom along with the property, moral, and family rights it involves. On the other hand, this higher public order must do so as an institutional sphere wherein individuals exercise the further freedom of determining the totality of right which now includes the institution of this self-ordering activity as its ruling organ.

This institution is the sovereign state whose sphere of politics builds the crowning order of public freedom. It has this ultimate character not just because it gives all the structures of interaction a necessary realization through its own activity, but because its sovereign rule allows the whole into which it unites them to be self-determined as well. Within its political domain, individuals accordingly enjoy their highest, most concrete freedom, for the institutional practice of the required state can only consist in a certain mode of self-determination of its members. To animate such a state, the mode in question must be the participation of citizens in self-government, determining through their own free action the totality of right in which they exercise not only this political freedom but their personal, moral, family, and social freedoms as well.

Any liberal or socialist state that reduces government to an administration of civil law and/or public welfare fails to meet these requirements, as does, of course, any fascist state that subordinates politics to natural determinations. Although the valid sovereign state must ensure civil freedom, it does so by giving civil institutions the law and power to enforce property and family rights and social welfare and not by becoming an instrument of civil society with no political ends of its own. On the contrary, the sovereign state acts for its own sake since what it does in resolving the dependence of civil society is order itself as the self-ordering unity of the reality of freedom. Because the state's self-determining activity incorporates all the other structures of freedom as secured components of the whole it governs, it only reaffirms the unconditioned character of its own rule in providing the conditions for their existence. In this way, political unity asserts itself as an end in itself that must be maintained as such if civil society is to have its own law and authority through freedom. When the state achieves this total sovereignty, it can realize self-government without failing to realize the other structures of right just as it can secure their freedoms without yielding the independence needed for its own.

By contrast, civil government, the welfare state, and all regimes based on class interest subordinate politics to social ends. This automatically strips the state of the self-grounding autonomy needed not only to realize political freedom but to enable civil society to realize its own social justice. When this happens, self-government is reduced to administration, bound to carry out aims that the state has not determined for itself. The resulting politics suffers from the same deficiency afflicting civil institutions; namely, the inability to establish freely its own law and authority instead of having it independently given. So long as that condition persists, the entire order of right lacks the unconditioned character justice requires.

To escape that decisive limitation, the state must constitute a free political domain radically distinct from the civil society it grounds and sustains. The basic outline of such a body politic lies already at hand.

In the first place, the state must be an association whose members interact within its proper sphere not as civilians pursuing their particular interests but as citizens determining government policy as the end of their own individual action. For that policy to be something they can freely will, the state in which they act must itself be the existing structure of their political freedom to govern themselves. On that basis, politics unifies the universal will of state authority with the particular wills of its citizens without any opposition between them. While individuals exercise their respected rights as citizens by determining the general policy of the government, the state has its own sovereign legitimacy for them by being the institutional reality of their individual political freedom. Here the self-determination of the citizen is participation in self-government because the political order has as its end self-rule and not particular interests or public welfare as in the "politics" of civil government, class rule, or the welfare state.

At the same time, the state can be this sovereign sphere of self-government only if it does not cancel the social freedom of interest or any of the other relations of right. If it did so, it would set itself against its own members in their capacities as persons, family members, and civilians, engendering an irreconcilable conflict of right against right. The basis of political unity would thereby be destroyed, and freedom would be deprived of any total existence. To avoid such self-destruction, the just state must accommodate all other freedoms within its domain and secure their right through its own rule.

In accomplishing this, however, the state must preserve its own sovereignty by preventing any of these component spheres of right from subordinating politics to their own ends. If the order of right is to be determined by freedom rather than externally imposed, the state must ensure that its citizens exercise their freedoms of personhood, moral subjectivity, family life, and social involvement without letting these undermine their political freedom.

For this reason, the state has the right and obligation to restrain and punish the arbitrariness of conscience when its moral acts violate the laws of the state. So, too, the state can rightfully demand that its members risk their lives and particular personhood when required for the defense of the political freedom of national sovereignty, which alone guarantees personhood in general.

Similarly, the state must lord over civil society in a dual way. On the one hand, the state must provide civil institutions with the law and authority they require to ensure social justice. To accomplish this, the state must first enact two types of law relative to civil society. One consists in the administrative law that determines the jurisdiction and organization of the public enforcement of civil right and welfare, and the other in the body of civil law that civil institutions administer in securing the property and family rights of individuals while guaranteeing their satisfaction of their needs through action of their own choice. Having legislated both of these, the state must then ensure that civil institutions act in accord with the law it has imposed on them and that they have at their disposal the means enabling them to do so. Only under this *political* supervision can it be assured that civil institutions are able and compelled to carry out their *social* regulation of the economy.

By itself, however, the intervention by the state in civil society for the sake of social justice does not automatically prevent class struggles, economic power, and other factors from overwhelming politics. These factors may still subordinate government policy to some social interest and thereby undermine the opportunity of citizens to exercise self-rule. For this reason, the state must also intervene in society on purely political grounds to keep civil society in its subordinate position and preserve the autonomy of political freedom.

This requires measures at least as radical as those undertaken by civil authority to enforce social justice. The most obvious one, and by no means the least important, consists in state action against political corruption, which basically consists in individuals fraudulently using government office for their own private gain. Such action must be complemented by the more sweeping task of insuring that the social conditions of political action do not give certain citizens an advantage over others in participating in politics. Insofar as achieving publicity for political programs, organizing political groups, and mounting political campaigns each requires significant private means and labor, the state must take positive measures to provide all citizens with equal access to the social resources needed to engage in politics. Only when this is actually achieved is political action free of social privilege and properly universal.

In this regard, the state secures the conditions for its own political freedom by mediating itself with civil society. Through its two modes of intervention, one for social and the other for purely political ends, the state insures that its citizens' freedoms as persons, moral subjects, family members, and interest-bearing civilians are realized in unity with the sovereignty of politics.

Nevertheless, what these relations do not provide is the actual institutional order with which the state mediates its own universal rule with the particular political wills of its citizens and realizes the specifically political freedom of self-government. The principal problem confronting political theorists and citizens alike is determining the valid structure of this order. Although the movements of our times have mainly turned their attention to the order of society or some other prepolitical "foundation" of the state, the order of justice requires that this political question have paramount importance.

If it be ignored through acceptance of the sanctity of existing constitutions, there can be no assurance that freedom has obtained the self-sufficient reality that the just state can alone provide. What lies at stake in determining the institutions of political freedom is thus not just whether self-government consists in parliamentary democracy, a federal system of participatory assemblies, or some other form, but whether right will exist on its own account and so achieve the unconditioned universality justice demands.

To resolve this problem of freeing right of foundations, capital and civil society must first be understood in their own limited reality, for if their boundary cannot be drawn, politics can have no sovereign domain of its own.

10
The Reason for Democracy

For as long as people have questioned the authority of the status quo by asking what justice is, the relation between reason and practice has figured as an issue of decisive importance in the legitimation of conduct and institutions. The quest for justice has unavoidably turned to their relationship in response to the dual problem of justification that no theory of justice can ignore.

This problem is both practical and theoretical. On the one hand, realizing justice presents the practical problem of justification, which consists in performing those actions and erecting those institutions that are justified not by current custom and opinion but in an unconditionally valid way. On the other hand, conceiving justice involves the theoretical problem of justification, which consists in arriving at ideas about justice that command universal validity. In both cases, reasons are called for—reasons to render conduct and institutions just rather than merely operative practice and reasons to render conceptions of justice justified truths rather than unjustified opinions.

Not surprisingly, philosophers who have attempted to conceive justice have traditionally located the reasons making actions just and theories true in reason itself. Insofar as reason is held to exhibit the unconditioned character, universality, and objectivity required for valid justification, what counts as reasons legitimating actions and theories is none other than the exercise of reason comprising rational argument.

If this leaves theory radically self-justifying to the extent that it moves from opinions to truth by relying on reason alone, it leaves action seemingly dependent upon reason for its measure and standard.

Whereas theory can be legitimated only by depending upon itself, action can be just only if it conforms to rational principle.

Yet action depends upon will, and willing is not thinking, any more than knowledge of justice is equivalent to the performance of just deeds and the existence of just institutions. Although justice can be done only through acts of will, the will has the power to do right as well as wrong so long as it is voluntary. If just action is action in accord with reason, then justice will consist in the activity of the rational will, which will be a will guided by reason and thereby justified by reason.

The rational will cannot be identical to the free will, however, if freedom is viewed as the liberty of choice natural to the will and reason is viewed as a faculty of binding principles whose truth is no matter of choice. On these terms, justice requires that freedom be restricted, for if the will is left to itself, there can be no guarantee that it will choose those actions in accord with reason. Yet, if the will is endowed with liberty of choice, then the only resource available to limit the freedom of the will and compel it to be rational is the will itself. Justice would therefore seem to be an ever elusive chimera, with no assured reality at all.

Theorists of justice have generally grappled with this antinomy of reason and willing by laying hold of one side to the exclusion of the other. One tradition of thought, initiated by Plato and Aristotle, has sought to secure the justice of rational willing by supplanting freedom with the rule of reason over the will. Another tradition has taken the opposite extreme and held justice to consist in the free sway of liberty realized in the democracy of majority rule. Although neither position can be sustained on its own terms, the complimentary collapse of their arguments suggests a third alternative that not only resolves the antinomy of reason and willing, but offers the only admissable justification of political democracy.

THE FAILURE OF THE CLASSIC EXCLUSION OF FREEDOM FROM POLITICS

The theory of justice that excludes freedom from the state in deference to the rule of reason follows a firm logic already uncovered by its first major advocate, Plato.

The starting point of this theory is the premise that reason prescribes goals for action whose achievement comprises the unconditionally justified conduct, the rational willing, constitutive of justice. If this teleological view be admitted, then justice will clearly require the performance of those set functions that fulfills these goals set by reason. Since these functions have fixed ends, each requires a corresponding expertise, disposition and excellence or virtue in performance to assure their best possible completion. Therefore, if the rational goals of justice are to be best achieved, then those best qualified by expertise, disposition, and virtue to carry out those functions that attain these goals must perform them.

To the extent that individuals are endowed with natural differences that affect their technical competence for these functions and to the extent that they have not all equally acquired the skills and knowledge suited to fulfilling each task with excellence, everyone's occupation should be appropriately prescribed rather than be left to personal preference or chance. Insofar as the various functions needed to achieve the rational goals of goodness each requires a plurality of individuals to perform in common their specific task, the community devoted to justice will be divided into necessary classes carrying out the different functions at hand. To insure the greatest good, individuals will belong to their class or classes not by choice but according to their capabilities to perform the corresponding functions. It should be noted that although Plato allots each individual to just one class, arguing that only such specialization guarantees the best performance of each task, it is not inconceivable that the same individual might be qualified for more than one task and perform several, so as to belong to several classes without prejudicing the rationally predetermined goals of justice.

Nevertheless, because individuals do have choosing wills, it cannot be guaranteed that they will join the appropriate classes and execute properly the functions they are best suited to perform unless a further function be exercised. This function is the ruling activity whose purpose is to safeguard the realization of justice by making sure that all the functions achieving its rational ends are performed by those individuals most fitted to do so. To carry out this ruling activity an additional class of individuals is needed, whose members must again be selected on ability and be required to serve their posts to guarantee the best possible rule. This class can well be called a guardian class, for its task consists in maintaining an order already determined by reason's prescription of the goals and corresponding functions of justice.

On this basis, the ruling function of the guardians is a purely administrative activity of overseeing the given framework in which its own function proceeds. The guardians do not decide what organization the state should have but simply implement the class organization eternally decided by reason. In this sense, the rule of the guardians does nothing but give each individual his or her due, for compelling all to perform the class activities they do best does produce the greatest justice for everyone *if* justice indeed consists in the fulfillment of predetermined ends.

Under such a regime, all freedoms that might interfere with achieving the set goals of justice would have to be precluded. If there is any rational hierarchy of needs and occupations, then market freedom must be restricted to prevent individuals from both satisfying whatever needs they please through commodity exchange and entering occupations through similar agreement irrespective of the tasks mandated by reason. Most importantly, all political freedom would have to be curtailed, since neither the goals of the state, nor its organization, nor the assignment of its different functions could be left to the will of all or any of its members, if the order of reason is to be automatically ensured. Democracy, thus, could not be tolerated, for there is no telling whether the majority will choose what is rational, when rationality in politics consists of fixed ends and activities.

Yet can political freedom possibly be so entirely excluded? Although the guardians may be able to use their power to restrict the political, market, and even household freedom of their subjects, can the guardians' own political freedom be curtailed without eliminating their necessary position as rulers? Is there not an irrepressible element of freedom rooted in the very structure of rule that gives whoever governs the state a sovereign will knowing no limitation other than that which it imposes upon itself?

Plato, for one, addresses this problem by calling upon reason itself. He recognizes that there must be something to guarantee that the guardians do restrict their actions to achieve the goals of justice and will what is rational. His solution is to appeal to reason and require that the guardians be philosopher-kings. It is not enough that they be administrators expert in the administrative science consisting in right opinion of the ends of justice and the functions fulfilling them. All that can be apprehended without understanding why these ends should be followed. The guardians must therefore be philosophers of justice, who also know the reasons *justifying* the ends of justice. Only then will they be compelled by the force of reason to recognize the legitimate authority of these goals.

This would be a solution if knowing what justice is in its full justification were identical with doing what is just. Yet Plato himself recognizes that willing and reasoning are different activities, that the philosopher can pursue thinking without ruling, that the philosopher must be compelled to rule. But who will compel philosophers to rule or guardians to philosophize when it is precisely the apex of command that must be rational? To be founders of the just state in speech or in deed guarantees nothing once the rulers are in place, lording over all others as well as themselves.

Plato's concerted attempt to secure the rational willing of justice by excluding freedom here collapses in face of the seeming bond between freedom and political rule. Although he seeks to conceive the just state as the embodiment of given forms of conduct antecedently apprehensible by the rulers imposing them, the structure of political dominion leaves justice realizable only insofar as the state contains a self-determining activity imposing order upon the order of which it is a part.[1]

If this leaves the total banishment of independent willing a political impossibility, it is hardly evident how political freedom can provide any more viable a solution to the problem of justice.

THE APPARENT OPPOSITION BETWEEN DEMOCRACY AND JUSTICE

By definition, the rule of freedom would appear incompatible with any normative order involving functions and ends prescribed independently of the will. Although the sovereign political will might well choose policies conforming to already established norms, the prerogative of its political freedom would seem to leave any such conformity a nonobligatory matter of choice. So long as the authority and power of government are taken to reside in a sovereign will free unto itself, what is and should be done cannot be ordained in any prior fashion by reason but only observed after the fact of the sovereign will's arbitrary decisions. Conceiving political freedom in terms of the sovereignty of the people's will, expressed in the democracy of majority rule, alters nothing in this indifference to set ends and functions. With the people left to choose as they will according to majority decision, there can be no telling what goals will be set or which activities will be executed to fulfill them.

Precisely for this reason, it would make no sense to raise objections against the political equality and lack of expertise of those who rule under such democracy. Since the majority can do as it pleases, citizens need no special qualifications. Instead of having to carry out preordained functions requiring certain skills, the people are in the position of first deciding what goals should be addressed and then how they shall be implemented. Accordingly, all individuals here need to exercise their political freedom is the choosing will they have by nature, provided they are neither severely retarded, insane, comatose, nor too young to choose. The need for special skills would only arise when it came time to administer what has already been politically decided.

The problem remains, however, of how political freedom can be justified in its own right. Since the exercise of political freedom cannot be counted on to achieve any prescribed norms, democracy simply cannot be argued for coherently as a means to an end distinct from itself. On the contrary, the defense of political freedom would appear to require the denial that there are any given ends to which politics should be subordinated. Historically, it is just such a denial of the authority of given ends that provides the point of departure for the legitimation of liberty classically inaugurated by Hobbes' rejection of any teleological conception of man.[2] Nonetheless, denying that there is a good life of given character may set the will free of external prescription, but this does not of itself vindicate freedom. Somehow, political freedom must be shown to be an end in itself if democracy is to have legitimacy.

The problem is that freedom's normativity seems ruled out from the start due to the very considerations that led Plato to try to exclude liberty from his ideal state. In a word, although the autonomy of the choosing will may be a necessary precondition of justice, the very fact that it allows for right as well as wrong action would seem to indicate that freedom cannot be an end in itself. If one extends this objection to political freedom, the conclusion seems to be that democracy cannot be justified, for either the will of the majority is oblivious to the distinction of right and wrong or it must be made to follow prescribed ends, which it cannot do without sacrificing its own autonomy.

Furthermore, even if political freedom were an end in itself, the exercise of democracy could not guarantee its own perpetuation. So long as majority decision has free sway, there is nothing to prevent the majority from supplanting democracy with another form of government. Thus, although the legitimation of democracy would seem to require the demonstrated illegitimacy of all prescribed restraints upon the will of the majority, the absence of such limits appears to leave democracy beyond good and evil as well as incapable of maintaining any commitment to its own form of rule.

In answer to these problems, the advocates of democracy have generally sought its redemption by introducing fixed guidelines to limit majority rule. These restrictions have been added to achieve two presumed requirements of justice that would otherwise go unfulfilled. First, democracy is to be limited so that majority rule is compelled to maintain rather than violate those functions besides democratic participation that can be considered ends in themselves. This would include the protection and furnishing of whatever nonpolitical activities and services are worthy of being matter of right. In this way, normatively valid property, moral, family, and social relations, together with the rights of the minority, would be guaranteed against the arbitrariness of the will of majority. Second, democracy is to be restricted so that majority rule remains the form of the government, no matter what the majority may wish.

In both cases, what supplies the needed restriction is nothing other than a framework of constitutionality, where the constitutional provisions setting down the limits of democracy are not subject to revocation or amendment by the will of the majority. Only if the limiting constitutional provisions have this fixed character, free from alteration by democratic decision and thereby irreducible to mere positive laws, could democracy be counted on to maintain itself or any other relation of right.

This recourse to constitutionality may save democracy from its own arbitrariness, but in doing so there would seem to be reinstated all the problems afflicting the theory of justice that relies upon the authority of given ends to make the will rational. The moment a nonamendable constitution gets introduced, the question arises as to who is to impose it without being subject to arbitrariness themselves? Although experts of justice are excluded from any privileged role within the democratic state, they would apparently be needed both to found the constitution as well as to oversee its realization by the existing democracy. Yet, if an expert founder and overseer is required to make democracy a justified political order, how can such a figure be counted on to will what is rational? Once again, the specter of freedom raises its irrepressible head to threaten the implementation of the fixed provisions that alone might permit political freedom to enjoy legitimacy.

Whereas the attempt to banish freedom from politics foundered by having to rely upon the will to make rule rational, the alternative project of legitimating democracy apparently arrives at a like impasse by having to impose fixed standards to bring reason to the will of the majority. Either way, rational willing seems to fall victim to arbitrariness, leaving political justice easy prey to the skeptical challenge of nihilism. The fundamental problem at issue is well clarified by examining the flawed advocacies of democracy that such disparate figures as Jefferson, Rousseau, and Lenin have provided.

THE FLAWED ADVOCACIES OF DEMOCRACY

Jefferson's advocacy of democracy is particularly instructive because he draws upon the two most influential traditions in the philosophy of justice, the praxis theory of Plato and Aristotle and the contractarianism of liberal philosophy, and in so doing, inadvertently testifies to how neither can lend support to democratic government.

In his letter to John Adams,[3] Jefferson adopts the classical ideal of aristocracy, arguing that the just state is one ruled by those individuals who are the most virtuous and talented. Indeed, so long as one accepts the teleological view that justice consists in the fulfillment of fixed ends through set functions, such a conclusion can hardly be avoided. Jefferson, however, departs from the Greek praxis theoreticians by maintaining that democracy is the best form of government because democratic election offers the greatest insurance that the best individuals will be selected to rule. Although Jefferson admits that the many may not always choose the best candidates but may be blinded by birth and corrupted by wealth, he still claims that, for the most part, the natural aristocrats, the wisest, most virtuous, and ablest men, will be elected into office. Just to be sure, he calls for a ward system of public education and for the abolition of entails and primogeniture to prevent a pseudoaristocracy from arising on the basis of social privilege.

Nevertheless, no matter what measures are taken to instruct the public and eliminate social disadvantage, there can be no guarantee who the majority will elect so long as it is free to choose as it will. As the Greeks well recognized, democracy cannot insure rule by the best any more that it can insure the passage and implementation of any set policies. Since all that majority decision necessarily entails is its own momentary exercise, Jefferson's defense of democracy as a means to aristocratic ends completely fails.

His advocacy of republicanism fares no better when he relies upon the principles of social contract theory. This is no more evident than in the Declaration of Independence. There, Jefferson reaffirms the liberal credo of Locke, maintaining that all men are born free and equal with inalienable rights to life, liberty, and the pursuit of happiness, that government is properly instituted to secure these rights, deriving its just powers from the consent of the governed, and finally, that the people have the right to alter or abolish their government whenever it violates its mandate and replace it with a new government that will protect their persons and property with the consent of the governed.

Significantly, the Declaration of Independence makes no mention of democracy and political freedom but limits its call for independence to the establishment of the civil government prescribed by contractarian theory. That government need not be democratic, for all it is charged with is securing the nonpolitical freedoms of property owners with their consent. As Locke himself points out in chapter 10 of his *Second Treatise On Government,* just civil government can take the forms of monarchy or oligarchy since, although its legitimate authority rests upon the consent of the governed embodied in the social contract, this entails not citizens' participation in self-government but only their right to select who will rule over them to protect their persons and property. In exercise of this right, they can choose themselves as rulers, but they can just as easily choose one or several individuals to govern them and even consent to a dynastic succession. Thus, it can come as no surprise that many of those who took up arms in support of The Declaration of Independence could later attend the Constitutional Convention fully expecting to enthrone George Washington as king of the United States of America.

Of course, as already indicated, democracy can qualify as a civil government provided that it not only enjoys the consent of the governed but also secures the nonpolitical rights of individuals that liberal theory locates in a state of nature. Because this state of nature is by definition any condition where no legitimate government exists (and not just some prehistoric state antedating the rise of civilization), natural right cannot possibly involve any exercise of political freedom. If it did, the state of nature would contain rightful political institutions that liberal theory maintains have legitimacy only as products of the convention of social contract. Consequently, the government that is contractually instituted to secure the liberty all people have a right to by nature has as its goal the realization of nonpolitical rather than political freedoms.

Liberal theory must therefore treat democracy not as an end in itself but as a means to something else. This, however, leaves democracy not only optional, insofar as other forms of government can secure nonpolitical freedoms, but potentially inadmissable in those cases where the majority decides to adopt policies violating the person and property of individuals.

As much as Jefferson wishes to promote the idea of republican democracy, the liberal premises of the Declaration of Independence actually lend support to the expendability of democratic rule. Because social contract theory conceives normative freedom not as the institutional practice of self-government but as the noninstitutional natural liberty of individuals, the justice it prescribes requires the enforcement of only civil rather than democratic rights.

The radical distinction between liberty and political freedom comes to a head most markedly when Jefferson attempts to extend the consequences of contractarianism to the constitutionality of his democratic republic. In his letter to James Madison of September 6, 1789 (pp. 261–66), Jefferson consistently argues that a constitution infringes upon the liberty of individuals if its authority rests on ratification by a preceding generation. In that case, he maintains, the members of the current generation are no more obligated to obey the constitution than to pay public debts accrued in the past. The reason is that neither debts nor constitution here issued from their consent, which is the sole source of their obligation, granted the legitimacy of liberty. Accordingly, Jefferson proposes that a constitution be valid only for the period during which those who participated in its ratification still comprise the majority of citizens whereas once that period elapses an entirely new constitution should be enacted with the same expiration feature. The problem is that Jefferson also asserts, albeit without argument, that the just state is a democratic republic approximating participatory democracy as much as possible by means of direct election of all state officials for short terms, complemented by a system of ward assemblies attending to local affairs (pp. 251, 269).

Clearly, Jefferson cannot coherently uphold both positions at once. If he accepts the right of each generation to determine its constitution with complete liberty, then he cannot also maintain his commitment to democratic government as the mandatory paragon of justice. The choice seems clear: Either one accepts the contractarian allegiance to nonpolitical liberty and forgoes advocacy of democracy, or one attempts to justify political freedom on its own terms without appeal to natural rights. Jefferson does neither and instead remains uncritically inconsistent.

Rousseau, by contrast, has an awareness of the underlying difficulty and attempts to meet it head on. His approach, however, is akin to squaring the circle, for Rousseau seeks to justify democracy by demonstrating that it is an end in itself because it is the only reliable means for securing nonpolitical liberty. Although Rousseau remains loyal to the social contract conception of the primacy of natural rights and the corollary notion that government is legitimate insofar as it protects person and property with the consent of the governed, he is well aware of the problems arising from the instrumental character of the liberal state. Rousseau recognizes that so long as civil government is merely a means to an end distinct from its own political activity, there can be no guarantee that the state will fulfill its mandate, nor that there will be any resources with which to judge violations objectively and counter them. Locke's appeal to the judgment of the people provides no remedy, for how will the people be able to convene and judge with authority? Even if the people could be assembled, insoluble problems remain. If unanimous consent of the people is required to pass judgment on the conduct of government, no judgment of censure will likely be forthcoming so long as the officials in question are members of the "people" themselves. If, on the other hand, majority decision is relied upon, the door is left open for a tyranny of the majority in violation of civil freedom. Finally, if each individual is free to rely upon his or her own judgment, as Locke suggests,[4] to determine when government no longer commands obedience, the authority of the state becomes subject to the rule of individual arbitrariness—which is precisely what civil government was established to prevent.

For Rousseau, the solution to these difficulties lies in bringing direct democracy to the legislative power of civil government. If sovereignty is invested in a general will that acts by making law according to the majority decision of an assembly of all citizens, then, Rousseau maintains, government will automatically achieve its legitimate end of protecting persons and property. The reason Rousseau offers for why the general will can do no wrong is that it consists in citizens exercising the genuine freedom of willing law upon themselves. This precludes injustice both because no will can injure itself and because all acts of the general will, being acts of legislation, apply equally to all individuals as legal subjects. In virtue of its democratic legislating structure, the general will presumably prevents any particular will from subordinating state rule to its own interests at the expense of others. Since the general will enjoys universality in the two senses of emanating from all and applying equally to all, Rousseau concludes that it cannot help but secure the common good. Consequently, the democratic legislation of the general will would appear to be unconditionally just and hence attain the dignity of an end in itself.[5]

Rousseau's line of argument would be persuasive *if* the common good to be achieved were nothing other than the democratic legislating comprising the activity of the general will. In that case, the general will would automatically realize justice. Rousseau, however, still ties the common good to the realization of prepolitical liberty. Despite the fact that he goes one step beyond contractarianism by identifying freedom with obedience to law that is not just self-imposed (as in Kantian autonomy) but codetermined by the wills of all other citizens, he maintains that the general will should fulfill the aims of social contract and protect person and property with the consent of the governed. As a result, Rousseau is forced to admit that democratic legislation will not automatically achieve the common good (see Book II, ch. 3, and Book IV, ch. 1). Because the latter has a fixed predetermined content distinct from the activity of the general will, the general will must be externally directed to make those laws that are just, rather than those that serve a particular faction or are detrimental to all. Since the general will is nonetheless sovereign, this direction can only take the form of persuasion—persuasion exercised by a powerless "legislator" who suggests laws for adoption by the general will and fosters faith in a "civil religion" to convince the citizens to will what is rational (see Book II, ch. 7, and Book IV, ch. 8).

Here Rousseau's justification of democracy comes to the point of collapse. The need for a legislator and civil religion demonstrates that the justice of the general will lies not in its democratic structure but in the conformity of its legislation to independently determined rights. Further, this conformity is endemically jeopardized by nothing other than the sovereignty of the general will, a sovereignty that gives it license to legislate justice into the ground.

If Lenin does not share Rousseau's allegiance to liberal principles, his defense of workers' democracy is similarly problematic. In *State and Revolution* Lenin offers the democratic ideal that has become the canonical prop for the apologists of "people's democracies" the world over. What is theoretically important about the political injustice of such regimes is not simply that they have substituted party dictatorship for "workers democracy" but that the latter ideal is inherently contradictory.

Lenin proposes his conception of workers' democracy as the just alternative to parliamentary democracy. Relying upon a bevy of quotations from Marx, Lenin condemns parliamentary democracy as bourgeois democracy because so long as there is a capitalist society, he maintains, the private owners of the means of production will possess the overwhelming preponderance of wealth affording them privileged access to the instruments of political activity, such as the media and campaign resources. Under such circumstances, democracy turns into bourgeois democracy, and the bourgeoisie becomes a ruling class able to impose its interests upon the state even though there are universal suffrage, freedoms of speech and assembly, and the elimination of all political privileges directly tied to class affiliation.[6]

What should supplant parliamentary democracy, whose rule of the majority is actually a screen for rule of the few, is the dictatorship of the proletariat, whereby, according to Lenin, the working class will exercise political rule through a democracy limited to its own members. Although this excludes citizens of other classes from political participation, it secures genuine majority rule since, Lenin claims, the members of socialist as well as capitalist societies are overwhelmingly workers. Further, although the working class is but a particular group, its interest is universal in character, having no other goal than the elimination of class distinctions, the withering away of the state, and the emergence of classless communist society. Accordingly, whereas bourgeois democracy violates political justice by using the show of a universal rule as the instrument of a particular social interest, workers' democracy possesses legitimacy by both realizing majority rule and subordinating government to a particular social interest that is properly universal (p. 80).

The fatal flaw in Lenin's argument is that workers' democracy is incompatible with the revolutionary goals of communism. Following Marx and anticipating Max Weber and most contemporary social and political scientists, Lenin holds that the state is purely instrumental in character, comprising nothing more than the privileged institution holding the monopoly of coercive power over society. As such, politics cannot be an end in itself, for power for its own sake is empty and meaningless. Rather, the state has meaning by serving as a means to independently determined ends—ends that Lenin traces back to class interest, given the economic determinism of his reading of Marx. On these terms, the state is rendered an instrument of class domination that allows one class to oppress another thanks to the force of political power. Accordingly, politics not only has no legitimacy of its own, but the state becomes an inherently unjust institution of domination that should be done away with. Hence, the goal of the dictatorship of the proletariat is not to establish the just state, which is here a contradiction in terms, but to eliminate class divisions in society and thereby eliminate the basis for any state whatsoever (pp. 18–19, 75, 90).

This means that workers' democracy is not an end in itself but only justifiable to the degree that it follows the road to communist society by taking those social measures that progressively undermine the economic bases of class divisions. Workers' democracy, however, will not automatically implement such policies so long as the proletariat is at liberty to choose as it pleases. Furthermore, since the goal of the revolution is antecedently prescribed by "scientific socialism" independently of any exercise of political freedom, the rule of revolutionary experts, schooled in the incorrigible truths of Marxism, would presumably be more reliable in any case.

Thus, as much as Lenin seeks to legitimate workers' democracy as the genuine form of majority rule, he cannot allow it free reign so long as he maintains his teleological commitment to the construction of communist society. As a result, Lenin falls back upon a "solution" that borrows equally from Rousseau and Plato. Just as Rousseau introduced a legislator and civil religion to bring the people to reason and Plato made philosophers guardians of the polis to instruct their subjects in the good life, so Lenin calls upon the vanguard party and its ideology to guide the proletariat. Since the goal of the revolution is not workers' democracy or any form of government but a communist society knowable by virtue of Marxist "science," Lenin's vanguard cannot be a mass party controlled by the rank and file and thereby subject to their arbitrariness. It must rather be a political elite, schooled in the wisdom of dialectical materialism, which alone purportedly qualifies its members to be true guardians of the revolution.

Prior to the seizure of state power, the vanguard party can only rely upon persuasion to influence the working class, and to that end, it employs a mass line like a civil religion to cajole a proletariat more susceptible to ideological faith than the rational apprehension of "scientific socialism." After the revolution, however, the vanguard party is in a position to go beyond Rousseau's powerless legislator and adopt a role more like Plato's ruling class. Under the imperative of achieving the "rationally" prescribed goals of Communist society, the party has no choice but to free itself of subordination to any constituent assembly, workers' soviets, or trade union movements, and make itself the ultimate arbiter in society and state, vigilantly restricting the political as well as social freedom of the working class whenever necessary to forward the transition to communism.

The results, which have made familiar history ever since the Bolsheviks liquidated the workers' soviets and trade unions, testify to nothing less than the inexorable conflict between workers' democracy and Communist rule. Whereas liberal principles can be realized without political freedom, the Communist future has no need for democracy whatsoever. By reducing the state to a disposable tool of preordained social ends, Lenin and his epigones have undercut all reason for political freedom under the dictatorship of the proletariat.

As for the redeeming goal of the workers' state, when Lenin provides a glimpse of the awaited order of communist society, where the working day, the market, classes, and the state have all been superseded, he can only offer the promise that habit will insure that individuals take what they need in harmony with one another (pp. 81, 93). Habit might be the midwife of virtue, as Aristotle would say, but so long as humans have a choosing will it is hard to imagine how habit could guarantee any type of justice without recourse to the ruling agency of political authority. In the social and political void of associated producers, where humanity has been reduced to its species being by shedding market and state, what is left is a hobby existence of purely private activities, be it fishing in the morning, painting in the afternoon, philosophizing in the evening or whatever. There, at the end of history, democracy is as out of place as any other public endeavor.

Clearly, if democracy is to be defended, the paths of Jefferson,

Rousseau, and Lenin cannot be followed. Nevertheless, the common failures of their arguments point directly towards the one and only vindication of democratic government. What their examples suggest are the following three requirements for the justification of democracy:

1. Democratic political freedom must be an end in itself rather than merely a means to independently determined ends.
2. The matters that fall under the prerogative of democratic decision must be unsusceptible to any antecedent prescription by reason. Otherwise, justice would require that these matters be handled instead by experts administering rationally preordained policies enjoying a validity independent of what the majority may will.
3. The democratic process must be bound by nonamendable constitutional provisions requiring the state to maintain its own democratic workings as well as to secure whatever nonpolitical relations have validity of their own.

In order to understand how these requirements can be met without reintroducing the antinomies of reason and willing afflicting the traditional conceptions of justice, it is appropriate to begin with the last requirement first and work back to the solutions of the other two, upon which the justice of democracy ultimately depends.

DEMOCRACY, CONSTITUTIONALITY, AND THE DIVISION OF POWERS

In the face of the inherent arbitrariness of majority rule, constitutionality is necessary to limit democratic decision-making and make possible its normativity. At stake in constitutionality are two imperatives already apparent in the failed attempts to justify democracy. Because majority rule of itself offers no guarantee that the majority will maintain democracy, there must be constitutional provisions requiring democratic decisions to respect and preserve democratic freedom. Otherwise, democracy is in a position to violate its own principle. Similarly, since majority rule need not respect other relations of justice, there must be constitutional provisions obligating democratic government to recognize and enforce all rightful activities and institutions besides that of democratic rule. Although these two imperatives refer to the distinct spheres of political and nonpolitical right, they can converge to the extent that the maintenance of nonpolitical relations of justice are themselves preconditions for the exercise of democratic freedom.

For instance, if certain individuals are deprived of their elemental right to have inalienable ownership of their own bodies, as occurs whenever slavery exists, those individuals have no opportunity to act in their own names as participants in democratic government, let alone in any other rightful capacity. Similarly, it could be argued that in an unjust society, where social disadvantage leaves some groups with privileged access to the resources needed for political action, democratic freedom can have no more than a formal reality as the public mask of oligarchy.

In any event, whether nonpolitical relations of justice be preconditions of political freedom or not, their enforcement can only be guaranteed under democracy if the will of the majority be bound by prescriptions it can neither alter nor rescind. Just as the principle of democratic rule can be secured only if it is not subject to but master of all positive legislation, so democracy can claim the normativity of being consonant with nonpolitical justice only if it is subject to nonamenable constitutional provisions spelling out every relation of right that should be unconditionally upheld.

In this light, the United States Constitution can be doubly faulted. On the one hand, it falls subject to critique for failing to guarantee such nonpolitical matters of justice as securing equal opportunity for all by eliminating social disadvantage and unemployment. On the other hand, it stands reprimandable for allowing constitutional amendment. Although the ordained amendment procedures involve more than acts of Congress, the very allowance of amendment undermines the distinction between constitutional and positive law by giving citizens the right to change the Constitution however they will. So long as this right is retained, the Constitution offers no firm commitment to political democracy or any other relation of justice. However hallowed it may be, constitutional amendment legally permits anything from prohibitions of budget deficits and abortion to genocide or religious rule, provided enough citizens are willing to push such measures through the amendment procedures. Admittedly, constitutional amendment can permit peaceful reform when the constitution is itself unjust and worthy of change. This has been the case with the U.S. Constitution, which has needed amendment to eliminate such injustices as slavery and the political disenfranchisement of women. Nevertheless, the only ultimate purpose of constitutional amendment can be to establish the just constitution, which should be nonamendable to guarantee that the relations of justice it prescribes are not dismantled with impunity.

Although talk of the nonamendable character of the just constitution may seem foreign to citizens accustomed to living under unjust constitutions in an age of widespread nihilism, this feature of political justice is indicative of how the just constitution, if there be such a thing, is an object of reason. By virtue of being just and not merely operative, such a constitution would be unconditionally valid and thereby invariable and universally prescriptive. Even if, following Aristotle, one were to recognize that existing conditions may not everywhere be ripe for the best regime, the just constitution would still provide the invariable standard for judging what kind of regime would be the best possible under given circumstances. The just constitution would accordingly be rationally justifiable, for it would share the qualities of universality, objectivity, and unconditionality that reason must exhibit if it is to be a source of justification in questions of truth and justice. As such, the just constitution would be transparent to reason and a proper object of political philosophy.

If, by contrast, one abandons all reference to the unconditionally best regime while maintaining normative commitments, one falls into the absurdities of those who, following Gadamer, have absolutized the role of prudence in Aristotle's ethics and politics to the exclusion of reason. In view of the unmasked assumptions of much traditional theory, it is not without appeal to make this move and argue that all standards are conditioned by the historically limited cultural frameworks within which human reflection operates, such that all normative judgments are relative to given particulars and given conceptual schemes. The problem with this position is that it makes an unqualified claim of its own concerning the ultimacy of prudence at the very same time that its unconditional advocacy of prudential judgment rules out any final pronouncements concerning the situation of theory and practice.

Aristotle, it should be noted, is fully aware of this self-referential inconsistency of any absolutization of finitude and therefore grants prudence its essential role within ethics and politics without reducing all discourse on conduct to prudential judgments about what must be done here and now. Accordingly, he can speak of *oikos* and *polis*, citizenship and constitution, monarchy and tyranny, aristocracy and oligarchy, polity and democracy, the difference between illegitimate and legitimate regimes, and choice, virtue, means of conduct, and prudence itself all as universal categories of the philosophy of praxis without falling into hopeless contradiction. Naturally, it can be argued whether Aristotle has correctly applied these categories in their full universality when, for example, he excludes women, slaves, laborers, and all who are not household masters from citizenship and thereby fails to make political and social unity coextensive. To treat this as a normative problem, however, automatically transcends historical concerns by raising the issue of what justice per se demands, which is very different from engaging in the reflective equilibrium of asking what would be compatible with certain prevalent modern views. Although one can always adopt the posture of nihilism and question whether justice as such is possible, this does not prevent all talk of the just constitution from referring to something that, if it be, can only be addressed by reason and political philosophy. Since the legitimacy of democracy is tied to constitutionality, it makes sense to consider, even if only hypothetically, the character of the just constitution as it bears upon the rationale for democracy.

In this regard, it might appear that the need of democracy for constitutionality testifies to the impossibility of justifying majority rule, given the putative rationality of the just constitution and the apparent irrationality of democratic decision. Actually, the reverse is the case, for the rational character of the just constitution gives good reason for precisely the type of rationally opaque prerogative democracy involves.

Under constitutionality, government is charged with nothing other than realizing the constitution, for the latter's provisions should prescribe all those activities and relationships that are unconditionally just. Government must accomplish this, however, in face of changing circumstances in society, politics, and foreign affairs, which are concerns of justice and must therefore be taken into account in implementing the constitution. Consequently, although the just constitution may have an *a priori* determination, prescribed by reason, its realization in practice involves applying its rationally determinate provisions to a given, changeable reality that can only be known through experience. This provides the basis for positive legislation, for without positive laws, enacted in reference to the factual situation of the nation, the statutes of the constitution cannot be acted upon in any general yet determinate fashion.

What allows for toleration of democratic perogative is precisely the resulting predicament of positive legislation. Under constitutionality, positive law cannot be an object of reason; it can only be an object of judgment. Since the constitution contains all those rules that are invariably valid and rationally prescribable, what is left to positive legislation is supplying rules, obedience to which will implement the rational strictures of the constitution in the current state of affairs. Insofar as the reality at hand cannot be preordained by reason but only perceived after the fact in experience, the formulation of positive law requires an act of judgment burdened by subjectivity in two respects. On the one hand, the perception of the given situation is subject to all the limitations upon factual knowledge that preclude any final objective certainty. Just as in evaluating evidence in a court of law, discretion must eventually be relied upon to decide whether the facts have been accurately and honestly reported, whether they are complete or representative, and whether they have been properly interpreted. On the other hand, once the facts have been established, subjective discretion must be called upon again to judge how the laws should be determined to best implement the constitution. Reason alone may be capable of specifying the constitution but not the particular measures by which it is to be applied in every possible situation. Thus, as much as lawmakers must use reason to apprehend the constitution and rely upon experience to understand the reality that is to be constitutionally governed, composing the appropriate laws requires an act of judgment going beyond what reason prescribes and perception observes. As with interpretations of facts, this judgment lies outside the limits of reason and requires the contribution of subjective discretion if any determination is to be made at all.

This means that positive legislation is insusceptible to the rational prescription that would rule out democracy as a candidate for the just state. Because knowledge of the factual state of affairs and formulation of the laws properly addressing it are both opaque to reason and dependent upon subjective judgment, there can be no privileged wisdom providing for absolutely correct laws nor any privileged experts in legislation. On the contrary, anyone with a mature mind and will is competent to exercise the judgment required for positive legislation. Exactly because the content of positive law cannot be determined with any absolute truth, it is both permissable and unavoidable for positive law to be determined by political opinion rather than by the political wisdom of a philosopher-king or vanguard party. Since positive laws cannot be rationally deduced from constitutional principles, legislative debate is always an open-ended prospect where no speaker can claim unqualified truth. Therefore, so long as there are no other intervening regulations, the weight of political opinion is the only factor that can give one opinion rather than another the authority to ordain the law.

Here, within the limited realm of positive legislation enacting laws to realize the constitution in the given situation, no policies or goals have any *a priori* command other than the constitution itself. If there is any terrain for democracy, it would have to be in this legislative arena in which given ends, set functions, and experts have no relevance.

Clearly, no class, group, or individual can claim any privileged role in fulfilling the task of positive legislation. Even if one were to follow Marx and grant the proletariat a universal interest in accord with justice —that is, a rational interest determinable by philosophy,—this would not make the working class any more reliable than any other legislator. Determining what laws should be enacted to promote its rational interest would still involve subjectively perceiving the prevailing situation and subjectively judging how to apply the rationally knowable proletarian interest to that state of affairs. As a result, not only would the legislative programs of workers be as various as subjective discretion allows, but individuals of other classes might just as easily advance legal proposals more propitious to proletarian interest than those of any workers or their self-anointed guides. Just as knowledge of an interest cannot provide an unequivocal determination of the positive laws serving it best, so the political opinions of individual legislators cannot be derived from their social roles, even if the latter give them an objective interest that they seek to promote.

If these considerations indicate how democracy is at least compatible with positive legislation, the subordination of such law-making under constitutionality immediately raises the issue of a division of power, an issue that must be confronted by any advocacy of majority rule. This is basically because the very distinction between constitutional and positive law, required for the justification of democracy and justice in general, rests upon not just the nonamendability of the constitution but the separation of two governmental powers from the legislature as well. One of these is a branch of government exclusively empowered to authorize the laws proposed and voted upon by the legislative power, an authorization stamping them as constitutionally valid and thereby first rendering them the actual law of the land, commanding obedience and enforcement. Then there must be a further branch of government with exclusive authority to execute the authorized laws.[7]

If, in place of such a division of powers, the legislature could both formulate laws and authorize them, then constitutionality would have no reality, for the legislature could certify any law it made to be constitutional no matter how much it actually violated the constitution. Furthermore, even if a separate authorizing power existed, if the legislature could execute the authorized laws as it saw fit, it could make their enforcement take any form it chose in utter disregard for the constitutional expectations of the authorizing power. Either way, a democratic legislature would be able legally to eliminate virtually every limitation of constitutional government and make the will of the majority unbeholden to any law or principle of justice.

Of course, the same danger of absolute domination arises if the authorizing or executive powers are combined with any other branch of government. If, for instance, the authorizing power were permitted to formulate the laws it approves for execution or execute what it authorizes, it would be able to rule without any constraints. For this reason, the authorizing power should be limited solely to approving or rejecting laws drawn up independently by a separate branch of legislation. Although this makes the authorizing power the effective head of state, since its certifying decision alone allows government actions to be performed in the name of the state, it leaves the apex of authority otherwise powerless. Unable to determine either the content of the laws it rejects or approves or how authorized laws are to be executed, the head of state can here do nothing more disruptive than leave government momentarily stalled by refusing to authorize any proposed laws.

Under such conditions, the division of powers achieves the organic unity which constitutionality requires for its very maintenance. To be properly differentiated form one another, no organ of government should be able to exercise its characteristic power without the complementary constitutional activity of others. When the legislature cannot make its laws valid without the assent of a separate authorizing power, the authorizing power has nothing to certify without the preceding legislation of the lawmakers, and when the executive cannot govern without authorized laws to implement, no particular will can substitute itself for the universal will of the state as a whole. The state is instead only able to act through the co-determination of all its separate powers.

If democracy is to enjoy constitutionality and with it any hope of validity, it must be structured in accord with such a division of powers. That is not the case with the democracy prescribed by either the U.S. Constitution or the participatory council democrats such as Pannekoek and Arendt.

Under the U.S. constitution, the authorizing power is not properly separated from the legislative and executive branches of government. Both the President and the Supreme Court exercise the power of authorizing laws, the former by signing or vetoing bills of Congress, the latter by judging the constitutionality of laws at issue in cases coming before it. Their powers of authorization, however, are not as exclusive as those of a head of state should be, for Congress can override the veto of the President, whereas the Supreme Court can only pass judgment on those laws that figure in cases appealed to it. This means that Congress is in a position to authorize its own laws and exercise virtually unlimited power so long as presidential vetoes are overridden and legal challenges have not made their way through the judicial system to the Supreme Court to test the constitutionality of those laws. In addition, the President is also the chief executive, which means that an element of the authorizing power is conflated with the executive branch of government. Although these structural problems have so far not led to the usurpations they permit, the danger of legal despotism will remain so long as constitutional change is not undertaken.

This danger is no less present in the proposals for participatory council democracy that have been made in light of the historical experiences of the Paris Commune, the 1905 and 1917 Russian revolutions, the Spanish Civil War, and the Hungarian uprising of 1956. Hannah Arendt presents the idea of council and democracy in its strongest form by purging it of the oligarchical element of class dictatorship at the hands of which worker councils have suffered in theory and practice. She proposes a pyramid of councils, resting on democratic assemblies open to all who wish to participate. These have jurisdiction over local affairs and elect members to the next level of assemblies, which have their own more encompassing jurisdiction and elect members to the succeeding assemblies, until finally the whole edifice is crowned by a supreme council acting on a national plane.[8] Although the entire structure incorporates successive demarcations of authority, these demarcations involve the vertical differentiation of varying degrees of local, regional, and national authority according to the principle of federalism rather than a horizontal separation of powers limiting political prerogative at each level of rule. With a federation of participatory assemblies the legislative, authorizing, and executive powers of government are conflated at every stage, offering no institutional means for preventing assemblies from doing as they please. Although the different jurisdictions of each successive assembly are presumably defined prior to their respective engagements in political decision-making, the absence of any additional governmental organs leaves nowhere to appeal when assemblies violate their own mandate and conflict with other levels of political council or other nonpolitical relations of justice. Under such a council system, every citizen may have the opportunity to govern in person at a local level, but none enjoys the safeguards of constitutional rule that a separation of powers makes possible.

THE ABIDING PROBLEM: CONCEIVING DEMOCRACY AS AN END IN ITSELF

If all these considerations set ground rules to which democracy must conform if it is to have legitimacy, they do not themselves justify democracy as the proper form of government. Constitutionality and the separation of powers may be basic prerequisites of political justice, but democracy is certainly not required for their existence. Similarly, positive legislation may entail an irreducible element of subjective discretion making democracy permissable, but that does not mean that this discretion need be exercised democratically. Indeed, it might simply be a matter of indifference how positive laws are made, provided that there be a division of powers in accord with constitutionality.

Therefore, if democracy is to qualify as the just regime, worthy of exclusive advocacy, it must not only satisfy the requirements of constitutionality and separation of powers, not to mention the relations of nonpolitical justice that should be constitutionally guaranteed, but also be the only realization of constitutional government that is unconditionally valid. For this to be the case, democratic rule must be an end in itself. Only then would democracy be indispensable, since its justification would lie in its own existence rather than in the achievment of some independent goal that might be fulfilled by other means. Accordingly, the legitimation of democracy ultimately rests upon the demonstration that democracy, qualified by constitutionality, separation of powers, and respect for nonpolitical relations of justice, is nonetheless for its own sake.

What provides this demonstration is a threefold argument that eliminates equally the antinomy of willing and reason. It establishes first, that normativity consists in self-determination, second, that practical normativity or justice consists in the reality of freedom, and third, that political justice consists in democratic self-government.

NORMATIVITY AND SELF-DETERMINATION

Traditionally, the candidates for truth and justice have been distinguished from mere opinion and operative practice either in virtue of some privileged givenness or by being determined by some privileged determiner. The recurring recourse to given determinacy in establishing the validity of theory and practice has arisen out of a common pair of judgments. It has been widely asserted that justification ultimately requires some nondeducible self-evident reason to provide firm ground for what is to be justified. Otherwise, it has been held, argument is left resting upon hypothetical assertions, with the result that any conclusions are equally hypothetical and therefore indistinguishable from unjustified opinion. Similarly, it is commonly affirmed that since the holding of opinions and the maintenance of institutions and modes of conduct testify only to their being and not to their validity, truth and justice must be sought not as they are conventionally determined through subjective artifice but as they are by nature, according to the given determinacy that comprises their objective, justified content. Guided by these judgments, the quest for truth and justice characteristically proceeds by asking the parallel questions "What is?" (in the sense of "What is the given determinacy or nature of reality?"), and "what is the Good?" (in the sense of "What is the given determinacy or predetermined structure of conduct and institutions comprising justice?"). With normativity taken to lie in given determinacy, the sought-after answers are supplied through the appropriately passive activity of contemplation, where reason immediately apprehends, rather than mediately constructs, the first principles of reality and justice providing the privileged givenness on which all else is grounded and demonstrably knowable.

This whole approach to theoretical and practical justification is plagued by the sceptical objection that every candidate for first principle, be it of reality, justice, or even knowing, is equally unjustifiable precisely because its given determinacy cannot be supported without introducing some reason whose mediating role undermines the candidate's putative immediacy as first principle. It might appear that a proposed first principle might still be justified by showing that all else does follow from it. Such a demonstration, however, would require prior knowledge of both what is the totality of reality or justice that must be deduced and what comprises valid deduction. If that knowledge depended, like all else, upon the first principle, the demonstration would fall prey to a vicious circularity where what is to be proven is presupposed by its proof. If, on the other hand, such knowledge could be had independently of the first principle, it would contradict the latter's presumed primacy as the sole source of justification.

What these problems suggest is that whenever normativity is based in some given determinacy, the latter has its privileged status not by virtue of its given content but by being posited or determined as such by whoever has ascribed it its foundational validity. Although this outcome certainly undercuts classical metaphysics and its corollary theories of the Good, it does not leave theory and practice in the clutches of skepticism and nihilism. Another approach to truth and justice lies at hand, for if no given content can provide justification, it is natural to presume that what makes something true or just must lie in its being determined by the proper determiner.

Not surprisingly, the attempts to conceive truth and justice in terms of given determinacy have historically been supplanted by precisely such an approach of establishing validity in determined determinacy. With regard to the quest for truth in general, this has taken the form of transcendental philosophy. Rejecting the immediate apprehension of given reality characterizing metaphysical contemplation, transcendental inquiry instead conceives objectivity not directly but indirectly as something constituted or determined by some condition or other, be it of knowledge, reference, or meaningful speech. Whether the transcendental condition takes the form of the structure of consciousness, intentionality, *Dasein*, ordinary language, or the hermeneutic situation, it always provides the privileged determiner that determines what is valid and knowable as such.

In the theory of justice, on the other hand, determined determinacy has been adopted as the standard of normativity by the liberal tradition. Liberalism rejects the authority of given teleological ends, such as the pattern of a Good Life involving prescribed virtues, given means of conduct, and rule by experts, and instead grants legitimacy only to what the will determines in its exercise of liberty. Here, justice does not lie at hand as a predetermined form awaiting embodiment but rather issues from social contract or some other procedure of construction, whereby government has validity not by corresponding to what is good by nature but by being willed into being by all and by permitting acts of any content whatsoever provided they are determined by the free choice of individuals without infringing on the free choice of others.

Although the turn to conceiving truth and justice in terms of determined determinacy proceeds from a critique of the foundational legitimacy of given determinacy, it falls victim to the same sceptical challenge simply because determined determinacy issues from a determiner whose own content is given prior to and independently of its act of determination. This is evident in how a transcendental condition is not constituted by its determination of objectivity, any more than the will of liberal theory owes its character to its own act of choosing. Thus, although transcendental conditions are introduced to avoid direct reference to reality, they themselves can only be characterized in just the same dogmatically direct manner as reality is contemplated by metaphysics, whereas the privileged determiner of liberal theory is a natural will, whose form is just as given as any teleological end.

Since every case of determined determinacy logically involves an element of given determinacy in the prior character of its determiner, there is no way any determined determinacy can be ascribed privileged legitimacy without resurrecting the dilemmas of first principles. In fact, every such determined determinacy is patently unjustified insofar as it is grounded upon a determiner that lacks the very quality of determined determinacy in which normativity has here been invested.

It might appear that the vulnerability of transcendental philosophers and liberal theorists to the same critique they rightly direct against metaphysics and teleological theories of justice entails the final triumph of theoretical skepticism and ethical nihilism, where all that remains is the edifying occupation of deconstructing theories and systems of justice so as to reveal the given assumptions on which they rest. As much, however, as given and determined determinacies do fail as candidates for normativity, the prevalent failure of thinkers to consider any positive alternative to them does not prevent the logical possibilities of determinacy from providing a third option. This option, which exhausts the alternatives for justification, is self-determined determinacy.

That self-determined determinacy, or freedom, could be the substance of normativity in theory and practice becomes readily plausible once one considers the problem of justification in truth and justice in all its simplicity.

At first glance the problem appears completely paradoxical. In order for knowledge claims or actions to be justified, something must be provided to certify that they are not unfounded opinions or behavior. What serves to justify them must itself be justified, for otherwise the normative validity of the knowledge claims or actions at issue would rest upon something with no basis of its own. This predicament, however, would seem to be an ultimately hopeless one, for every attempt to provide justification would require a prior reason to justify every successive ground of justification, resulting in an infinite regress that could only be ended by the provision of a putatively self-evident reason whose own authority could never be established.

Indeed, this problem is insoluble so long as one bases truth and justice upon some foundation, for then what is to be justified rests upon a ground that never can share the same normativity of being grounded by a foundation distinct from itself. What undermines all attempts to establish normativity in given or determined determinacies is just this dilemma of foundationalism.

When, however, one considers truth and justice as a whole, it is evident that the justification of truth cannot be sought outside truth any more than justice can be valid by virtue of what is not just. In other words, neither can be ascribed foundations without cancelling its normativity by conditioning it upon what is neither true nor right. This does not mean that knowledge claims and conduct can never be justified. It rather suggests that both truth and justice can only possess their constitutive normativity by being self-grounding. This, however, can only be achieved if what is true and what is just are determined by themselves rather than by any separate determiner or ground. In effect, truth and justice must have self-determined determinacy. Then both will not only be free of foundations but enjoy the universality and unconditioned character that validity involves. As self-determined determinacies, truth and justice would be universal and unconditioned not by lacking all content but by having a self-determined particularity independent of any externally given particular factors. Although thinking the truth and doing right may indeed involve any number of preconditions, such as the fortunate distance between the sun and earth, the peculiar bonding properties of water, a certain sequence of natural mutations, the structure of consciousness, the existence of language, the material means for survival, and so forth, all these allow for both truth and falsity and right and wrong without prescribing what are justified opinions and actions. This juridical problem would still remain in the province of what is universal and unconditioned—that is, in the province of freedom.

Of course, the intimate connection between truth and freedom has been recognized ever since the quest for truth was seen to require an autonomous reason rejecting the authority of given opinion and instead establishing by itself the validity of every element in its own argument. Reason, however, could never attain this radically self-justifying, self-grounding autonomy so long as it based its inquiry upon given or determined determinacies. In either case, its argument rested upon a foundation whose own content was accepted without justification. Reason becomes autonomous only when philosophical inquiry begins with no grounds or primitive terms and somehow presents a subject matter that presents itself, a subject matter self-ordered so that its form and content are results of its own development, a subject matter that is self-determined determinacy. Such a radically independent reason would be dialectical in the sense in which Hegel uses the term, for it would be a reason that takes neither its method nor subject for granted but operates in a systematic immanence where what comes into consideration are determinacies issuing from the absence of all reference to givenness as well as all transcendental constitutions. Indeed, dialectical reason and freedom go together, for the only subject matter that could be developed in a wholly immanent fashion would be self-determined determinacy, since it alone neither rests on givenness nor is determined by a distinct determiner.

Although what all this actually involves may appear unfathomable (see chapter 1),[9] especially against the backdrop of a philosophical tradition beset with the alternatives of foundationalism and skeptical relativism, the complementary impasse of these two options at least suggests that the program of a foundation-free dialectical reason warrants serious investigation. Fortunately, the corollary character of foundation-free justice is readily conceivable and may make more plausible the approach to justification it exemplifies at the same time that it clarifies the way in which democracy can be legitimated.

If justice, like truth, must consist in self-determined determinacy, then justice is no more and no less than the reality of freedom in the concrete sense of free action and all the institutional relations it involves. The significance of this characterization should be apparent. If both truth and justice are wedded to freedom, with truth tied to autonomous reason just as right is tied to the free will, then the antinomy of reason and willing is eliminated. To the degree that rationality has the character of self-determination, which it must have to escape the dilemmas of foundationalism, and self-determination is the structure of validity, the freedom of the will is no longer in any opposition to the rational will constitutive of justice. Instead, the rational will is nothing other than the free will, and, indeed, it has normativity only by being free, since what makes the free will valid is the same self-determined character that makes autonomous reason justified. Accordingly, there is no antinomy between reason and willing. Rather, there is a complete identity between rational, justified willing and freedom.

This identity of the rational will and freedom does not mean that justice consists in the reign of arbitrary choice any more than autonomous reason entails theoretical anarchy. Contrary to the assumptions of liberal theory, "free" arbitrary choice or liberty is not self-determination because the choosing will has a given structure that underlies every choice it makes and, conversely, because the alternatives among which it is at liberty to choose have their character given independently of the empty form of choice that is itself indifferent to the particular content of action. Instead of being self-determined, the will endowed with liberty actually operates as a determiner with a given character consisting in the natural will all selves possess, provided they are not physiologically or psychologically damaged. Thus, when the natural will chooses some alternative, it does not give itself a new form determined by its act but simply takes an action whose content adds nothing to the character of the agency performing it. That agency remains a will at liberty to choose what it pleases. In this respect, what the choosing will determines is not itself, for its own agency is in no way determined by its actions but precedes them all as a natural given. To be truly self-determined, the will would, instead, have to determine its own agency through its action, which is something the choosing will of liberty can never do, given its constitutive character.[10]

Similarly, any reason that proceeds by virtue of assertions arbitrarily made by a thinker is not autonomous, for both the method and content are determined by a reasoner whose own rationality, or, if one will, whose "communicative competence," exists prior to the process of reasoning as part of the given "nature" of the mind. Only when reasoning proceeds "dialectically," with a self-unfolding, self-determined content whose development is not prescribed by the given structure of consciousness, language, or any other condition that may necessarily underly the operation of thought, can arbitrariness be supplanted by autonomy of reason. This may appear to be an unrealized ideal, despite Hegel's attempt to present such reason at work in his *Science of Logic*. Yet it should be clear that if philosophy is not to take for granted its method or subject matter but account for both within its own inquiry, then it has no option but to leave the validity of its thought as undetermined by the whims of any given reasoner as by the prevailing norms of the culture in which it happens to be situated. Instead of being subject to any exogenous agency or rule, philosophical reason must determine its own topics and procedure to be worthy of the name. However this actually be accomplished, it is clearly incompatible with any reasoning whose validity is determined not by itself but by the natural language, author, or any other contributing factor by which it may concretely unfold as the thought of a real individual in some particular historical context.

Analogously, in order for willing to be self-determined, the character of the will must be willed into being through its own act so that *who* wills is determined in conjunction with *what* is willed. Accordingly, the free will is not something natural like the choosing will but rather an artificial, conventional agency whose own specific autonomy is a product of willing. An individual who wills in relation only to him- or herself or to nature cannot possibly exercise such self-determination, for every act of his or hers is no more than an act of a choosing self, whose liberty of choice precedes each and every volition as its determiner. When, however, individuals will in relation to one another, it is possible for them to engage in conventional roles, such as property-owner, moral subject, family member, member of society, and citizen, that can involve autonomous actions that determine the very institutional framework within which their specific agency is constituted. When institutions are so ordered that this occurs, individuals participate in modes of self-determination where their concomitant actions codetermine both the form and content of their wills (see chapter 9). For instance, in property relations, persons determine themselves in the artificial capacity of property owner through interrelated acts whereby they establish entitled possession for themselves by embodying their wills in some domain limited in recognition of the similarly established ownership of others. Although persons must make choices in disposing over property, they achieve genuine self-determination by thereby determining the nonnatural conventional agency they exercise as property owner.

Similarly, political self-determination would require an institutional framework where the role of citizen consists of codetermining the political order of self-government without which individuals could not exercise their agency as free citizens. Since justice consists in the reality of freedom, political justice would therefore require democracy to the extent that realizing the constitution can only be an exercise of freedom when all citizens participate in codetermining the legislation, authorization, and execution of the law that governs their own activity as members of the state. Insofar as constitutionality entails division of powers, the required democracy could not consist in direct participation of every citizen in all three branches of government. Rather, it would involve some arrangement where the legislature, head of state, and perhaps some element of the executive are democratically determined, albeit in such a way that the compositions of the legislative, authorizing, and executive wills are distinct from one another. Under these conditions, democracy could enjoy the status of being an end in itself, for it would comprise the political self-determination that is the ultimate raison d'être of the just state.

Naturally, these brief guidelines for the justification of democracy specify precious little of the actual structure of self-government. Whether democracy should involve participatory assemblies, proportional representation, federal organization, or other arrangements are questions left open by the identity of justice and freedom and the need for constitutionality and division of powers. Nevertheless, only the general validation of democracy allows these questions to be meaningfully raised as matters of paramount importance for citizens the world over. The strategy provided here for justifying democracy should suggest that the pursuit of these questions need not be in vain.

II
The Logic of the State

HOW SHOULD THE STATE BE CONCEIVED?

How should the state be conceived? Is it to be thought of as a natural thing? Or is the state something artificial, conceivable as an artifact produced by some exercise of technique? Or, is the state intelligible as neither a natural nor an artificial entity, but rather in terms of spirit, like the mind? The answer to these questions determines not only what we take the state to be, but what kind of normativity it can be ascribed, as well as what kind of science political theory can comprise.

Michael B. Foster, perhaps the most important British political philosopher of the twentieth century, has raised these questions with unique clarity in contrasting ancient and modern political philosophy as exemplified by Plato's *Republic* and Hegel's *Philosophy of Right*.*
Finally rejecting the political theories of both Plato and Hegel, Foster offers a radical idea of political sovereignty calling into question much of the tradition of political philosophy. Although his alternative proposal is ultimately flawed, Foster's reasoning paves the way for resolving the problems he uncovers. To arrive at this end, let us follow out the implications of Foster's argument for the conception of the state.

CONCEIVING THE STATE AS A POLIS

In conceiving the state, it is natural to characterize it in contrast to other forms of association, such as the family and market, which can

---

*Michael B. Foster, *The Political Philosophies of Plato and Hegel* (Oxford: Oxford University Press, 1968). Page references to this book will be given in parentheses throughout this chapter.

both precede its formation and stand distinguished from it once it emerges. Of course, once this route is taken, all depends on how the state is distinguished from these other forms of community.

Plato provides one basic option by defining the specifically political association of the polis in contrast to the economic community of the so-called City of Pigs introduced by Socrates in Book II of the *Republic*. The form uniting the City of Pigs is a division of labor and harmony of trades by which its participants satisfy their natural needs by exchanging the products of their complementary craft activities. This form of community is natural in two senses (15). To begin with, it issues conjointly from the natural needs of human agents, which are best satisfied through mutual cooperation, and from the natural distribution of talents, which assigns each individual a place within the division of labor to best satisfy the wants of the community. Second, the form of the whole is not the product of any conscious purpose, since each participant merely aims at producing the particular product of his or her trade, with no one aiming at producing the division of labor and system of exchange itself. Instead, the order of the City of Pigs is realized as a blind function of the natural necessities that set each individual in pursuit of a particular yet interdependent craft. Although all craft workers may consciously impose an antecedently conceived, particular form upon the material they work upon, a form that gives their product its own identity, none of their craft activities consciously imposes the encompassing common form of the division of labor upon the material that receives it—namely, themselves in their totality.

Lacking this reflexive activity, the economic community of the City of Pigs holds itself together like a natural organism, maintaining itself through complementary functions, none of whose operations depends upon knowledge of the form of the whole. Unlike the parts of a mechanism, whose identities are defined independently of their combination, the different trades of the City of Pigs function like bodily organs, defined in relation to the whole division of labor that includes them. They can realize their own perfection and sustain their particular craft activity and the lives of their practitioners only in conjunction with the exercise of the other trades. Hence, the interest of each is bound up with the interest of the entire community, just as the health of bodily organs depends upon the healthy operation of one another. When any trade begins to emancipate itself from its subordination to the organic interdependency of the whole, producing without regard for the need and products of other sectors, it undermines both the perfection of the whole and its own perfection, just as a diseased organ strikes at the health of the entire body upon which its own health depends (189–90).

Admittedly, the unity of markets is not, strictly speaking, natural in both these respects. Although the system of exchange and division of labor defining a market economy involve an interdependency that is not produced as the conscious end of any of the economic activities it contains, markets need not be based upon the satisfaction of natural needs through a division of labor organized in terms of the natural talents of its members. Instead, markets may address the satisfaction of artificial luxury needs, exceeding all natural requirements, and permit individuals to pursue crafts that need not correspond to their given aptitudes. Plato points to this possibility in describing the transformation of the City of Pigs into a fevered city, where the economic community breaks free of the limits of natural need and engenders a market in which want knows no bounds and wealth is pursued without limit. However, the introduction of the artificial element of conventional, luxury needs and the occupations directed to their satisfaction does not itself introject a political element. Rather, Plato introduces the idea of political association by adding to the economic order a ruling activity of guardianship designed to restore the health of the City of Pigs by controlling the fever of artificial needs and satisfactions, whose frenzied pursuit of limitless wealth creates imbalances and conflicts undermining the community from within and without.

Significantly, this new political occupation is conceived as a craft activity aiming at consciously reimposing the original division of labor and system of exchange that arose in serving the natural needs to which its pursuits were limited. In this respect, the community that now contains the political element of guardian rule still involves the natural unity of the division of labor defining the City of Pigs. However, because this unity is now realized by virtue of being known and willed by the ruling guardians, the community has acquired an entirely different character. Instead of remaining a natural organism, whose unity is neither an artifact nor a structure of mind, the political community now exists by containing an activity consciously aiming at realizing the form of the whole. Whereas the members of the City of Pigs were united merely in accord with a given form, the members of the political community are united by a knowledge and purposive willing of this form (63).

We can thus follow Foster in acknowledging that Plato has discovered an essential feature of politics; that the unity of the state is not something natural in character. If the unity of a natural thing indeed depends upon the presence of form, whereas the unity of products of art depend upon their form being known and purposively imposed upon a given matter (16), Plato would seem to have further established that rule is a craft and that the political community is an artifact. As such, the problem of realizing the ideal polis is no different than bringing into being any other product of art. The form of the ideal polis exists as a timeless object of thought, prior to any possible embodiment. To bring it to tangible realization, its maker, the ruler, must simply obtain knowledge of its form and then instantiate it in light of this knowledge. Yet can the state be coherently understood as a product of political craft, as Plato maintains? The state may not be natural, but is it merely artificial?

Plato's reliance on a craft model in understanding the state rests on several points that might not appear to be definitive of political association. To begin with, he conceives political unity to have a natural form, given antecedently to the ruling activity that imposes it. This allows the ruling activity to operate by realizing an antecedently apprehended form, like any craft activity. Further, insofar as Plato premises the rule of guardians upon a political class division, he construes political activity as a preeminently nonreflexive relation between ruler and ruled, where the ruler imposes the form of the state upon the antecedently given, politically passive material of the subject class. In this respect, ruling again follows the model of craft, where the technical act imposes its preconceived form upon a given material distinct form both the activity and the craftworker who performs it. In fact, one could say that the nonreflexive form of craft elicits the equally nonreflexive craft of rule. What calls for the external supervision of the guardians is that the craftsworkers impose form upon a material other than themselves and therefore cannot restore the harmony of their division of labor once market fever disrupts it (22).

This relation between the nonreflexivity of the subject and ruling crafts does set the ruling activity apart form all other arts. Whereas every craft within the economic community has for its end some specific product—which, as a particular, can be an object of desire—

the end of the ruler's activity, the form of the polis, can only be an object of reason. Because it comprises the form ordering all particular desires and the activities satisfying them, it is not the object of any want but rather the precondition for the satisfaction of each and every one. Representing the universal system of desires and satisfactions, the form at which rule aims transcends the particulars of desire by being the universal grounding them, and thus it is solely an end for reason (17).

This singular mark of the art of rule, however, does not free it of the cardinal features of craft activity, of being purposive and informative in character, for rule here remains determined by an antecedent form that is both the end of the rulers' activity and the essence of its product (180). As a purposive activity, rule is governed by reason's prior prescription of the form to be realized. As an informative activity, rule is confined to realizing this intelligible form in an independently given matter, which, being sensible and particular, is opaque to rational conception and hence cannot be created by technical art (180). Since the form imposed by rule is not the product but the antecedent guide of the activity it informs, this form can be distinguished as essence from the historical accidents encumbering each individual state, just as the essence of any artifact can be discerned from the accidental particulars that differentiate one artifact from others produced according to the same plan. By conceiving the state as the product of political craft, it therefore becomes possible to differentiate formal, essential, universal, and intelligible aspects from material, accidental, particular, sensible features that are irrelevant for comprehending the nature of the state. Hence, to the extent that the state is an artifact, it can properly be the object of an a priori political theory such as Plato undertakes (183).

These ramifications of extending technique to politics might seem illicitly founded upon the aforementioned assumptions that the form of the state is natural and that there is a distinction between ruler and ruled. The former assumption seems refuted by the conventional character of states, reflected in their historical rise and fall and diversity of regime, whereas the later seems refuted by the possibility of democracy, where ruler and ruled are one and the same. Yet these objections can be met, at least in a preliminary way. The conventional character of states need not dispel the inescapable fact that every ruler rules within and, to some extent, in accord with a preexisting constitution, be it written or unwritten. In this respect, ruling always operates in regard to an antecedently given form, determining the ends and procedures by which its role is defined. Similarly, whether the political regime is democratic or not, the state always governs in a nonreflexive fashion over society and household, just as it always involves some distinction between officeholders and nonofficeholders, even in the most participatory of democracies.

THE SELF-TRANSCENDENCE OF POLITICAL CRAFT

Nevertheless, even if these ripostes hold sway, the activity of rule possesses a basic feature that not only sets it apart from every other craft but finally transcends the whole framework on which technique rests. As Foster points out, rulers do not simply engage in the nonreflexive activity of imposing form upon a material other than themselves. Although in relation to the subject class they govern, the rulers impose an order to which they are not subject, the natural order of the division of labor, the rulers equally preside over a political community whose form includes not only craftworkers, but auxiliaries and rulers as well (22).

In response to this feature, Plato first suggests that the form uniting rulers and subjects within the polis is imposed by Socrates and his interlocutors, the founders in speech of the city. Their verbal foundation still seems to fall within the model of craft, both because these interlocutors know and impose the constitution of the polis upon a city to which they do not belong and because their founding activity allows the rulers to practice their nonreflexive administration of subjects within a framework their ruling activity can presuppose rather than establish. Yet, as Plato admits, so long as interlocutors rather than rulers construct the constitution of the polis, it remains but an ideal, a city in speech still awaiting realization. The political unity ordering rulers and subjects alike can only be realized if, as Plato finally proposes, rulers ascend to the knowledge of the founders in speech and, as philosopher-rulers, impose the form of the polis upon all, themselves included (24).

Once this occurs and rulers attain knowledge of the form of which they themselves are a part of the matter and engage in imposing that form upon themselves, ruling transcends the character of art, just as political unity transcends the character of an artifact. Instead of comprising an art imposing a given form upon a given matter, rule here acts upon itself, producing not an artifact but an entity containing within itself a purposive self-informing activity responsible for determining and sustaining the unity of the whole. For Foster, this transformation signifies that the rulers cease to be a ruling class and become a sovereign body, exercising a power of constitution-making ingredient in, rather than presupposed by, their governance. In this capacity, they no longer ply statescraft within the given confines of a polis but now govern within a state, which is distinguished from both natural object and artifact by containing the activity of a sovereign will (26).

Yet cannot what here defines the state be reincorporated within the paradigm of technique along the lines of Aristotle's example of a doctor who cures himself? An artifact may not contain the art that produces it in the way that the state contains its own artificers (31), but does not a self-curing physician combine art and artifact in a single being? Such a doctor seems to duplicate the reflexivity of rule by being both the practitioner of medicine, imposing the form of good health, and the patient receiving the imposed form. There is, however, a fundamental difference. What the doctor imposes upon him- or herself is a regained natural form of health, given independently of medical practice (30), whose own essence is dictated by the nature of human health, prior to any healing act. In the state containing a sovereign will, there is no reimposition of a given natural form. If, as Foster suggests, the rule of the sovereign will incorporates constitution-making within itself, there can be no order antecedent to the self-founding activity distinguishing the state.

THE NATURE OF SOVEREIGNTY

Yet if the state is neither a natural thing nor an artifact and its sovereign will is not an activity of craft, how are the body politic and rule to be categorized?

Foster provides four interrelated suggestions: 1) The sovereign will is *causa sui;* 2) the state is individual in essence; 3) the unity of the state consists in ideality rather than organic unity; and 4) the virtue of the state lies in freedom rather than the justice of natural form. By virtue of these features, Foster maintains, the state falls outside the realms of nature and artifice and hence cannot be the object of a science of natural law or causal determination (26). Instead, the state falls within the realm of spirit and must be subject to the type of study appropriate to that historical sphere. To comprehend what this implies for the nature of the state and political philosophy, these four categorizations must be examined in turn.

To begin with, the sovereign will is *causa sui*—that is, self-cause—to the degree that the state enjoys its constitutive sovereignty by containing within itself the power to mandate its own constitution (26). Unlike the form of natural things and artifacts, the essence of sovereignty is not an idea to which particular realization is an accident, adding nothing to its nature. Because the sovereign state contains and exercises the power to determine and realize itself, the particular realization it gives itself is indissolubly part of its essence. In this respect, the state is like God in the ontological argument and well deserving the sort of divine attributes the body politic has attracted since Hobbes spoke of that mortal divinity (26).

Granted that the state is self-cause, it follows that its essence must be individual rather than universal. With the particular realization of the state part of its essence, the body politic cannot be like a natural object or artifact, whose essence can be conceived as a form shared by all members of its kind. If the state were universal in essence, its particular existence, in which all features unique to it reside, would be extraneous to its nature. However, if the self-active aspect of sovereignty makes it part of the essence of the state to be realized, then that essence must include the individual, in terms of which realization occurs (26).

This individuality of the body politic has important ramifications for how the sovereign will operates. If we follow Foster in understanding the reflexivity of rule to mean that the sovereign will not only commands the law but constitutes the state (188), then the sovereign will departs from the rationally guided activity of craft to exhibit two features of a creative will. First, in willing the law and constitution of the state within which it rules, the sovereign will is not directed upon a given end, since what it wills is a political order first determined in being realized. Hence, the sovereign will cannot be subordinate to a prior prescription of ends by reason (188). Second, in realizing the state to which it belongs, the sovereign will creates a body politic that has neither a natural existence independent of this its enactment nor an ideal nature that had awaited embodiment.

According to Foster, this creative, rather than merely informative, character of the sovereign will entails that the state does not have an organic unity such as Hegel ascribes to it (188). In what Foster regards as the Hegelian view, the state is sovereign by possessing an organic unity that makes the state internally one by realizing the supremacy of the state over any power within it and externally a unit by providing for the independence of the state from any power without it (188). What is specifically organic about such a unity is that the different elements within the state are all relative to the whole to which they belong, realizing their own perfection only in contributing to the perfection of the whole and thereby to the well-being of its other components. In political terms, this signifies that both the branches of government and the institutions of society are organs of state, subservient to the sovereign authority wielded through the whole.

The problem, however, is that by having an organic unity, the state cannot contain a single element exercising absolute power over the rest. For, if internal sovereignty consists in the subordination of each element to the whole, no single power in the state can be the source of its sovereignty. Just as the health of an organism is not a function of one organ but destroyed by disease when one organ subordinates the rest to itself, an organically united state loses its defining sovereignty if one of its components manages to dominate the others (189). Yet if the organically united state cannot contain a sovereign element within itself, how can it retain any sovereignty? Does it not sacrifice the self-informing element of rule, which, by virtue of its conscious determination of the whole to which it belongs, distinguishes the state as something more than either a natural organism or an artificial thing?

Hegel, Foster observes, seeks to overcome this dilemma by making the head of state the ultimate instrument, if not the source, of the realization of sovereignty. However, because Hegel's head of state is a constitutional monarch who can do no more than dot the "i" of the measures presented to him, assenting to a determination of political will he can neither initiate nor alter, Hegel's head of state does not provide a power to create law and constitution, the power by which sovereignty is defined (191). Nor does Hegel's introduction of a parliament fill the gap. For instead of conceiving parliament as an organ for the creation of law, Hegel restricts it to an instrument of enlightenment, whose legislative act provides only an elaboration of a rationally predetermined constitution that itself mandates the workings of parliament (193). The limits of organic unity provide little alternative. For so long as the state remains an organic unity, it cannot enjoy real sovereignty, if, as Foster maintains, the state is only sovereign by containing a will creating the political order (188).

Granted that organic unity cannot be ingredient in the sovereign state, how else can the body politic be characterized, beyond being self-cause and individual? As Foster maintains, freedom is the remaining key, providing the state with its generic excellence and unifying principle.

FREEDOM AND SOVEREIGNTY

With the state distinguished by containing a sovereign will, rendering the body politic self-cause and individual, the virtue of the state cannot reside in the embodiment of natural form defining Platonic justice (44). The reflexivity of rule instead makes the actualization of freedom central to the state's perfection and calls for a radical transformation if the body politic is to become in accord with its concept. Freedom commands this centrality in several respects.

First, the self-activity of sovereignty renders a division of political classes antithetical to the concept of the state. Given the reflexivity of rule, the need for a subject class as the recipient of the activity of a ruling class is eliminated. With rulers imposing order upon themselves and their own activity, there is no reason why all cannot engage in the same self-rule (44). The body politic is accordingly no longer characterizable as a community containing a particular class imposing form upon the whole. The structure of sovereignty renders any distinction between rulers and subjects a vestigial relic of a community that has failed to realize the full import of political association. Only by eliminating all residue of a subject class does the body politic become in accord with its concept. In so doing, it transforms itself from a polis into a state, which by containing a sovereign will, equally becomes an association able *as a whole* to impose form upon itself (47). This makes the state a free community, providing its members with the specifically political autonomy of being subject to an order that they have all imposed upon themselves.

This establishment of political autonomy entails a redefinition of the subject. To begin with, the subject is no longer a recipient of form, defined as subject opposed to predicate, where the subject's essence is to be that given substrate in which predicates inhere. Instead, the subject now figures as subject of a self-informing activity, distinguishing the subject from objects that are mere recipients of form (50).

In addition, the political subject is now essentially endowed with a distinct faculty of will and not just reason or desire. This follows from the positive character now essential to law in the state. Because the sovereign will creates its law rather than embodying rules antecedently prescribed by reason, state law cannot be determined apart from its particular enactment. Hence, the essence of law here lies in its positive, imperative character, making it more than an intelligible proposition, whose worth lies in its conformity to reason. Since law commands what should be, whereas theoretical cognition and desire address what is, law is directed to neither but to the will of the legal subject. As subject to the law of the sovereign will, the citizen thereby faces imperatives whose significance lies beyond what is given to reason or desire, imperatives that can only be authored and answered through an exercise of will (134).

In both respects, as creator of law and as subject to the law, the citizen is the agent of an activity of freedom. As the creator of law, the citizen participates in such organs of politics as the institutions of free speech, universal suffrage, parties, and parliament (187). These are not organs of government in the sense of instruments by which rulers impose order upon their subjects. Rather, they are means by which the sovereign will exercises power over the organs of government, whose administration is here subsidiary not to the eternal prescriptions of reason but to the reflexive self-ruling activity of politics (188).

Admittedly, the state does retain art in the functions of government. To the extent that government acts in pursuit of given ends directed by knowledge and has as the given matter of its administration non-officeholding citizens who are governed but do not govern, the organs of government possess the purposive and informative character corresponding to the craft conception of rule (187). Accordingly, government is subject to a division of labor, rendering it an organically united system of specialized administrative functions (163). Hence, the Platonic appeal to political art is appropriate in this domain but fails as a general political conception by conflating the body politic with government administration. This conflation is fundamentally mistaken because government administration is not identical to the ruling activity of the state but rather is subordinate to the sovereign will that gives government its ends and authority. Consequently, even though every state involves the submission of governed citizen to government administrator, this submission is only relative, since it actually is predicated upon the subordination of government administration to the authority of the governed's own political will (187).

By providing citizens the opportunity not just to enter service in government administration but to participate in creating the laws under which they are governed, the organs of politics thus provide a freedom very different form that enjoyed in a polis. Although, following Foster's analysis, the citizens of a polis are politically free in the sense of sharing an equal right to rule, they do not possess any right to make the law that they are required to administer in their possible role as ruler. For, with rule structured as if it were a craft, imposing a preconceived form upon a given matter, law can no more be created by the ruler than the laws of medicine can be made up by the physician (220). When, however, citizens can participate in the organs of politics of a state, they win the right of commanding the laws that government must enforce, an opportunity proper not to the rule of a polis but to the sovereign of a state (200).

Hence, in being administered by government, citizens are subjected to an order that they have codetermined in their capacity as participants in politics. Yet even this does not exhaust how freedom comprises their life in the political realm. Indeed, simply in obeying the law, citizens must exercise an autonomy transcending the limits of political art. For, as Foster observes, the universality of legal command requires that citizens use their own discretion in determining how they can realize the law in their particular situation. In this sense, obeying law is not equivalent to having form imposed upon one. Just as the unity of the state is only realized by containing an agency both knowing and willing its order, so obedience to law requires not just conformity of action to a given rule but activity determined by knowledge of the law as well as by an act of will making its own purely positive contribution.

Significantly, this specifically political autonomy of creating and realizing self-imposed law is not a condition for preserving the economic order of society; nor is it necessitated by any principle that social order is essential to the well-being of individuals (35). As Foster points out, all these prepolitical relationships can be maintained without political sovereignty, which is why foreign conquest can leave them all undisturbed. This expendability of political freedom as a means to nonpolitical ends reflects the purely self-contained validity sovereignty brings to the state. By being *causa sui* and individual, the free community of the state must be the source of its own legitimacy, for not only is it not the necessary condition of other forms of association, but it does not realize independently given values.

In what way can the state provide for its own legitimacy? Is it found, as Foster's argument seems to suggest, in the state's realization of its own perfection, something it can only do by eliminating all difference between ruler and ruled and freeing itself of submission to all given laws?

If the perfection in question were common to each and every state, this would seem to imply that the state has a given essence, allowing an evaluation of each particular state in terms of how well it has lived up to its universal potential. Yet any such standard would seem to violate the individual, self-caused character of the state. If the state is to be understood and critiqued, its constitutive individuality must be confronted.

A REVOLUTION IN POLITICAL THEORY?

Does confronting this individuality require what Foster prescribes—namely, a revolution in political theory involving the same conceptual transformation undergone by biology in adopting the theory of Darwinian evolution and by aesthetics in accepting Romanticism's recognition of the creativity of artistic genius and the individuality of the work of fine art?

In the case of biology, as long as living things were conceived to have their identity in a timeless, specific essence, they could be the objects of a nonhistorical science that relied on a conceptual ordering of species and genera, heuristically revealed, but not juridically grounded in empirical observation (175). Any natural history would then be confined to recording the inessential features clothing the particular realizations of the essences of living things, features adding nothing to an understanding of their natures and accessible only by observation (175). However, once natural species are discovered to be products of a temporal development, with identities that are anything but immutable, biology becomes subject to the historical understanding that had previously been restricted to its inessential aspects. With the Darwinian revolution, living things became comprehensible only in terms of a nonteleological evolution of species, where the temporal succession of species is not a progressive realization of antecedently given ends revealed to reason but rather an establishment of types whose character can be found nowhere else but in observation of their individual existence. Although the evolution of the species may be thought of as presenting a progress, it does not distinguish between higher and lower species in terms of any ideal distinct from both. Rather, the only ranking evolution provides is one of increasing complexity, where the advanced species enjoy their higher rank by incorporating the structures of the lower ones. Excluding all reference to antecedent essences and determining the nature of living things by their individual existence, Darwinian science could be said to take seriously the notion that living things are creatures rather than artifacts or natural embodiments of given form (175).

The modern Romantic conception of art similarly overthrows the classical view, which conceived technique as the whole rather than a subordinate element of art and thereby construed the artwork as an artifact whose excellence lay in its mimesis of an antecedently given form. Accordingly, the classical conception left all the creative features of art, such as the uniqueness of the artwork and the artist's failure to conceive it beforehand, to chance or miracle (183). By contrast, the Romantic conception recognized the work of fine art to be a product of imaginative creation, governed by no preconceived end and exhibiting an individuality allowing of no distinction between an essential idea and the accidents of its embodiment (185). Although artistic creation, like every human activity, does not achieve pure creation but requires materials and some technique, its greatness is not a matter of technical skill but one of imaginative creativity for which technique is only a vehicle (186). Hence, a critic who judges an artwork by some standard conceived apart from the individual work misunderstands its character, ignoring that because the artwork is fundamentally a created object, its essence is not discernible from its existence (185)—which is to say that its "meaning" cannot be conceived apart from its sensuous apprehension (202). This, however, does not eliminate all art criticism; rather, it mandates that the work of art can only be criticized in reference to itself (187). By the same token, although art history cannot be conceived teleologically, in reference to a distinct end to which works of art progress, it can be viewed as a development. As in the natural evolution of the species, art eras can be understood as developing out of one another without progressively embodying some goal determined apart from them all (203).

What would it mean for political theory to undergo a similar transformation in light of the individual, self-active character of the state?

To begin with, any Platonic theory conceiving the essence of the state apart from the historical accidents of its particular embodiments would have to be ruled out (169). Instead, the state would have to be treated as the object of historical understanding.

This need not involve a debasement of political theory, if the limitation to historical understanding involves no abandonment of a higher cognition. Whereas a historical understanding had to be confined to the accidents of the state when the essence of politics was considered rationally derivable, once the assumption of a universal essence of the state is discarded, and with it the possibility of a speculative political science, a historical understanding obtains license not only to address all features of politics but to be the only appropriate cognition for obtaining knowledge of the state (173).

This applies equally to the normative dimension of politics. So long as the right of the state was derived from some timeless standard, like natural law, the historical understanding of politics had to be confined to the sources of the state's power, rather than its right. Once, however, sovereignty is acknowledged as the source of its own norms and legitimacy, the "natural law" giving it its right becomes a product of historical development, allowing historical understanding to address the source of the state's authority as well as the source of its power (187). For Foster, this means that the stages of a speculative deduction of the concept of the state, such as that found in Hegel's *Philosophy of Right*, need not be rejected out of hand. Although all pretence to their logical necessity must be discarded, the stages can be retained provided they are understood as the historical realities they and any other political "essentials" by nature are. Accordingly, abstract right should be comprehended as nothing more than Roman law, morality as Lutheran pietism (174), civil society as modern capitalist society, and the state as a modern republic.

This does not render politics unintelligible, let alone beyond all critique. To the extent that the state represents a work of creation (201) rather than an artifact, it can be understood as being part of a political history comprising a development—like that linking artistic periods—which nevertheless has no teleological character (203). This allows for a twofold critical treatment. A state can be understood by its historical context, judging the necessity of its features in terms of the temporal interests of its period (171). On the other hand, a state can be evaluated in the way in which a work of fine art is susceptible of criticism: not in reference to any standard definable apart from the work but in view of the work's own internal requirements, as understood by a historical appreciation of its individual existence and the historical character of the norms it imposes upon itself (187).

Such an outcome seems inescapable in those aspects of political reality, such as its positive law, where there is no possibility of any conceptual derivation. Such measures can only be accepted on the basis of a historical rather than a philosophical explanation, one that perceives the exigencies of the particular state here and now, as addressed in anticipation by lawmakers and in retrospect by political historians (171). However, can the same be true of all dimensions of politics and all political theory, including the very discourse about the state that Foster has conducted? There may well be no return to a Platonic political theory of conceiving the state in terms of embodied form, but does that mean that reason must abandon politics to historical understanding?

CONSTITUTIONALITY AND SOVEREIGNTY

Whether political philosophy must undergo the revolution Foster champions depends on the answer to two questions: 1) Is reason, as Foster maintains, incapable of conceiving the individuality and associated self-activity by which the state is defined? 2) Is the sovereignty differentiating the state from natural things and artifacts to be conceived in terms of the creative willing to which Foster appeals?

A definitive answer to the first question lies well beyond the scope of this discussion. Yet it bears asking how Foster could present his own arguments on the nature of the state if reason were powerless to conceive individuality and its adjunct features. For what else is Foster doing but conceiving the idea of the state when he characterizes it as *causa sui*, individual, and a structure of spirit? Although he may consider the body politic he conceives to be something historically realized only in modern times, that does not alter the fact that his analysis has consisted not in historical description but in a thinking about the nature of political rule and the unity of the state.

THE LOGIC OF THE STATE

That Foster reaches his conclusions on purely conceptual grounds suggests of itself that perhaps his whole analysis of sovereignty has gone astray. What decides the matter is the relation of constitutionality to the self-realizing activity of rule. Can rule incorporate the activity of political foundation that determines the constitution? And can the state contain an element within itself that stands above all constraint as a sovereign will? Unless an affirmative answer can be given to each of these questions, the abandonment of political theory to historical understanding loses its reason for being.

In regard to the first issue, Foster is well aware that the activity of political rule can be distinguished from the activity by which a state is founded and given its constitution. After all, the constituting will exercised by the founders of a state does not act upon itself or belong to what it founds. Instead, it produces a state resulting from the expenditure of its founding act. However, Foster maintains that the political will sustaining the founded state is as creative as the will that determined the constitution under which the sovereign will rules. Just as Descartes maintains in the Third Meditation that all created things require for their preservation the continued exercise of the same power by which they were created, so Foster maintains that the sovereign will animating the body politic engages in the same activity of creation that was exercised in the state's original foundation (192). In other words, the sovereign will relates to the will of the state's founders as divine providence relates to divine creation of nature (193). However, the sovereign will does so not merely by creating the state anew but by being included in the state that it creates and preserves. Accordingly, to still employ the idea of a creative will, Foster must admit that the state is, properly speaking, *self-created* by the sovereign will (193).

Retention of an identification of the sovereign will with a creative will might seem warranted provided the sovereign will is not absolutely bound by the constitution that defines its working but has the power to amend it. In that case, the sovereign will could appear to be subject to a constitutional framework that it creates and imposes upon itself. Yet even in this case, the analogy is problematic. Although a creative will is not a demiurge, imposing given form upon given matter, it still does not exhibit the reflexivity generic to political rule. A creator wills into being something other than itself. Hence, a creator is not self-determined by an act of will. Rather, a creator figures as an antecedent determiner of a creation that is no more self-determined either, since it owes its character to the prior act of the creator bringing it into existence. Although these features indeed make it possible to describe the founding will of the state as a creative will, they preclude any identification of rule and creation. For in contrast to any creative will, the sovereign will is already situated within the body politic whose rule it determines, whether or not it enjoys the power of constitutional amendment. Even when it engages in statutory amendment procedures and imposes upon its future actions an altered constitutional framework, the sovereign will remains subject to a given constitution its current actions always presuppose and never fully create. In making amendments, the sovereign will must observe the antecedently determined amendment procedures as well as the other constitutional provisions determining its ruling agency. On the other hand, after making new constitutional statutes, the sovereign will rules once more within an antecedently given framework defining the supremacy of its role and all its prerogatives. At either stage, the sovereign will diverges from a creative will by ordering the political whole to which it belongs and doing so within a framework it neither antedates nor brings into being.

Although this means that, contrary to Foster's argument, the state is not characterized by containing within itself its founding will and the power to lay down its own constitution, this does not mean that the state is indistinguishable from a polis, embodying given form in a way making possible a Platonic political theory. The ruling activity may always be subject to a given constitution framing its role, but rule is still a reflexive activity that imposes political order upon itself with an irreducible positive element of its own.

To understand this, the relation between the reality of the state and its constitution must be comprehended. The constitution may be enacted by an act preceding the actual existence of the state, but the realization of the constitution as more than a piece of paper or moribund custom depends upon the engagement of political activity residing in the legislative, authorizing, and executive functions that themselves depend on the activities of nonofficeholders and officeholders alike. Hence, although all of these political activities presuppose the constitutional order within which they proceed, that order has no existence apart from their engagement.

Moreover, these political activities realize the constitution they presuppose only by stepping beyond its universal statutes and making positive laws, particular authorizing judgments about the constitutionality of such legislation, and particular decisions on how to enforce these laws. All these measures, called for themselves by the constitution, require reactions to the given state of the nation that cannot be derived from the reason embodied in constitutional statute but require independent acts of will. Consequently, the realization of the constitution presupposed by political activity is coeval and codetermined by acts of will that cannot be understood in terms of any embodiment of predetermined form. The constitution indeed figures as what the state is implicitly or in itself, but the constitution's own reality as the defining framework of an actual state depends upon a political activity knowing and willing the constitution, positing it as what it is in itself by virtue of a self-referential activity by which citizens impose their political association upon themselves. For this reason, the constitution does not function as the given form of an artifact or natural object or as a foundation robbing political activity of its constitutive freedom. That freedom remains the defining feature of political unity, albeit stripped of the trappings of the creative will with which Foster has clothed it.

Freedom, understood as self-determination rather than the positing of a given determiner, retains its constitutive role, on the one hand, insofar as constitutionality in no way eliminates the vestigiality of a distinction between ruler and ruled. Because the positive acts of will by which the constitution is realized are activities that determine the political order to which political agents are always already subject, rule is fundamentally self-rule. The requirements of a division of powers and the technical side of executive functions may entail a distinction between the agents of government and those who are governed. Yet this distinction retains the relative character Foster appropriately notes, due to the subordination of government to the will of the sovereign, which is none other than the political agency that imposes the realized constitution upon itself.

On the other hand, the rulers who impose constitutional order upon themselves do so in an irreducibly positive manner, whereby the political context their rule presupposes is equally coeval with their political activity. Consequently their self-government is an exercise of political freedom, whereby the very agency of every citizen is actually determined through the activities sustaining the context by which their political roles are defined. In this way, the state consists in a self-activity involving political self-determination, whereby citizens determine their own political role precisely by willing the constitution within which they operate. If, instead, they exercised a creative will, their agency would cease to be self-determined, for the creation of their act would be determined by an act lying prior to it and their creative agency would be the given condition rather than the self-determined product of their activity.

This is why the state, as a structure of political freedom, cannot contain within it a will sovereign in the sense of being free from all constraint and literally possessing the power to lay down the constitution. If any will or wills within the state enjoyed this context-free liberty, the body politic would no longer be committed to realizing existing institutions of political freedom. If only some citizens possessed this license, the sovereign will would subject others to an order that is not self-imposed. On the other hand, if such a sovereign will were wielded by the will of all, its creative character would mean that citizens never interact within existing institutions of political freedom but always exercise an antecedently determined agency, willing what is not yet at hand. This may absolutize the power of choice, setting it free of all institutional limits, but it deprives everyone of the self-activity in which self-determination resides.

The sovereign will must rather be a constitutional will, which signifies that it consists in the codetermination by all citizens of the body politic within which their self-government can alone proceed. Then, the constitution does not figure as a given foundation, in opposition to the legitimacy of self-determination. Because the reality of the constitution is coeval with the self-government of citizens, their willing of the institutions of political freedom within which their political activity must always be situated is nothing but an exercise of self-determination, determining the reality of the framework that grounds their own political agency.

Consequently, the individuality of the state is not at odds with its having a universal structure that can be conceived apart from the particular acts of will by which it is realized. Its political campaigns, positive laws, and executive measures may be accessible only to a historical cognition and the sort of criticism to which works of fine art are subject. Yet its constitution can still have a universal character transparent to conceptual thought. As Foster's own argument exemplifies, this universal character is not something that excludes the structure of self-cause, of that whose existence is its essence, of that which is unconditioned, self-determined, and individual. Far from being opaque to thought, such a structure may well be what is most akin to the workings of autonomous reason. When Aristotle conceived the absolute as self-thinking thought rather than as a creator defined by a purely positive act of will, he already suggested how the reflexive activity of self-cause had a form that was individual yet not foreign to reason. By the same token, what Foster sees as Hegel's fault neglecting the conceptual ramifications of the doctrine of creation in deference to those of the doctrine of trinity may be a mark of strength. If one conceives individuality in terms of creation—that is, in terms of what is determined by a given determiner, or what Hegel would call a "Logic of Essence"—it ought to come as no surprise that a theory accepting this image should treat what is individual as conceptually unintelligible. If, by contrast, individuality is conceived in terms of self-determination, as Hegel attempts in his Logic of the Concept, it may well be made intelligible in ways not so foreign to much of Foster's own account. In that case, political theory can rise above the hermeneutics of art criticism and secure a nonhistorical understanding of the just state.

12
The Theory and Practice of the History of Freedom: On the Right of History in Hegel's Philosophy of Right

THE IMPLAUSIBILITY OF A PHILOSOPHY OF HISTORY

Hegel's philosophy of history has long been dismissed as a genial retelling of the recorded past that must be condemned for imposing an *a priori* conception of historical development upon the intractable givenness of historical fact. Although subsequent thinkers have offered their own schemes of history, Hegel's theory has won notorious fame as the most paradoxical of all. According to common view, Hegel not only constructs history from concepts in unparalleled detail but conceives past history as a history of freedom while subjecting the course of events to a preconceived necessity lying outside the conscious determination of the agents of history.

If the latter suggests a suspect contradiction in the particular content of Hegel's conception, his general project of a philosophy of history has been perceived to be fatally flawed in light of the corollary ontological and epistemological grounds that seemingly exclude any *a priori* theory of history whatsoever.

To the degree that history is made by individuals with wills allowing for a novelty unbeholden to the cycles of natural necessity, the aggregate result of what they all choose to do over time would appear to entail an arbitrariness as devoid of necessary universal order as it is opaque to conceptual thought. If indeed history results from the combined actions of individuals who enact and tear down institutions according to how they choose to relate to one another, then what is historical involves utterly conventional activities that individuals pursue in their plurality rather than natural functions whose unwilled alterations, such as aging, may have a universal order but no historical character. Accordingly, not only can no individual action in history be preordained, but no historical "meaning" can be deduced from it, since its historical significance will depend upon how all others decide to act in conjunction with it. Because their concomitant actions proceed on the same terms, historical reality seems to present a continuum of an endemically all-sided arbitrariness. This situation of overdetermined willfulness would appear to leave historical action in an insoluble ethical predicament. Whereas each individual has an ethical responsibility before history, by having the possibility of precipitating historical change through acts influencing what others do, the historical effect of each deed is ultimately determined by the actions others choose. If this leaves assignment of responsibility problematic, it also means that any pattern to the succession of events and enacted institutions is simply a matter of circumstance that can only be perceived after the fact. No matter what conditions prevail, the very structure of historical action seemingly precludes there being any final guarantee that individuals will not act so as to overthrow existing regimes, enact novel formations, reestablish previous forms, or perpetuate the status quo.

Even the very continuation of history would appear to be subject to chance. For if history can only be made by a plurality of willing individuals and if the natural preconditions of their existence can be eliminated either as a result of their own chosen actions or of natural events, then the continuity of history is itself a matter of contingency. That the sun will burn out, that galaxies may collide, and that we possess the ability to bring about nuclear or ecological holocaust would seem to indicate that history has not only no necessary past but no necessary future at all.

If this arbitrariness infesting the structural reality of history precludes any sure conformity between what happens in history and *a priori* schemes of historical development, the way in which historical reality is given to our knowing seems to preclude any philosophical knowledge of it as well.

Since the facts of history lie at hand in the form of observable ruins, received documents, and the testimony of the dead and the living, knowledge of what has happened is caught in all the dilemmas of an interpretive knowing that has no criteria for judging the truth of its object other than ones it stipulates for itself. As in a court of law, where, as Hegel himself points out, the facts of the case can only be known beyond a reasonable doubt,[1] so in face of the givenness of history, all certainty of historical knowledge has nothing more to rest upon than faith in the honesty and accuracy of available testimony, faith in the prudence of interpretations of given records, and faith in the representative character of the chosen data to which historical understanding applies itself. Because all these operations of subjective judgment first render recorded history an object of investigation, no theory concerning historical fact could provide universal truths; it could provide only subjective constructs, concluded from subjective assumptions determining what is putatively given.

Thus, the philosophy of history undertaken by Hegel would appear to be ruled out as much by the conditions for knowing history as by the character of historical reality itself.

There is, however, a central feature of Hegel's discussion of history that raises questions as to whether the above objections to an a priori theory of historical fact have any application to the philosophy of history Hegel has pursued. This feature is the striking circumstance that Hegel treats history as a theme of the philosophy of right, conceiving it as the third and final section of the determination of the state, which brings his development of right to a close. What this placement suggests is that Hegel somehow sees fit to include history as a topic of the theory of justice so as to develop a conception of history that is not an *a priori* scheme of what has occurred or will occur but part of a normative theory of what ought to occur.

At first sight, this novel inclusion of history within the theory of justice appears particularly strange, since Hegel equally maintains that the relations of right must be determined in their concept and cannot derive their content from what happens to be given in history. As he points out time and again, the mere historical existence of institutions testifies only to their being and not to their legitimacy (*PR,* par. 2 and note to par. 3). How then can history, so burdened with facticity, have any place in the normative theory of what right ought to be?

Although few discussions of Hegel's philosophy of history have asked this question, only when it is answered can the genuine significance of Hegel's theory of history be appreciated. By addressing how and why history enters as a legitimate theme of the philosophy of right, one sees not only that a conceptual theory of history is possible but what its subject matter must be.

JUSTICE AND THE PROBLEM OF FOUNDATIONS

Paradoxically, what compels Hegel to secure a place for history within the orbit of right is the unprecedented radicalism with which he bars historical givenness from playing any role in determining the content of justice.

Unlike so many of his followers, Hegel realizes that no historical age can directly serve as a criterion for judging relations of right. All those, for instance, who immediately take modernity as a standard and speak synonymously of what is "progressive" and "just," fail to recognize that modern reality has no normativity on the basis of its contemporaneity but only insofar as its institutional order is intrinsically just. Since modern relations are not given facts of nature, governed by laws independent of our wills, but historically enacted structures open to question and change, if they do not accord with concepts of right, a revolution may be called for not in the science of justice but in existing institutions.

What makes Hegel's rejection of all historical justification so radical is that it is tied to the recognition that no given content of any sort can mandate what ought to be either in theory or in practice. Although theorists of justice have traditionally alternated between grounding justice in nature and convention, Hegel considers both options equally untenable on just this point.

Because justice involves what may legitimately occur through the voluntary actions of individuals, it cannot consist in what happens according to nature independently of their wills. Although natural relations provide necessary preconditions for individuals to exist and be able to engage in willing, the very fact that natural relations are given, rather than willed into being, means that they cannot prescribe what is just but can only comprise a normatively neutral domain presupposed by all action, whether right or wrong.

Although justice is thus not given by nature independently of willing, it cannot be determined by given convention as a set of operative rules of behavior. Convention can no more be a source of normativity, Hegel realizes, because compliance with given rules only means that behavior is rule-governed and not that it has legitimacy deserving respect. Admittedly, since justice is not a relation of nature but something willed into being, it does exist only by convention. Nevertheless, for relations among individuals to have the normativity distinguishing them from ordered behavior, they must neither be relative to nor legitimated by the particular conditions of their enactment. This must be so because what is just ought to hold regardless of any particular circumstances that do not already involve relations of justice commanding the same respect. If relations of justice were relative to some factor that was not just itself, they would be conditioned by something unjust and immediately forfeit their normative character as what ought to be.

For this reason, justice has an unconditioned universality indissolubly linked to an independence from givenness, be it natural or conventional. What is just is universally valid in that it is justified under any circumstances that do not themselves comprise relations of justice. Only when the particular features of a given state of affairs already enjoy the normativity of justice are they worthy of entering into determining what practice ought to be followed. Consequently, the universality of justice is unconditioned insofar as relations of justice can only be legitimately limited by what falls within justice itself.

This means that no factor given independently of just willing can mandate the content of justice. To have normativity, justice simply cannot have its measure or ground in something other than itself. Justice must rather be its own ground and somehow legitimate itself without reference to any outside standard.

Although this insight is already implicit in Plato's and Aristotle's notion that justice exists for its own sake and no other, Hegel brings it to its full consequences.

To begin with, he recognizes that for justice to be its own ground, it must have no foundations. The basic problem with both natural right and conventionalist theories of justice is precisely that they give justice foundations, either by grounding it in natural law, deriving it from some procedure of construction (as in the case of Rawls), or by appealing to convention. In so doing, they commit the fallacy of determining justice by something other than itself, thereby making it relative to something outside of justice and canceling its putative legitimacy.

Hegel, on the contrary, is aware that the problem of foundationalism must be overcome, and overcome not only with regard to justice but with regard to truth itself. In both theory and practice, justification can be secured only when all unlegitimated givens are deprived of any determining role. In Hegel's view, the problem with metaphysical and transcendental philosophies is that they develop their conceptions with unargued assumptions concerning reality and the conditions of knowing, just as natural right and conventionalist theories of justice determine it on the basis of given factors and principles whose own justice lies out of account. As Hegel argues in the *Science of Logic*,[2] if philosophy is to concern itself with truth instead of opinion, it cannot take up its subject matter and method as givens determined outside and prior to its own inquiry. If they are to be justified and not arbitrarily assumed, then they must be accounted for within philosophy. In other words, philosophy, like justice, cannot have any foundations.

What provides the needed elimination of foundations in theory and practice is not the alternative offered by theoretical and practical holism. Although the holist position aptly recognizes the parallel problems of foundationalism in questions of truth and justice, all it offers in answer is a reduction of theoretical and practical normativity to matters of pragmatic agreement within an ongoing open-ended conversation of humanity.[3] That, however, only reinstates the foundational dilemma by rooting theory and practice in the pragmatic structure of discourse of whose irreducibility holists are inexplicably certain. In conceiving the latter as the ultimate basis of all justification, theoretical or practical, holists not only metaphysically assume that their notion is an accurate account of the reality of conversation but make it a transcendental ground determining the formation of all normative claims.

Hegel, on the contrary, recognizes that foundationalism can be overcome not by reverting to a sceptical conventionalism but by taking seriously the problem of freeing theory and practice from givenness.

In the case of theory, Hegel reasons that philosophy can escape the foundational dilemma of unjustified assumptions only by being totally self-grounding. To have this radical independence from all that has not already been philosophically established, philosophy must proceed from no determinate ground whatsoever. This can be achieved, Hegel realizes, only if philosophy begins from indeterminacy, an indeterminacy signifying the absence of all presuppositions concerning both reality and knowing as well as the content and method of philosophy. From that starting point, philosophy can succeed in grounding itself so long as it is systematic, developing both its entire content and method solely by virtue of what gets determined within its own development. Instead of moving from one topic to another by virtue of arbitrary reflections upon what is taken to be given, philosophical discourse must be self-determining, for only by unfolding with total immanence can it avoid relying upon extraphilosophical assumptions to generate its subject matter and the order of its consideration. Since the immanent development of systematic philosophy proceeds from indeterminacy, its initial self-determination will not be that of some given content but self-determination per se, which is what Hegel calls the "Idea."

In the case of practice, however, a specific content is already at hand; namely the relations of willing individuals to one another. Although the theory of justice addresses the specific dimension of their normativity, which cannot be derived from any prior conditions, justice nevertheless has as its necessary material condition the existence of nature and willing selves. In Hegel's *Philosophy of Nature* and *Philosophy of Spirit*, which follow successively upon his development of the Idea, he claims to have accounted for these nondetermining preconditions of justice without violating systematic immanence. Now, addressing justice itself, Hegel recognizes that the problem consists in how the relations among individuals, involving all that nature and selfhood imply, can achieve the added self-grounded character giving them the unconditioned universality justice requires.

Not surprisingly, the answer that allows justice to be distinguished from mere convention is similar to that which allows truth to be distinguished from opinion. Because justice, like philosophy, can have no foundations but must be its own ground, the relations of justice must be determined entirely through their own process. Since they cannot be prescribed by any independently given factor, the relations of justice must be wholly self-determined. This means that the one and only substance of justice is relations of freedom among willing individuals. Freedom can alone provide normativity in practice, because what is self-determined has unconditioned universality precisely by being determined through itself rather than through any given particular condition.

Accordingly, Hegel concludes that the theory of justice is the philosophy of right. It is philosophy both because, in their systematic immanence, philosophical concepts exhibit the same self-determined character as justice and because the independence of justice from given circumstance leaves it beyond the grasp of the positive sciences, which investigate only what is given to them. On the other hand, the theory of justice is the philosophy of right, and not the philosophy of goodness and prescribed virtues, to the degree that rights consist in the objectively respected exercise of freedom. Since freedom is the substance of justice, the philosophy of right has as its subject matter nothing but the self-determined reality of the freedom of individuals, which Hegel appropriately calls the Idea of the free will, insofar as the Idea is self-determination per se.

Consequently, if history is to have any legitimate place in the philosophy of right, it must be by virtue of the character of freedom in which justice consists.

HISTORY AS A MATTER OF FREEDOM

In the first instance, what ties history to right is the nonfoundational character freedom must have to be the substance of justice. Because justice is its own ground, freedom cannot be conceived as a principle out of which the relations of justice are derived. If this is done, freedom gets reduced to a determiner of something other than itself, the derivative relations of justice, whereas these equally lose all self-determined character by being determined by a principle of freedom prior to and separate from them. Thus, not only do the derivative structures of justice fail to exhibit the self-determination that would grant them legitimacy, but the principle of freedom lacks a genuinely self-determined character of its own.

Because freedom is here construed as a prior principle determining something other than itself, it stands as a given structure whose act of determination adds nothing new to its character. Since the particular content that gets willed thus falls outside the principle of freedom, that freedom is merely a given universal capacity to choose among independently given alternatives. As such, the freedom in question is a natural capacity of liberty—natural in that its own exercise of willing determines neither its own given form nor the particular contents from which it is at liberty to choose. Consequently, freedom, taken as the principle of justice, has no normativity of its own, for its very liberty is conditioned both by whatever given array of alternatives lie before it and by the givenness of its own capacity to choose.

Hegel is well aware that the freedom of justice cannot be reduced to a prior principle of liberty and that the attempts of classical liberal theory to construct justice on such a basis are fatally flawed from the start. He realizes that so long as the structure of free willing be located in a natural capacity with which all people are born or in a faculty of a noumenal self, freedom and justice will stand apart and forfeit their common normativity.

Hegel accordingly concludes that normative freedom cannot be a natural or egological given but must rather consist in the enacted relations of justice themselves. In contrast to liberty, the freedom of justice must be at one with the self-determined relations among individuals comprising the structures of right. Although Hegel does not deny that individuals are endowed with choosing wills irrespective of their relations to one another, he recognizes that actual self-determination can only be achieved in interactions among individuals where what they will has its particular content not through factors given independently of their freedom but by virtue of what they will towards one another.

In effect, just as the normativity of justice requires that freedom be its substance, so self-determination requires that freedom be identical to right. If the will is to escape the heteronomy of liberty and have a particular end specific to freedom, it must individuate itself through its own act, exhibiting a content exclusively its own as well as a form common to the will in general. Hegel recognizes that the only way the will can accomplish this is by entering into a contrastive relation to other wills, wherein each is able to individuate itself as a particular instance of a commonly realized structure of willing. In order for this to occur, the relation among wills cannot be a given condition imposed upon their willing, for then, the particular content of each will would not be self-determined but determined through a contrastive relation that none has willed into being. Consequently, free wills must will their relation to one another as part of their own self-determination and do so such that the relations they enter into with others are voluntarily willed by the latter as well. This means that self-determination irreducibly involves an interaction among individuals, where each wills its own particular end and relation to others by simultaneously honoring the self-determinations these others will as part of the same relationship. As a result, freedom is itself a structure of right, comprising complementary self-determinations linked through a mutual respect securing each objective reality.

That freedom, the substance of justice, so consists in enacted interactions among individuals directly sets right in relation to history. If, as Hegel has argued, freedom is not given by nature or by virtue of the self but arises only when individuals choose to interrelate in a certain way, then the domain in which right comes into being is none other than history. Although this does not make historical occurrence a criterion of justice, it does mean that history cannot be a matter of indifference for the theory of justice. The very nonfoundational character of justice leaves it to history alone to realize what ought to be. No natural law or propensity of the self can bring justice into being so long as freedom is itself an enacted structure of interaction. Consequently, the philosophy of right must certify that freedom can emerge in history if its own conceptions of right are not to be ideals incapable of coming into being.

Accomplishing this has nothing to do with the impossible task of conceiving in an *a priori* fashion what has happened or will happen in history. Rather, what lies at stake is conceiving what historical change must occur for justice to come into being. Since justice is the reality of freedom, that question is one of conceiving how freedom can arise within history. It is for this reason that the philosophy of history Hegel develops within the philosophy of right essentially is and must be a history of freedom. Strictly speaking, the problem of this history is a purely normative matter whose resolution is completely independent of past and future events. Indeed, the question of freedom's emergence is not even limited to the particular destiny of homo sapiens but concerns a universal development of what ought to be that is applicable to any setting where there are individuals with wills. Although Hegel himself does not properly emphasize this point, his whole discussion of spirit, which includes justice, has little about it that is species specific. He well recognizes that any attempt to determine thinking and willing through the natural particularities of species being would involve violating their universal nonnatural character. It may be true that the self is necessarily embodied in an animal organism, but that does not mean that the only such organism that can possibly possess a mind and will is a featherless biped. Conversely, simply being a homo sapien does not mean that one has a will and mind with which to enter into relations of right, as is evident in the cases of the comatose, the severely retarded, and the insane.

Accordingly, the problem of history that legitimately enters into the philosophy of right is a question not of how people have erected or can erect structures of freedom but of how any thinking and willing selves can do so. Although this problem can readily be seen to emerge from the philosophical consideration of justice, what is less apparent is that anything philosophical can be said about its resolution. For if the conventional character of history leaves the actual course of events a matter of willful contingency, how could the historical emergence of freedom ever have any universal form?

There are two factors that caution against such scepticism and suggest that Hegel's attempt to conceive the coming into being of freedom is not a hopeless task.

First, no past, present, or future events can mandate by themselves what must occur for justice to come into being. Their very own facticity precludes their playing any necessary or prescriptive role. Consequently, the task of establishing how freedom can emerge in history involves no immersion in the historical facticity that lies outside conceptual determination.

Second, the two termini circumscribing the problem of freedom's emergence are conceptually available, granted the possibility of a systematic philosophy of nature and spirit. On the one hand, the philosophical conceptions of nature and individual selves, such as Hegel offers in his philosophy of nature and subjective spirit, comprehend the material with which historical development proceeds. As such, the conceptions of nature and individual selves provide the philosophically transparent starting point from which the coming into being of freedom must be conceived. On the other hand, the endpoint of the development at issue is given by the conception of justice itself. The structures of freedom conceived within the philosophy of right are precisely the terminus whose emergence from the givenness of nature and individual selves comprises the whole history of justice's coming into being. What the normative history of freedom addresses is nothing other than how these relations of right can arise from those preconditions of history. For this reason, Hegel can only take up the question of the history of freedom at the end of the philosophy of right after having worked out all the relations of right in which freedom consists.

Thus, when the problem of the history of freedom arises, both the starting point and conclusion of that history are already conceptually at hand in the systematic determinations of nature and self and of right, respectively. What remains to be determined is how, through convention, the latter can come to be from the former.

Admittedly, the starting point at hand—namely, the reality of nature and the plurality of selves—offers no more to guide the emergence of justice than the ever present possibility that individuals, endowed with choosing wills, may at some point simply choose to interact in ways that conform to all the relations of right and do so in a natural setting where geographical, temporal, and other natural differences will add their own particular cast to that conformity.

If there is to be any more definite development to the history of freedom, it must therefore be due to the structure of its endpoint: the reality of justice. The content of the relations of right must mandate in a conceptually determinate way how they themselves can come into being if Hegel's enterprise is to be taken seriously. Otherwise, the philosophy of history will be left with nothing more to do than repeat the truism that freedom can arise whenever individuals choose to act in accord with justice.

THE POLITICAL CHARACTER OF THE HISTORY OF FREEDOM

Hegel is well aware that what alone can concretize the history of freedom is the concreteness of justice. Justice, on its part, must be concrete, for only be being a totality unto itself can justice have the ungrounded character required for normativity.

Unlike modern thinkers such as Hannah Arendt and Jürgen Habermas, Hegel realizes that the interaction of freedom cannot be construed as a noninstitutional ideal of unrestrained reciprocal recognition that serves as the legitimating principle for all organs of public life. Doing so only reinstates the foundational dilemmas of liberal theory, once again separating freedom from the reality of justice and supplanting self-determination with the positing of a prior principle.

To have normativity, the structures of freedom must instead comprise every relation of justice. This means that freedom must not have its measure in a single regulative interrelationship but rather consist in a self-grounded system of specific interactions. Although Hegel grants that freedom can be spoken of in general, he recognizes that to do so legitimately requires a categorical development of self-determination per se that properly falls within systematic logic rather than the philosophy of right. In contrast, the Idea of the free will involves no general determination of freedom but rather a sequential development of the different spheres of right. According to Hegel, the structures that so build freedom's total reality are the distinct interactions of property relations, morality, the family, civil society, and the state. If this be accepted, then the coming into being of freedom entails the very determinate matter of generating all these different structures together in the particular relationship that allows them to be a self-grounded totality.

As a consequence, the relationship among the different spheres of right is of primary importance in understanding the manner in which they may arise. In Hegel's conception, this relationship has a dual character common to the elements of any self-determined whole.

One the one hand, the different spheres of right stand in an order of increasing complexity, in which the less determinate relations form the structural prerequisites incorporated by those that are more determinate. This ordering follows that of the conceptual development of right, which proceeds from abstract right to morality, the family, civil society, and the state, precisely because no relation can be systematically considered if its presupposed component elements have not already been accounted for.

In this ordering, abstract right comes first insofar as it is the most elementary structure of freedom, incorporating no others in its own relationship while being presupposed by all the rest. By themselves, property relations simply involve individuals laying their wills in different particular entities that they mutually recognize as the entitled domains of their respective persons. Moral, family, social, and political relations may give the disposal over property added dimensions relative to their own contexts, but they do not themselves constitute the property relations among persons. Rather, all these other structures of right presuppose the existence of property, for if individuals do not already have recognized ownership of at least their own bodily facticity, without which they are slaves, there is no way their activity can recognizably express their own will to others and allow them to engage in any further exercise of right.

Although this leaves moral relations subsequent to property relations to the degree that no individuals can be held responsible for their actions if they do not belong to them, morality falls second in line since acting on conscience means acting independently of what family, social, political, or any other objective relations may mandate.

Family relations, by contrast, come third, for they involve adult individuals who already enjoy personhood and moral subjectivity but do not interact within the family through social or political institutions. Individuals may legally marry and divorce and otherwise employ civil law to regulate their family affairs, but this does not determine the being of the family, but only gives it a publicly protected form of legality.

Civil society follows upon the family in that it incorporates the plurality of households within the domain of its economic, legal, and other social activities. It precedes the state, however, because none of its affairs contain the self-governing activity of politics, whose constitutive sovereignty requires that it come last as the sphere of right, presupposing all others by ruling over them.

What makes this ordering relevant to the history of freedom is that it reveals how each sphere of right can exist independently of those that incorporate it, but only if those it encompasses exist as well. For instance, property relations can arise historically without being accompanied by moral relations, households based on freedom, a civil society, or a self-governing state, whereas civil society cannot come into existence until individuals have won their rights as persons, moral subjects, and free family members.

In view of these separate requirements, it is possible to distinguish hypothetical stages in the emergence of freedom consisting in periods when the spheres of right that have so far been enacted are 1) property relations alone, 2) property and morality, 3) property, morality, and the free family, 4) property, morality, the free family, and civil society, and finally 5) the free state that incorporates all the other spheres of right within itself. In those periods when certain spheres of right are lacking, the alternative institutions would be determined by factors other than freedom and could conceivably take any of the countless forms that such illegitimate natural determination might take.

If this provides an *a priori* morphology of the possible way stations in the history of freedom, it also indicates that the emergence of justice is preeminently a political history. Contrary to the Marxist vision of the just society that terminates a socially determined history, it is here the coming to be of the just state that alone brings into being the totality of freedom.

The self-governing state can play this role not only because it incorporates all other structures of right within its dominion but because through its autonomous rule, it makes their realization a product not of historical accident but of an activity of freedom falling within justice itself. By securing the property, moral, family, and civil rights of its citizens in conformity with the exercise of their political freedom, the free state thus makes right fully self-grounded by providing a sphere of politics whose freedom posits all the other structures of freedom in reproducing its own.

Due to this totalizing character of the just state, the coming to be of freedom not only has a free political order as its ultimate result but equally encompasses the possible stages of political development that allow all the necessary structures of self-government to arise. The history of freedom accordingly entails a political morphology differentiating forms of government according to how fully they realize the political institutions of freedom.

The resulting typology has a very different status than that in traditional theories of justice. In general, prior to Hegel, forms of government were discussed as a proper theme of political theory rather than as a matter of history.[4] Hegel, by contrast, recognizes that because the just state must be unconditionally universal, it can comprise but one invariable form of government. As Hegel notes, its separate powers may exhibit monarchical, oligarchical, and democratic features, but as a whole, the just state has but one form, that of freedom (see *PR*, note to par. 273). Accordingly, the normative theory of politics gives an account of the just state as such and not of different forms of government. The normative history of freedom, however, requires their treatment, and it is precisely in that context that Hegel takes them up, recasting the classic forms of government—namely, tyranny, oligarchy, democracy, and monarchy—as possible stages in the development of political freedom.[5]

Although it may be granted that these different forms of government can be conceptually characterized with respect to their varying realization of the institutions of political freedom, this characterization in no way mandates that they must appear in a fixed sequence or that the just state requires any of them in particular as a real precondition for its emergence. All these forms provide is the range of naturally determined body politics that may precede the rise, or, for that matter, follow the fall, of the just state. In particular, their catalog leaves undetermined through what act, if any, the just state can be founded.

This problem of foundation is obviously of key importance in the coming to be of freedom, for it comprises the development that brings this becoming to a close.

What does shed light on this question is the totalizing character of the just state. It entails a second ordering of the structures of right that is virtually the inverse of the first order of ascending complexity that led from abstract right to politics. This further ordering occurs in terms of the actuality of the state. By virtue of its own activity, the emergent state stands not simply as a result of the less concrete structures of right, which can arise before it and which its own rule presupposes. Rather, through its own resultant sovereignty, the state exists as their one and only ground, giving them all a secured realization that none can supply for itself.

In his development of abstract right, morality, and the family, Hegel makes quite clear how they all lack the resources either to determine objectively what each individual is due or to adjudicate disputes, punish wrongdoers, and provide retribution for victims. Without appeal to a higher public authority, persons cannot resolve cases of nonmalicious wrong, fraud, and crime anymore than family members can enforce household obligations and rights to which they are entitled (see *PR*, pars. 82ff., 102, and 176). As for moral subjects, Hegel shows that conscience can never arrive at an objective fulfillment of morality, for all it has to determine the good is its own subjective discretion (*PR*, pars. 137–41).

The case of civil society is ultimately no different. Although the social institutions of civil law and the public administration of welfare do enforce the property, family, and economic rights of individuals, civil society contains neither the legislative power to make the laws carried out within it nor the elements of constitutionality that can give its public institutions the authority they require.

Only a self-governing state can provide these lacking features through freedom, instead of leaving them be supplied by illegitimate factors independent of right. In so doing, the self-governing state frees itself from the presuppositions of the other spheres of right by positing them as elements emanating from its own sovereign rule.

Finally, what seals the independence of the just state is its constitutionality. Such a state rests on nothing but itself insofar as the measure of its own governing activity lies within it in its constitution. Accordingly, the just state grounds not only all other relations of right but itself as well. Through thus dual achievement, logically foreshadowed in the Idea's totality of categories, the sovereign constitutionality of the state realizes freedom as a self-grounded whole, just as normativity requires.

This foundation-free character of just politics adds a final specification to the history of freedom. Because the coming to be of justice ultimately entails founding the free state and because the free state is constitutional, the history of freedom must conclude with the enactment of the just constitution.

THE PERPLEXITIES OF CONSTITUTION-MAKING AND THEIR MEANING FOR THE HISTORY OF FREEDOM

Although Hegel does not dwell upon constitution-making in his thematic discussions of history, he does deal with its problems in his treatment of the state constitution itself. There he raises the principal issues that make constitution-making so central and perplexing a problem for the normative history of freedom.

Paradoxically, the importance of constitution-making in the emergence of justice directly reflects its utter unimportance in legitimating the structures of right. Clearly, the coming to be of the just state is something different from its actuality, and, as Aristotle points out in Book I of the *Politics,* conceiving the former is quite a separate task from determining the latter. In light of Hegel's critique of all normative foundationalism, the separation between the founding and the legitimate actuality of the just state is complete. To have normativity, the state must be self-grounding, and this it achieves when it exists for its own sake as the self-determined totality of right that has its standard of legitimation within itself in its own constitution. Accordingly, what makes the state just cannot be the manner in which it came into existence, but the structure it actually has. Since that actuality must be an end in itself to be just, any attempt to base the state's legitimacy in the procedure of its creation automatically undercuts its normativity by grounding it in something other than its own constitutional politics. For this reason, all procedural theories of justice, be they social contract conceptions or not, are incapable of determining political freedom and must be discarded.

Hegel recognizes that the radical demarcation of the state's legitimation from its coming into being means that the founding of the state is not itself a relation of right but a matter of history, subject to all the contingencies that involves. Furthermore, he realizes, the self-active character of the just state excludes constitution-making from its own domain of political freedom. For politics to have the normativity of action for its own sake, the end that citizens freely will must be nothing other than the realization of self-government—which is the very framework in which they engage in political action in the first place. To exercise political freedom, the citizen must already be situated within the constitutional institutions comprising self-government. What gives them their normative character as organs of self-rule is that the only way citizens can act in their context is by governing themselves and thereby willing that context itself.

The willing into being of the constitution, however, is by its very character an unconstitutional act, exercised by agents who do not will their constituting action as an end in itself but as a means for producing something that does not already exist—namely, a new political order whose own constitutional activity is completely distinct from the constituting activity responsible for its foundation. Therefore, enacting a constitution is not an activity for its own sake, enjoying the special normativity of political action, but one of making, which acts in explicit indifference to its own given context in order to will another as the authentic framework of justice.

In this regard, any government that gives one, some, or all citizens the power to determine the constitution destroys the justice of the state. It introduces into the political domain a willing that does not act for its own sake, realizing the constitutional order in which political freedom consists, but instead exercises an unrestrained arbitrariness that makes government whatever it pleases. If one takes seriously Hegel's foundation-free concept of politics, one is forced to conclude that there can be no power of constitutional amendment in the just state. This must be excluded not only because it would leave the structure of the state subject to the arbitrariness of choice but because the just constitution is, as such, unconditionally universal and hence valid under all circumstances. Only an unjust constitution deserves to be amended, and the only legitimate object of its amendment can be the enactment of the just constitution, which needs no alteration.

For these reasons, what falls within the prerogative of self-government is the legislation, authorization, and execution of positive laws that do not alter the constitution but realize it in face of those conditions relevant to justice that are inherently changeable, such as foreign affairs, the state of the economy, and so on.[6] Citizens are legitimately free to determine all matters of positive law, but that freedom exists only through the just constitution, which is itself no matter of choice. Political legislation has the task of making inherently alterable, rescindable laws, which, as such, deal with what is open to change itself. Here, as Hegel points out (see *PR,* par. 301), personal opinion, rather than reason, comes legitimately into play. The changeable conditions that require legislation can be perceived only in given experience, whereas the framing of laws in response to the perceived situation must rely on the discretion of subjective judgment to determine laws that apply the conceptually determinate constitution to the particular circumstances at hand. The just state thus has a history of its own consisting not in the enactment or alteration of its constitution but in the positive legislation and governing that proceed on its basis. By contrast, the power legislating constitutions falls outside the just state. As Hegel remarks in his lectures on the *Philosophy of Right*,[7] that power is history itself—the history of freedom's emergence that precedes the history of the just state's own positive legislation.

Although this conclusion follows readily enough from the very character of constitutional government, the relegation of constitution-making to history seems to call into question the constitutive autonomy of the just state and with it, the history of freedom consisting in its emergence. The very fact that political freedom does not include the right to determine the constitution would appear to contradict the self-determined character the state must have to be normatively valid. For if political action cannot determine the constitutional order of the state but must receive it from history, then it would seem that the political order is not self-ordering but preordained by the prior historical action that brings the constitution into being. How, then, can the state retain normativity when, instead of being self-determined, it appears to be naturally determined in the sense that its own form is given independently of political freedom?

The whole project of justice here seems to collapse in an insurmountable antinomy. If justice is to come into being and the philosophy of right is to be more than speculative fiction, then there must be a history of freedom culminating in the enactment of the just constitution. Yet, if the state can issue only from a preceding process of constitution-making, it would appear that the state can never have the self-determined character required for normativity. In other words, the very way the just state must arise makes it impossible for the state to be just.

There is but one solution to this dilemma, a solution already at hand in Hegel's concept of the free state. In a word, the state can be both self-determined and the product of a historical constitution-making if its constitutional order is one that comprises a regime of self-government whereby citizens freely will the realization of those same institutions in which they must already stand in order to exercise the right of political self-determination. Even though their activity is here restricted to enacting, authorizing, and executing positive laws, it realizes the constitution as a state existing for no other sake than its own self-government. Therefore, political freedom has itself as its end here, as the continual product of its own activity, if only by coinciding with and conforming to a constitution it can never bring into being but must always already possess.

On these terms, the historically enacted constitution is itself but a meaningless piece of paper unless citizens actually engage in the practice of constitutional self-government, which alone allows politics to be a self-activity consisting in the exercise of political freedom. Instead of ruling out one another, the foundation of the just state and the normative actuality of the state are inseparable correlates. The just constitution has not come into actual being unless it stands realized in a political order of freedom, whereas the state cannot have the legitimate constitutionality it needs to be self-grounded, unless history has provided it with its constitution. The character of each is such that it is simply impossible for there to be one without the other. Thus, the just state is and can only be both self-determined and dependent upon history for the enactment of its constitution.

This unavoidable solution to the ostensible antinomy of constitution-making thereby redeems the history of freedom, but at the same time, it introduces a further feature that, at first sight, is utterly perplexing. Hegel stresses it time and time again in claiming that, properly speaking, the constitution of the just state cannot be made at all (see *PR*, note to par. 273 and note and addition to par. 274). This seems to be a contradiction in terms, since the constitution is not a natural given but a product of convention that must be enacted to come into being. Hegel is well aware that the constitution, as the objectively recognized conceptual specification of the state, can be enacted only by being willed into being. He nevertheless argues against thinking of the constitution as the product of making because he realizes that it cannot come into existence simply by virtue of the willing of a single agency.

Although a Napoleon or a Stalin may unilaterally impose his constitutions for a republic or a people's democracy, no such imposition can make a constitution the internal standard of a just state on the force of its own command alone.

On the one hand, a constitution can have no reality as that of a just state if the nonpolitical structures of right—namely, the valid relations of property, morality, the family, and civil society—are not in place themselves and the process of their formation is something quite separate from the ordaining of a constitution that preeminently determines the political order.

On the other hand, no unilaterally willed constitution can have a just reality if the prospective citizens of the state do not engage in constitutional self-government but instead treat the constitution as a piece of paper signifying either the decree of illegitimate domination or the unobserved fiction of a powerless regime. Only the multilateral actions of citizens can comprise the self-ordered state and guarantee that the just constitution is that in actuality.

For these reasons, Hegel can rightly say that the founding of a just constitution is the product of the development of the entire life of a citizenry, involving the eventual multilateral enactment of all spheres of right (*PR*, note to par. 273 and par. 274). Although at some point a constitution will have to be made, this act will found the just state only in conjunction with the political recognition of citizens and their establishment of free personal, moral, household, and civil relations among themselves. Then, the enactment of the constitution will indeed usher in the culminating stage of the history of freedom, for it will have proceeded upon the liberation of all spheres of right from natural determination and their reconstitution as structures of freedom. By combining these two sides of liberation and constitution, the founding of the state will comprise the genuine revolution—not the revolution that rises out of social necessity to impose a new class rule in preparation for the withering away of the state but the revolution that strips away all grounded, conditioned modes of interaction and then constitutes the positive reality of freedom in its political totality. The normative history of freedom has this as its end, for the emergence of justice involves nothing else.

SYSTEMATIC VERSUS INTERPRETATIVE HISTORY

Certainly, Hegel's discussion of history does not limit itself to the systematic problems of freedom's coming into being. In the *Philosophy of Right* and especially in the *Lectures on the Philosophy of History* he turns to the recorded facticity of human history and considers its significance in regard to the history of freedom. Often it seems as if Hegel has conflated the two and deduced particular events from the requirements of what must occur if justice is to come into being. If this were what Hegel was doing, his discussion of various peoples and epochs would fall victim to the problem of metaphysical construction.

There is, however, a dimension to Hegel's treatment of recorded history that escapes this confusion. Although the *a priori* theory of history that falls within the philosophy of right is a normative conception having no direct relation to the course of human events, it can serve as a framework for interpreting that course to the degree that human history has given rise to the universal structures of right.

There may be no necessity that the development of humanity ever bring justice into being, but if modernity, for instance, happens to have realized important features of property relations, morality, the free family, civil society, and constitutional self-government, then the *a priori* concepts of the history of freedom can have a descriptive power in the interpretation of past events. Nevertheless, such an interpretive discussion is not an exercise of systematic philosophy but only an exercise of interpretation, bound to all the limits of any hermeneutic situation. It involves an application of rational categories to a perceived facticity that must rely on subjective judgment to make connections as much as in the making of positive law. If one recognizes this decisive limitation and distinguishes the interpretation of recorded history from the conception of the history of freedom, both can make their respective contributions without conflicting with one another.

In view of this, it is important to note that Hegel begins his *Lectures on the Philosophy of History* with the declaration that they follow from the *postulate* that there is reason in history.[8] If this is to be understood in a nonmetaphysical way, it signifies that Hegel intends to engage in an *interpretation* of past history, proceeding from his own subjective estimation that Western history has been a history of freedom's emergence and can therefore fruitfully be discussed by applying the systematic concept of the history of freedom to the perceived facticity of recorded events. Accordingly, the resulting discussion does not properly fall within the philosophy of right as a systematic theory of how justice can come into being. Rather, it falls outside philosophy entirely as an interpretive application of philosophical concepts to facts that must be experienced and related to be known.

For just this reason, one can argue endlessly over Hegel's interpretation of the past without ever reaching unequivocal answers. Where subjective judgment must be employed to reach conclusions, the unconditioned normativity of conceptual thought can never be attained. Nevertheless, Hegel's interpretations cannot be ignored in deference to his systematic arguments, for we as citizens must similarly orient ourselves to the facticity of modernity and judge to what extent its history has been a history of freedom and what remains to be done. As thinkers, it is our task to conceive the structures of right in the self-grounding discourse of philosophy. As citizens, it is our responsibility to erect and safeguard a self-grounded state of freedom. Because the reality of justice can always be overturned if enough individuals choose to do so, the history of freedom is always an open one in practice. It may be theoretically conceivable once and for all, but its realization in practice is an ever present political task.

Although the history of freedom falls within time, it holds valid for all eternity. Therefore, no matter where we stand in the order of events, we have the opportunity to redeem the transience of our practice by enacting the timeless conventions of justice. Only then will we have made history in which there is reason.

Notes

1. ROUTE TO FOUNDATION-FREE SYSTEMATIC PHILOSOPHY

1. See Willard Van Orman Quine, "Two Dogmas of Empiricism," in *From A Logical Point of View* (New York: Harper and Row, 1963); and T. S. Kuhn, *Structure of Scientific Revolutions* (Chicago: University of Chicago Press, 1970).

2. The varieties of transcendental philosophy that have dominated the twentieth century have shown through their own example that these assumptions apply not merely to the Kantian formulation of noumenal subjectivity but equally to any transcendental condition, no matter what content it may have. In this regard, the problems of Husserl's egological transcendental theory are no different than those of the ordinary language theory of the late Wittgenstein, the hermeneutic transcendentalism of Gadamer, or the ideal language theory of the early Wittgenstein, Habermas, and Apel, and French structuralism.

3. G. W. F. Hegel, *Phenomenology of Spirit*, A. V. Miller, trans. (New York: Oxford University Press, 1977), pp. 46–47. Subsequent page references to this work will be given in the text, with the abbreviation *PS*.

4. Husserl falls into this dilemma by claiming presuppositionlessness for intentionality, although he effectively admits that the phenomenological reduction should itself be the object of a transcendental constitution, like any other content. See, for instance, Edmund Husserl, *The Crisis of European Sciences and Transcendental Phenomenology*, David Carr, trans. (Evanston: Northwestern University Press, 1970), pp. 176, 206, 210. Husserl fails to recognize that the apodicity of the constituting ego is undermined by the infinite regress that results from each transcendental act being constituted itself. Precisely because each description of a transcendental constitution requires a constituting act to account for its own execution, no presuppositionless constituting structure can ever be reached.

5. Although Fichte, the young Schelling, and Husserl sought to eliminate the last vestiges of metaphysics by conceiving the transcendental structure as self-constituting, none of them recognized that when the constituting act of the ego is its own constituted object, the intentionality of the ego collapses.

6. See Hans-Georg Gadamer, *Truth and Method*, G. Barden and J. Cumming, trans. and eds. (New York: Seabury Press, 1975); and Richard Rorty, *Philosophy and the Mirror of Nature* (Princeton: Princeton University Press, 1980).

7. Among the few works in Hegel literature that take up the problem of the relation between the *Phenomenology of Spirit* and systematic philosophy are Kenley R. Dove, "Hegel's 'Deduction of the Concept of Science,'" *Boston Studies in The Philosophy of Science*, vol. 23 (Dordrecht, Holland: D. Reidel,); and by the same author, "Hegel's Phenomenological Method," *The Review of Metaphysics* (June 1970), vol. 22, no. 4; as well as William Maker, "Hegel's Critique of Absolute Knowing" (Ph.D. dissertation, New School For Social Research, 1978).

8. Among the more notable examples of this misinterpretation are those found in Karl Marx, *1844 Manuscripts*, Martin Milligan, trans. (New York: International Press, 1964); Soren Kierkegaard, *Philosophical Fragments*, David Swenson, trans. (Princeton: Princeton University Press, 1967); Ernst Bloch, *Subjekt-Objekt* (Frankfurt am Main: Suhrkamp, 1972); Georg Lukács, *History and Class Consciousness* Rodney Livingston, trans. (Cambridge: MIT Press, 1971), and *The Young Hegel*, Rodney Livingston, trans. (Cambridge: MIT Press, 1976); and Jurgen Habermas, *Knowledge and Human Interests*, Jeremy J. Shapiro, trans. (Boston: Beacon Press, 1971).

9. G. W. F. Hegel, *Science of Logic*, A. V. Miller, trans. (New York: Humanities Press, 1969), p. 48. Subsequent page references to this work will be given in the text, with the abbreviation *SL*.

2. DIALECTICAL LOGIC AND THE CONCEPTION OF TRUTH

1. See "Two Dogmas of Empiricism" in Willard Van Orman Quine, *From A Logical Point of View* (New York: Harper and Row, 1963).

2. See Aristotle, *Nicomachean Ethics*, Book VI, ch. 6, and *Posterior Analytics*, Book I, ch. 2.

3. So it is that Engels lists as the three most general laws of nature, history, and thought three laws of dialectics: the law of the transformation of quantity into quality and vice versa, the law of the interpenetration of opposites, and the law of the negation of the negation. (See Frederick Engels, *Dialectics of Nature* J. B. S. Haldane, trans. (New York: International Publishers, 1960), p. 26.

4. LOGIC, LANGUAGE, AND AUTONOMY OF REASON

4. See A. J. Ayer's *Logic, Truth, and Language* (Middlesex England: Penguin Books, 1982).
5. Quine, "Two Dogmas of Empiricism."
6. See Plato, *The Republic*, Book VII, 533c–d, and Aristotle, *Nicomachean Ethics* and *Posterior Analytics*.
7. G. W. F. Hegel, *Science of Logic*, A. V. Miller, trans. (New York: Humanities Press, 1969), pp. 82–83.
8. *Ibid.*, p. 838.
9. It is in light of this that Hegel does not deal thematically with reason and philosophy in his *Science of Logic* but rather treats them as topics of *Realphilosophie*, properly conceivable in the *Philosophy of Spirit*, which presupposes both dialectical logic and the *Philosophy of Nature*.

3. CONCEIVING SOMETHING WITHOUT ANY CONCEPTUAL SCHEME

1. Aristotle, *Metaphysics*, Book Gamma, ch. 4, 1006b9–10.
2. *Ibid.*, 1007a13–15.
3. *Ibid.*, 1007a33–35.
4. Immanuel Kant, *The Metaphysical Elements of Justice*, John Ladd, trans. (Indianapolis: Bobbs-Merrill, 1965), p. 18, n. 11.
5. Immanuel Kant, *Critique of Pure Reason*, N. K. Smith, trans. (New York: St. Martin's Press, 1965) A245, p. 263.
6. G. W. F. Hegel, *Science of Logic*, A. V. Miller, trans. (New York: Humanities Press, 1969), p. 82. Subsequent page references to this work will be given in the text, with the abbreviation *SL*.
7. Hegel discusses these objections in remarks 3 and 4 to chapter 1 of the *Science of Logic* (pp. 93–105.)
8. "Nothing" and "nonbeing" do not designate different categories, for negation of being is the same indeterminacy that nothing and being each comprise. Nonetheless, "nonbeing" is useful in analyzing determinate being, since it connotes how in the unity of being and nothing, nothing is immediately different from being.
9. G. W. F. Hegel, *Wissenschaft der Logik: 1. Band, 1. Buch; Erstausgabe von 1812* (Gottingen: Vandenhock and Ruprecht, 1966) p. 49.
10. Immanuel Kant, *Logik*, in *Werke VI* (Frankfurt am Main: Suhrkamp, 1968), A147, pp. 525–26.

4. LOGIC, LANGUAGE, AND THE AUTONOMY OF REASON

1. Aristotle provides one magistral argument after another to show how this is so in Book Gamma of his *Metaphysics*.

2. G. W. F. Hegel, *Logic*, W. Wallace, trans. (Oxford: Oxford University Press, 1978), para. 159.
3. G. W. F. Hegel, *Philosophy of Mind*, W. Wallace and A. V. Miller, trans. (Oxford: Oxford University Press, 1978), para. 440.
4. *Ibid.*, para. 535.
5. G. W. F. Hegel, *Phenomenology of Spirit*, A. V. Miller, trans. (New York: Oxford University Press, 1977), p. 49; G. W. F. Hegel, *Science of Logic*, A. V. Miller, trans. (New York: Allen and Unwin, 1969), pp. 49, 51, 69.
6. Immanuel Kant, *Critique of Pure Reason*, Norman Kemp Smith, trans. (New York: St. Martin's Press, 1965), B256, p. 233.
7. *Ibid.*, B232, p. 218.
8. Hegel, *Philosophy of Mind*, paras. 381, 411–13.
9. *Ibid.*, Zusatz to para. 423, paras. 424–35.
10. See paras. 458–62 in Hegel's *Philosophy of Mind*.

5. THE APOTHEOSIS OF INTERSUBJECTIVITY

1. Alexandre Kojève, *L'Introduction à la Lecture de Hegel* (Paris: Editions Gallimard, 1947).
2. See P. F. Strawson, *Individuals* (London: Methuen, 1959).
3. Immanuel Kant, *Critique of Pure Reason*, Norman Kemp Smith, trans., (New York: St. Martin's Press, 1965), B274–79, pp. 244–47.
4. G. W. F. Hegel, *Philosophy of Mind*, W. Wallace and A. V. Miller, trans., (Oxford: Oxford University Press, 1978), paras. 458–62.
5. *Ibid.*, paras. 424–30.

6. HEGEL VERSUS THE NEW ORTHODOXY

1. Because the new orthodoxy has a unified position that can most fruitfully be discussed in its own right, independent of an analysis of its particular representatives, it is here addressed as an argument, without textual references to the innumerable presentations it has been given. For this reason, all subsequent references to the Hegel interpretation of the new orthodoxy consist in explorations of how the new orthodoxy can and must interpret Hegel to buttress its position. Since it is the logic of this interpretation that counts, citations from representatives of the new orthodoxy are not and need not be provided.
2. Richard Rorty, *Philosophy and the Mirror of Nature* (Princeton: Princeton University Press, 1980).
3. Thomas Nagel, *The View From Nowhere* (Oxford: Oxford University Press, 1985).
4. G. W. F. Hegel, *Phenomenology of Spirit*, A. V. Miller, trans. (New York:

6. HEGEL VERSUS THE NEW ORTHODOXY

Oxford University Press, 1977), p. 49; G. W. F. Hegel, *Science of Logic,* A. V. Miller, trans. (Humanities Press, 1969), pp. 49, 51, 69. Subsequent page references to these works will be given in the text, with the abbreviation *PS* or *SL.*

5. See also Kenley R. Dove, "Hegel's Phenomenological Method," *The Review of Metaphysics* (June 1970), vol. 22, no. 4; William Maker, "Hegel's *Phenomenology* as Introduction to Science," *Clio* (1981) no. 10.

6. Donald Davidson, "On The Very Idea of A Conceptual Scheme," in *Inquiries into Truth and Interpretation* (Oxford: Oxford University Press, 1984), pp. 183–98.

7. G. W. F. Hegel, *Philosophy of Mind,* William Wallace and A. V. Miller, trans. (Oxford: Oxford University Press, 1978), paras. 413–23. Subsequent references to this work will be made in the text, with the abbreviation *PM.*

8. Alasdair MacIntyre, *After Virtue* (South Bend, Ind.: University of Notre Dame Press, 1981).

9. *Ibid.,* p. 245.

7. CAN PHILOSOPHY HAVE A RATIONAL HISTORY?

1. It is along these lines that Arthur C. Danto reduces history to a construct of narrative in his *Analytic Philosophy of History* (Cambridge: Cambridge University Press, 1965).

2. Hegel's famous comments on the relation of philosophy to its age in the preface of the *Philosophy of Right* have provided a touchstone for absolutist historicism.

3. Among the most prominent thinkers who have judged modernity to have a universal, rational character are Hegel, Marx, and Max Weber.

4. Leo Strauss has made an analogous argument in his critique of the various forms of historicism in chapter 1 of *History and Natural Right* (Chicago: University of Chicago Press, 1953).

5. Immanuel Kant, *The Metaphysical Elements of Justice,* John Ladd, trans. (Indianapolis: Bobbs-Merrill, 1965), p. 5.

6. *Ibid.,* p. 6.

7. *Ibid.*

8. THE LIMITS OF MORALITY

1. Michael J. Sandel aptly describes this project as it pertains to justice in *Liberalism and the Limits of Justice* (Cambridge: Cambridge University Press, 1982), pp. 175ff.

2. See Charles Taylor, *Hegel* (Cambridge: Cambridge University Press, 1975), pp. 368–69.

3. *Ibid.,* p. 376.

4. Leading expositions of this view include Alasdair MacIntyre's *After Virtue* (South Bend, Ind.: University of Notre Dame Press, 1981); and Bernard Williams' *Ethics and the Limits of Philosophy* (Cambridge: Harvard University Press, 1985).

5. For an elegant reconstruction of these moves in Hegel's account, see Robert Bruce Berman, *Categorical Justification: Normative Argumentation in Hegel's Practical Philosophy* (Ph.D. dissertation, New School For Social Research, 1983), pp. 155ff.

6. G. W. F. Hegel, *Philosophy of Right*, T. M. Knox, trans. (New York: Oxford University Press, 1967), par. 115. Subsequent references to this work will be made in the text, with the abbreviation *PR*.

7. Robert Berman has raised this suspicion in conversation.

8. G. W. F. Hegel, *Vorlesungen Uber Rechtsphilosophie*, Edition Ilting (Stuttgart-Bad Cannstatt: Frommann-Holzboog, 1974), 4:308. Subsequent references to this work will be made in the text, with the abbreviation *VR*.

9. See Berman, *Categorical Justification*, p. 155, and Kenley R. Dove, "Logik und Recht bei Hegel," *Neue Hefte für Philosophie*, no. 17, 1979. p. 105.

10. See Richard Dien Winfield, *Reason and Justice* (Albany: SUNY Press, 1988), p. 179.

11. G. W. F. Hegel, *Philosophy of Mind*, William Wallace and A. V. Miller, trans. Oxford University Press, 1978), par. 505. Subsequent references to this work will be given in the text, with the abbreviation *PM*.

12. As Hegel says, the content is not yet objectively rational (*VR* 3:377).

13. G. W. F. Hegel, *Werke VII* (Frankfurt am Main: Suhrkamp, 1970), note to paragraph 123, p. 231.

14. Taylor, *Hegel*, p. 376.

15. This analysis is offered in Robert Berman, *Categorical Justification*, pp. 159–60.

16. See *ibid.*, p. 160.

17. Hegel purports to systematically conceive these alternatives by treating in succession hypocrisy, moral probabilism, willing good intentions to justify evil, acting on conviction to sanction evil, and finally, moral irony. To what extent his account succeeds can be seen in what follows.

18. As Kenley Dove points out, this same task informs the project of legal positivism. See Dove, "Logic und Recht bei Hegel," p. 108.

19. Michael B. Foster, *The Political Philosophy of Plato and Hegel* (Oxford: Oxford University Press, 1968), p. 87.

20. Foster advances this view in *ibid.*, p. 83.

21. *Ibid.*, pp. 83–84.

22. *Ibid.*, p. 89.

23. *Ibid.*, p. 89.

24. *Ibid.*, p. 90.

25. *Ibid.*, p. 90.

10. THE REASON FOR DEMOCRACY   301

26. Taylor, *Hegel*, p. 431.
27. See Winfield, *Reason and Justice*, pp. 74–77, 117–65.

9. CAPITAL, CIVIL SOCIETY, AND THE DEFORMATION OF POLITICS

1. Admittedly, this conflation of social and political domains can fall either way for political economy, depending on whether emphasis is placed on civil society or civil government. Rousseau, for example, chooses to reduce all proper society to the activity of civil government, and thus, in his *Discourse on Political Economy*, he conceives political economy as nothing but the business of public administration.
2. Adam Smith, *The Wealth of Nations* (New York: 1937), p. 14.
3. For a discussion of these problems, see Richard Dien Winfield, "Freedom as Interaction: Hegel's Resolution of the Dilemma of Liberal Theory," in L. S. Steeplevich and D. Lamb, eds., *Hegel's Theory of Action: Proceedings of the 1981 Meeting of the British Hegel Society* (New York: 1982).
4. Hannah Arendt has analyzed these developments at length in both *The Origins of Totalitarianism* (New York: Harcourt, Brace, Jovanovich, 1973) and *On Revolution* (New York: Penguin, 1976).
5. See Richard Dien Winfield, "The Social Determination of Production: The Critique of Hegel's System of Needs and Marx's Concept of Capital (Ph.D. dissertation, Yale University, 1977).
6. For a discussion of these problems, see Richard Dien Winfield, "The Social Determination of the Labor Process from Hegel to Marx," in *The Philosophical Forum* (Spring 1980), vol. 11, no. 3; and in greater detail, Winfield, "The Social Determination of Production," part 3.
7. Karl Marx, *Capital* (New York: International Publishers, 1967), 3:819–20.
8. See Arendt's discussion of Engel's remark in *On Revolution*, p. 276.
9. Marx and Engels, *Basic Writings on Politics and Philosophy*, Lewis S. Feuer, ed. (New York: Peter Smith, 1959), p. 254.
10. Plato, *The Republic*, Book VI.
11. See Aristotle, *Nicomachean Ethics*, 1094a–1181b, esp. 1113a33–35, 1176a3–34, 1176bb25; and *Politics*, 1252a–1342b, esp. 1284a3–34, 1288a27–28, 1288a32–64.
12. See G. W. F. Hegel, *Philosophy of Right* (New York: Oxford University Press, 1967), paras. 82ff and 102.
13. *Ibid.*, paras. 136–40.
14. Karl Marx, *Capital*, vol. 1, chs. 6 and 7.

10. THE REASON FOR DEMOCRACY

1. M. B. Foster develops this point in detail in his sadly neglected work, *The Political Philosophies of Plato and Hegel* (Oxford: Oxford University Press, 1968).

2. It is important to note that although liberal theorists reject any teleology applicable to the individual will, their postulation of the right of individual liberty leaves politics a means to securing a prepolitical freedom, effectively precluding any successful defense of democracy.

3. Cited in John Sommerville and Ronald E. Santini, eds., *Social and Political Philosophy* (New York: 1963), pp. 266–70. Subsequent page references will appear in the text.

4. See John Locke, *Second Treatise on Civil Government* (New York: 1952), ch. 10.

5. See Jean-Jacques Rousseau, *The Social Contract* and *Discourse on the Origin of Inequality*, Lester G. Crocker, ed. (New York: 1967), *Social Contract*, Book I, ch. 7, and Book II, ch. 4. Subsequent page references will appear in the text.

6. V. I. Lenin, *State and Revolution* (Moscow: 1965), pp. 14–15. Subsequent references will appear in the text.

7. Hegel is one of the few thinkers to have proposed this type of division of powers. Among most other theorists, the authorizing power is either left unmentioned or combined with the legislature, whereas the executive power is supplemented by a separate judiciary branch whose administration of the law actually falls completely within the generic function of the executive. Although Hegel lays the groundwork for a properly organic division of powers, his own characterization of them is marred by two major errors. On the one hand, he fails to separate civil society from the state in a sufficiently radical way and instead injects estate relations into government so that political powers get alotted as matters of social privilege with different classes assigned direct political functions. See, for example, paragraphs 291, 303–8, and 312–13 of Hegel's *Philosophy of Right*, T. M. Knox, trans.. (New York: Oxford University Press, 1967). On the other hand, Hegel does not fully divide the powers of government and ends up disrupting the just organic unity of the state by allowing the head of state and the executive power to participate in legislation and rendering the estate assembly a largely advisory body (see para. 300 of the *Philosophy of Right*.

8. Hannah Arendt, *On Revolution* (New York: Penguin, 1965), pp. 282–84.

9. For some discussion of the nonmetaphysical, nontranscendental character of autonomous reason, see William Maker, "Understanding Hegel Today," *Journal of the History of Philosophy* (July 1981), vol. 19; "Does Hegel Have a Dialectical Method?" *The Southern Journal of Philosophy* (Spring 1982), vol. 20, no. 1; and Richard Dien Winfield, "The Route to Foundation—Free Systematic Philosophy," *The Philosophical Forum* (Spring 1984), vol. 15.

10. How liberal theory conflates self-determination with determined determinacy is analyzed in Richard Dien Winfield, "Freedom as Interaction: Hegel's Resolution to the Dilemma of Liberal Theory," in Lawrence S. Stepelevich

and David Lamb, eds., *Hegel's Philosophy of Action* (New York: Humanities Press, 1983).

12. THE THEORY AND PRACTICE OF THE HISTORY OF FREEDOM

1. G. W. F. Hegel, *Philosophy of Right*, T. M. Knox, trans. (New York: Oxford University Press, 1967), para. 227 and its addition. Subsequent references to this work will be made in the text.

2. G. W. F. Hegel, *Science of Logic*, A. V. Miller, trans. (New York: Humanities Press, 1969), pp. 67ff. ("With What Must the Science Begin?").

3. For a leading example of the holist position, see Richard Rorty, *Philosophy and the Mirror of Nature* (Princeton: Princeton University Press, 1979), part 3.

4. Plato is an exception to the rule, and in Book VIII of the *Republic*, he accounts for the different forms of government in terms of the history that results from the dissolution of the ideal polis.

5. G. W. F. Hegel, *The Philosophy of Mind*, W. Wallace, trans. (Oxford: Oxford University Press, 1971), note to par. 544.

6. Admittedly, in paragraph 298 of the *Philosophy of Right*, Hegel suggests that positive legislation contributes to the further becoming of the constitution. This development is consistent with constitutionality and the unconditioned universality of the just state only if it involves the further *realization* of the constitution in relation to changing circumstances rather than an actual alteration of the constitution itself.

7. G. W. F. Hegel, *Vorlesungen Uber Rechtsphilosophie*—vol. 4, K.-H. Ilting, ed. (Stuttgart-Bad Cannstatt: Fromman-Holzboog, 1974), p. 696.

8. G. W. F. Hegel, *The Philosophy of History*, J. Sibree, trans. (New York: Dover Press, 1956), p. 9.

Index

Absolute Idea, 32-33, 107, 109, 286
Absolute Knowing, 19, 24-25, 26, 27-31, 102, 105
Absolutely good man, 186
Abstract right, 189-190, 191, 192, 263, 283
Accumulation of capital, 202
Administration of law, 165-66, 205-6
Analytic philosophy, 87-88
Analytic-synthetic distinction, 40, 51
Antifoundationalism, 1-2, 100-1
Apel, K.-O., 91, 295
Apogogic argument, 78
Arendt, H., 188, 239, 282, 301
Aristotle, 37, 38, 40, 89, 255, 269; defense of the principle of contradiction, 78, 297; defense of the theory of substance, 58-60; ethics and politics, 186, 218, 224, 231, 234-235, 275, 287
Authorizing power, 238-39
Automation, 181
Autonomous reason, 245
Ayer, A. J., 39

Berman, R., 300
Bloch, E., 296
Bureaucracy, 176, 182

Capital, 171, 174-75, 179, 198-202, 203
Capitalist, 200
Cartesianism, 99
Character, 97, 219

Child rearing, 193
Citizen, 213, 248, 259
Civil freedom, 195-96, 208
Civil government, 173-74, 178, 213, 225, 227, 301
Civil religion, 228, 231
Civil society, 5, 164, 165, 169, 173, 194, 195-98, 263, 284, 286
Classes, 183; class interest, 183, 214, 229, 237; political classes, 251-53
Coherence theory of truth, 81-82, 88, 106-9
Colapietro, V. M., 91
Commodity relations: commodities, 189-190, 196; commodity exchange, 197-98, 199, 202-3; commodity production, 197, 200; inability to secure civil justice, 202-5
Communism, 179-83
Communist society, 181, 230-31
Communitarianism, 135
Competition, 200
Concept, 79
Conceptual scheme, 62-64, 100, 101, 107-9
Conscience, *see* morality
Consciousness, 82-86; as given subject matter of phenomenology, 26, 28-29, 104
Constitution: constitutional amendment, 233-234, 266, 288; constitutionality, 223-24, 232-40, 248, 265-68, 286;

Constitution (*Continued*)
   constitution-making, 265-266, 287-91; as an object of reason, 235
Contemplation, 241
Corporatism, 183
Crime, 138, 166, 169, 190, 203, 286
Critique of epistemology, 101-5

Danto, A., 299
Darwinian evolutionary theory, 261-62
Davidson, D., 107
Declaration of Independence, The, 225, 226
Deconstruction, 100, 127–29, 243
Deductive reasoning, 37-41
Democracy, 221-48, 254 bourgeois democracy, 180; and constitutionality, 223-24, 232-40; critique of, 229; justification of, 6, 222-23, 224-32, 240; participatory democracy, 239-40; "people's democracy", 229; of social democracy, 178-79; workers' democracy, 229; wrong defenses of, 224-32
Democratic centralism, 182
Descartes, 265
Determinacy: accounting for, 3, 32, 49-51, 55-75; categories of, 64-75, 297
Dialectical logic, 2, 4, 38, 45-53
Dialectical materialism, 38-39
Division of labor, 174, 250, 251, 259
Divison of powers, 237-40, 248, 257, 267, 302
Dove, K. R., 296, 299, 300

Economic determinism, 121, 180, 189, 230
Economic disadvantage, 202-5, 207, 210, 233
Edifying philosophy, 1, 20, 100, 243
Engels, F., 38, 181, 296
Estates, 183
Ethical community, 141, 151, 153, 155, 163, 164, 166-67
Exchange value, 197
Executive power, 238-39, 259-60
Exploitation of labor by capital, 199, 200, 202

Family, 151, 164, 165, 169, 192-94; civil enforcement of family rights, 205; family freedom, 192-94, 220; and the history of freedom, 283-84
Fascism, 5, 183-84, 213
Fetishism of commodities, 180, 197-98
Fichte, J. G., 18, 28, 41, 296
First principles, 15, 40, 119, 241-42
Formal logic, 2, 14, 37-41, 78
Foster, M. B., 6, 162, 166, 249-69, 300, 301
Foundationalism, 1, 4, 5, 82, 99, 119, 244, 246, 275-76, 287; foundational epistemology, 4, 84, 86
Fraud, 138, 169, 190, 203, 286
Freedom: and justice, 185-86, 243-48, 276-77, 282-83; and justification, 185-86, 240, 241-48; as interaction, 186-89, 247, 279-80; as virtue of the state, 255, 258-61
Free enterprise, 204, 211

Gadamer, H.-G., 20, 62, 91, 234, 295
General will, 227-29
Good, the, 16, 241, 242
Guardian class, 219-20, 251-55

Habermas, J., 91, 188, 282, 295, 296
Habit, 96, 97, 231
Hegel, G. W. F., 2, 26-33, 49, 65, 100-1, 121, 136, 185, 191, 245, 269, 299; on civil society, 167; on consciousness, 110, 113; critique of transcendental philosophy, 17; on ethical community, 149, 163; on history, 111, 114, 271-93; on the history of philosophy, 112, 115-16; on language, 86-88, 97, 113; *Lectures On The Philosophy of History*, 6, 292; logic of being, nothing and becoming, 32, 49-51, 65-68; on master-slave relationship, 94, 97, 98, 110, 113; on morality, 5, 136-68, 300; *Phenomenology of Spirit*, 2, 19, 26-31, 92, 101-5; *Philosophy of Nature*, 277, 281, 297; *Philosophy of Right*, 5, 6, 7, 97, 111, 136-68, 249, 263, 273, 277-78, 280, 281, 289, 292, 299; *Philosophy of Spirit*, 84, 92, 93, 110-16, 277, 281, 297; *Realphilosophie*, 81, 83, 111, 297; *Science of Logic*, 3, 27, 30, 31-33, 49-51, 65-74, 79-80, 93, 101, 105-7, 109-10, 247, 269, 276, 297; on spirit,

INDEX

98; on the state, 149, 257, 302, 303; on thinking, 77-89
Heidegger, M., 62, 91, 110
Hermeneutics, 100, 269
Historicism, 120-23, 128
History, 271-72; descriptive philosophy of, 272-73, 292; of the institutions of freedom, 6, 280-82; meaning of, 273; of philosophy, 4, 115-16, 117-31, 271-74; political character of the history of freedom, 282-87; prescriptive philosophy of, 6, 280, 292
Hobbes, T., 186, 222, 256
Holism, 20, 99, 105-10, 121, 234, 276
Husserl, E., 18, 21, 41, 62, 91, 295, 296

Imagination, 87, 97
Imperialism, 177, 179
Indeterminacy, 297; as outcome of phenomenology, 25, 31; and self-determination, 32, 46, 48; as starting point of systematic philosophy, 31-32, 49-50, 65-67, 276
Individuality: and the concept, 79-80; and dialectical logic, 47, 79; of the free will, 187-88; of the state, 6, 255-257, 261, 264-69; of the work of fine art, 261, 262-63; *see also* Freedom; Self-determination
Inequality of wealth, 203, 207, 210
Interaction theory, 185-89
Internal realism, 100
International relations, 177, 179
Intersubjectivity, 91-98, 110-11
Intuition: intellectual intuition, 28; intuitive intelligence, 40-41; and language, 87
Invisible hand, 203

Jefferson, T., 224-27, 231
Justice, 217, 274-77; as the reality of freedom, 185-86, 240, 241-48, 275-78; teleological conception of, 218-20, 241-42

Kant, I., 18, 41, 42, 43, 62, 73, 83, 87, 91, 94, 124, 295; doctrine of the analogies of experience, 84-85; ethical theory, 95, 136, 187, 192, 228
Kierkegaard, S., 26, 80, 296

Kojève, A., 92
Kuhn, T. S., 14

Labor, 174
Labor power, 201
Labor theory of value, 174, 180, 197, 200
Laissez-faire, 175
Language, 82, 83, 86-89, 113-14
Law, 260; administrative law, 215; civil law, 165, 205, 206, 212, 215
Legality, 170
Legislative power, 237-39, 257-58
Lenin, V. I., 38, 229-32
Liberal theory, 5, 172-77, 186, 188, 192, 213, 242-43, 278-79, 282; and the defense of democracy, 225-29, 302
Liberty, 172, 174, 186-87, 195, 218, 242, 246, 278
Locke, J., 173, 186, 225, 227
Logic, 2, 35-36, 77-80; *see also* dialectical logic; formal logic; Transcendental philosophy
Lukács, G., 92, 121, 122, 296
Logical positivism, 39-40
Luxury, 251

MacIntyre, A., 92, 114, 300
Maker, W., 296, 299, 302
Market freedom, 220
Markets, 151, 165, 175, 196, 250-51
Marriage, 193, 194
Marx, K., 26, 80, 92, 121, 122, 229, 230, 237, 296, 299; critique of commodity relations, 197, 199, 200, 202; theory of capital, 179, 180, 198-200; theory of communist society, 180-81
Marxism, 177, 179-80, 189, 196, 198, 230, 284
Mathematics, 14
Mean of conduct, the, 185
Memory, 87, 97
Metaphysics, 14-16, 19, 27, 33
Modernity, 292
Morality, 135-70, 191-92, 263, 283, 286; action and deed, 139; ethic of conviction, 161; ethic of good intentions, 160-61; evil, 158; the good and conscience, 137, 150-55, 191; intention and welfare, 137, 142-50; inter-

Morality (*Continued*)
est, 144-45, 147; and legality, 164, 165-66, 170; moral agency, 95, 96-97, 141, 168-69; moral hypocrisy, 159, 162; moral irony, 159, 162; moral self-deception, 159-61, 162; probabilism, 160-61; purpose and responsibility, 137-42
Multiplication and refinement of needs and commodities, 196

Nagel, T., 298
Natural determination, 5, 171, 184, 199, 201, 291
Naturalized epistemology, 100, 101-5
Natural law, 186, 275, 280
Nazism, 184
Need: civil, 195-96, 204, 208, 209; market, 196, 204, 252, 253; natural, 174, 196; subsistence, 174, 196
Nihilism, 115, 234, 235, 242, 243
Nonmalicious wrong, 138, 169, 190, 203, 286

Ontological argument, 256

Phenomenology: as a form of transcendental philosophy, 21; as introduction to systematic philosophy, 2, 19-26
Philosopher-king, 186, 220-21, 236, 254
Philosophy, 13
Plato, 15-16, 40, 186, 218-21, 222, 224, 230, 231, 249-52, 254, 259, 263, 264, 266, 275, 303
Polis, 249-55, 260
Political economy, 174-75, 196, 301
Political freedom, 213, 214-15, 220, 221, 222, 248, 258-61, 267-68, 285; and constitutional-making, 265-67, 287-91
Positive law, 259; and constitutionality, 235-37, 240, 266-67, 288-89, 303
Positive science, 13-14, 15, 19, 21, 23, 35
Post-analytic philosophy, 100
Poverty, 204
Praxis, 234
Principle of contradiction, 38, 39
Procedural justice, 275, 287
Production process, 197
Proletariat, 122; dictatorship of, 180, 229-31; proletarian interest, 122, 182-83, 229, 237
Property relations, 96, 169, 247; civil enforcement of, 205; and the history of freedom, 283; as the minimal structure of right, 189-90, 283; and morality, 138-39, 164, 283; violations of, 138, 169, 190, 203
Public administration of welfare, 208-11
Public opinion, 176

Quine, W. V. O., 14, 36, 40

Race, 184
Rational reconstruction, 129-31
Rawls, J., 186, 275
Reason: justificatory role of, 35, 217; self-justification of, 35-36, 52
Reciprocal recognition, 188
Reflective equilibrium, 100
Relativism, 186, 245
Revolution, 167, 291
Right, 96, 98, 279; right and duty, 98, 140, 153, 168, 193
Romanticism, 261, 262-63
Rorty, R., 20, 91, 303
Rousseau, J.-J., 186, 227-29, 230, 231, 232, 300

Sandel, M. J., 299
Schelling, F. W. J., 18, 28, 296
Self-determination: logic of, 46-49, 79, 282; and normative validity, 46-48, 168, 185-86, 240, 241-48
Self-government, 258, 260, 267-68, 285
Sense-certainty, 26
Sign, 86-87, 113-14
Skepticism, 36, 53, 242, 243
Slavery, 138, 233
Smith, A., 174
Social contract, 226-27, 287
Social contract theory: and the defense of democracy, 226-29
Social democracy, 5, 177-79
Social interest groups, 206
Socialism, 177-83, 213
Socrates, 15, 117, 130, 131, 250, 254
Solipsism, 98

INDEX

Something, category of, 55-75
Sovereignty, 214, 215, 227, 255-61, 265-66
Species being, 280
Spirit, 256
State, 151, 169, 213, 214-15, 249-69, 284; genesis of, 287-291; relation between state and civil society, 171, 173, 177, 184, 211-16; relations between state and non-political associations, 164-65, 166, 213, 214, 232-33, 240, 249-54, 260-61, 284-86
State of nature, 172, 225-26
Strauss, L., 299
Strawson, P. F., 94
Subjective freedom, 165-66, 170
Substance, theories of, 58-61
Surplus value, 198-99
Synthetic a priori knowledge, 41, 42, 44
Systematic philosophy, 2, 25, 276-77

Taxation, 210
Taylor, C., 299, 300, 301
Thinking, 3, 77-89; and consciousness, 82-86; and language, 86-89; and logic, 77-82
Transcendental philosophy, 16-19, 61-64, 88, 92, 108, 242, 276, 295; self-elimination of transcendental argument, 19, 44-45, 64; transcendental condition, 16, 42, 44-45, 46, 57, 119, 242, 243, 296; transcendental logic, 2, 41-45, 46

United States Constitution, 233, 238-39
Use-value, 197

Vanguard party, 230-31, 236
Virtue, 96, 185, 219

Weber, M., 177, 230, 299
Welfare state, 178-79, 213
Williams, B., 300
Williams, R. R., 91
Winfield, R. D., 301, 302
Wittgenstein, L., 62, 91, 94, 128, 295
Worker self-management, 200, 207
Wrong, 138, 190, 286

For Product Safety Concerns and Information please contact our EU representative GPSR@taylorandfrancis.com
Taylor & Francis Verlag GmbH, Kaufingerstraße 24, 80331 München, Germany

www.ingramcontent.com/pod-product-compliance
Lightning Source LLC
Chambersburg PA
CBHW052149300426
44115CB00011B/1584